CINEMA & ARCHITECTURE

CINEMA & ARCHITECTURE

Méliès, Mallet-Stevens, Multimedia

edited by François Penz and Maureen Thomas

BRITISH FILM INSTITUTE

bfi

BFI PUBLISHING

First published in 1997 by the
British Film Institute
21 Stephen Street, London W1P 2LN

The British Film Institute exists to promote appreciation, enjoyment, protection and development of moving image culture in and throughout the whole of the United Kingdom. Its activities include the National Film and Television Archive; the National Film Theatre; the Museum of the Moving Image; the London Film Festival; the production and distribution of film and video; funding and support for regional activities; Library and Information Services; Stills, Posters and Designs; Research; Publishing and Education; and the monthly *Sight and Sound* magazine.

British Library Cataloguing-in-Publication Data
A catalogue record for this book is available from the British Film Library

ISBN   0-85170-578-2

Cover
top: *L'Inhumaine* 1924 *d.* Marcel L'Herbier, *des.* Mallet-Stevens
upper centre: *Mon Oncle*, 1958, *d.* Jacques Tati, *des.*, Henri Schmitt
lower centre: *After Hours* 1985 *d.* Martin Scorsese, *des.* Jeffrey Townsend
bottom: *Cold Lazarus* 1995 *d.* Renny Rye, *des.* Christopher Hobbs,
Digital image by Paul Richens, Martin Centre, University of Cambridge

Design and layout: François Penz, University of Cambridge, Department of Architecture
Digital imaging: Ian Hitchman, University of Cambridge, Department of Architecture

Printed and Bound in Great Britain

Contents

Notes on Contributors

David Bass is an architect practising in London. He teaches at the University of Cambridge and at the Architectural Association. He writes and lectures widely on a range of architectural and film-related topics. He started research on the essay featured in this collection while a scholar in Architecture at the British School at Rome.

Tim Benton teaches History of Art and Architecture at the Open University. He has contributed to courses on the Renaissance, the 17th century and the modern period. He has published extensively on twentieth century architecture in Britain and Europe, notably on the architecture of Le Corbusier. He leads a group of art historians and educationalists at the Open University investigating the potential of multimedia for distance teaching.

Nicholas Bullock came to Cambridge to read Modern Languages but changed to Architecture. He was one of the founder members of the Centre for Land Use Built Form Studies, now the Martin Centre, where he completed his PhD under Leslie Martin in 1972. He was then appointed a lecturer in the Cambridge School of Architecture where he now teaches; he has also lectured regularly at the Architectural Association since 1975. His interests in housing and planning led to the publication in 1984 with James Read of *The Movement for Housing Reform in Germany and France*. He is currently working on Modernism focusing on Great Britain between 1945–55.

Henning Camre is the Director of the National Film & Television School, UK. His professional background is as a Director of Photography (fiction and documentary) and a documentary film-maker. In 1982 he became Chair of the CILECT/TDC Board (Centre International de Liaison des Écoles de Cinéma et de Télévision). In 1989, Henning co-founded GEECT (Groupement Européan des Écoles de Cinéma et de Télévision). He has carried out a wide range of international film and television research, education and training initiatives and activities for CILECT and UNESCO, In 1996 he set up CREATEC (the Creative Media Arts and Technologies Centre) at the NFTS. Henning is a Chevalier de l'Ordre des Arts et des Lettres.

Diana Charnley is the Head of Screen Design at the National Film & Television School, UK. She trained at BBC Television on a variety of studio-based and location productions, covering period and contemporary design on drama, features and serials. After gaining experience on *Plenty* (GB, 1984, d. Fred Schepisi), Diana art directed the feature films *Defence of the Realm* (GB, 1985, d. David Drury); *Clockwise* (GB, 1986, d. Christopher Morahan) and *The Dawning* (GB, 1987, d. Robert Knights). Production Design includes *High Hopes* (GB, 1988, d. Mike Leigh) and *Meantime* (GB, 1983, d. Mike Leigh).

Michael Eleftheriades is an architect who trained at the Architectural Association. After practising at Michael Hopkins and Herron Associates, he launched Media Synthesis Ltd and AntiGravity Ltd in 1993. The companies specialise in custom software solutions, information technology integration, and developing applications for Personal Digital Assistants.

Odile Fillion is a film-maker and a journalist. She was co-editor of *Le Moniteur* from 1988–94 and collaborates with a wide range of magazines and journals. She has produced numerous videos portraying architecture for exhibitions and installations purposes. She published *La Ville, six interviews* (Le Moniteur, 1994) and more recently *espace = écran? les architectes et les images de synthèse* (Ina/Imagina, 1996).

Annie Forgia is an architect who first trained as a film maker at IDHEC (the Institut des Hautes Études Cinématographiques). She is a lecturer in Architecture at the Paris-Val de Marne School of Architecture. She is the founder and Chair of IMARA (Image Animée et Représentation Architecturale).

Christopher Hobbs is a Production Designer and Art Director for film and television. He is also a painter, sculptor and an author and illustrator of original children's stories. His Production Design credits include: *Velvet Goldmine* (GB, 1997, d. Todd Hayes); *Cold Lazarus* (BBC/Channel 4, 1995, w. Dennis Potter); *Neon Bible* (US, 1994, d. Terence Davies); *The Long Day Closes* (GB, 1991, d. Terence Davies); *Orlando* (GB, 1991, w/d. Sally Potter); *Edward II* (GB, 1991, d. Derek Jarman); *The Garden* (GB, 1990, d. Derek Jarman); *The Wolves of Willoughby Chase* (GB, 1988, d. Stuart Orme); *The Last of England* (GB, 1987, d. Derek Jarman); *Salome's Last Dance* (GB, 1987, d. Ken Russell); *The Phantom of the Opera* (GB, 1986, d. Ken Russell); *Gothic* (GB, 1986, d. Ken Russell); *Caravaggio* (GB, 1985, d. Derek Jarman) and *The Company of Wolves* (GB, 1984, d. Neil Jordan).

Gavin Hogben has taught architecture at Princeton and Yale Universities and been a visiting lecturer at the Graduate School of Design at Harvard University. Currently he lectures in history and theory and teaches a Diploma design studio at the University of Cambridge, Department of Architecture. Recently, his design studios have studied film and architecture as parallel realms of imagination and production, and investigated film-making as a practical design tool. He also maintains an architectural practice in London and New York.

Andres Janser is an art historian and a film historian. He is co-editor of *archithese* (an architectural bimonthly), to which he contributes regularly, and teaches at the Institute of the History and Theory of Architecture, ETH Zürich

Patricia Kruth is a 'professeur agrégé' of English, and a Fellow of Darwin College, Cambridge (1993–97). For several years, she lived and studied Film in the United States, particularly in New York City. She has taught both English and Film at high school and university level. From 1993 to 1996 she was the Director of the French Cultural Delegation in Cambridge (Cultural Service of the French Embassy), and she was a co-organizer of the 'Cinema and Architecture' Symposium. She is currently working on a book on *The Poetics of New York in the Films of Martin Scorsese and Woody Allen.*

Earl Mark has a background in Film-Making, Architecture, Mathematics and Computing. He serves as Director of Computer Technologies and as Associate Professor of Architecture within the School of Architecture, University of Virginia, Charlottesville. He has held prior teaching appointments at MIT, ETH Zürich, and as a teaching fellow at Harvard where he earned his PhD in Architecture. He is responsible for directing the development of computer based curriculum and facilities. He teaches, performs research, and has published in the areas of computer aided design, design simulation and design research.

François Penz is an architect who teaches at the Department of Architecture, University of Cambridge. He is a fellow of Darwin College and a director and co-founder of Cambridge Architectural Research Ltd. He co-organised two architecture film seasons at the Arts Cinema in 1991 and 1992 with the French Cultural Delegation in Cambridge and published *Computers in Architecture* (Longman, 1992).

Paul Richens is one of the first people to develop software for architectural design and has twenty five years' experience of the use of computers in a creative discipline. As a member of the Advisory Board of CREATEC, he has been instrumental in helping the National Film and Television School to develop its approach to digital media research. He is Director of the Martin Centre for Architectural and Urban Studies, the research arm of the Cambridge University Department of Architecture.

Zbigniew Rybczynski is an author, director and the Head of Creative Research and Development at CFB Centrum in Berlin. Following a Fine Arts education as a painter, Zbig was drawn to photography and film, believing that they represent the natural continuation of painting as a means of recording an image. His active film career began in 1969 at the State Academy of Film in Lodz, Poland, and since then his films have won numerous awards including an Oscar for *Tango* and an Emmy for Oustanding Achievement in Special Effects for *Orchestra*. Twenty-four years of experimental work in constructing video and film images from separate components have led Zbig to formulate principles of 'visual motion' and 'equations of the image' from which he is developing new techniques for creating visual images using digital technology. Since 1994, Zbig has been based in Berlin where he is developing new technology for CENTRUM as well as preparing his own feature film projects.

Joachim Sauter has a background in Graphic Design, Film-Making and Visual Communication. He was Professor of Digital Media at the Academy of Fine Art, Berlin (1991–1996). In 1988 he was a co-founder of ART+COM, Berlin, and has since become its Chair. ART+COM is an interdisciplinary group concerned with the integration of computer technology, communication and design. He holds the Max Ophuls, Lissitzky, Ars Electronica Interactive Art and Prisma Interactive Art Awards.

Maureen Thomas is a writer and the Head of Screen Studies at the National Film & Television School, UK. She is also Head of Script Development for the Icelandic Film Fund. Teaching includes: University College London, the University of Cambridge, the University of Victoria, Canada and the National Centre for Film, Norway. Her writing credits include: *Zuppa Inglese* (Pimlico Opera, 1993, story and libretto; composer Daryl Runswick); *The Greenlanders* (European Communications, 1993, 13-part TV adaptation of Jane Smiley's novel); *Goodbye 13* (Norway, 1995–96, d. Sirin Eide; LUCAS Frankfurter Guckkastenmannchen Award for Best Film, Frankfurt 1996; Best Youth Film, Antwerp 1997). She is a member of the DTI Technology Foresight Hitech panel subgroup on Creative Media. Maureen is specialising in developing and teaching interactive narrative drama at NFTS CREATEC.

Odile Vaillant has been in charge of 'Cinema & Architecture' at the Pompidou Centre since 1985, where she organised the *Cadre de Ville* festival on contemporary architecture. She edits the bi-monthly *Cinéma-Vidéo* magazine which highlights the Pompidou Centre audio-visual events and co-ordinates the films/videos programmes for the exhibitions concerning Architecture and Design on behalf of the Musée National d'Art Moderne. She published an article in *Le Cinéma et les autres arts* (Bibliothèque Nationale, Paris, 1995) and published *Le Décor au Cinéma* (Editions Séguier, Paris, 1996).

Helmut Weihsmann is an architectural historian, author of *Gebaute Illusionen, Architektur im Film* (Vienna 1988) and *Cinetecture*: *Architektur – Film – Moderne* (Vienna 1995), who has taught at the Hochschule für angewandte Kunst in Vienna since 1988. He has published and lectured widely in the United States at Columbia University, UC/Berkeley, SUNY/Buffalo, Rice University, Yale University and Virginia University. He has contributed to conferences including the F.W.Murnau Retrospective in Bielefeld, the Fritz Lang Retrospective in Torino, the Berlin Sommerakademie 1991, *Cine City* at the Getty Center in Santa Monica and frequently at the FU-Berlin conference. He was a founding member of the *film+arc* festival in Graz 1993.

Ian Wiblin is a photographer. From 1994–95 he was the Kettle's Yard Artist Fellow / Gonville and Caius College Artist in Residence at the Univesity of Cambridge. A book of his work, *Night Watch*, was published by Kettle's Yard in 1996. He has exhibited in Britain, Germany, Israel and Slovakia. He is a lecturer in photography at the University of Glamorgan.

Acknowledgements

As well as the University of Cambridge and the National Film & Television School, we should like to thank the Symposium's other sponsors, Apple Computer, the Arts Council of England, and the French Cultural Delegation in Cambridge, who had the vision to promote the new convergence. We offer our special thanks to the British Film Institute, the Centre Georges Pompidou, the Cinémathèque Française, the Centre National du Cinéma (CNC), the Cinémathèque Philips, Andres Janser, the French Ministère des Affaires Etrangères, the Museum of Modern Art (MoMA), Odile Vaillant, and Marion Houston (University of Cambridge, Department of Architecture) who have helped make this an international venture and supported us in our effort to achieve a historical as well as futuristic panorama.

These people have made it possible for us to start a forum for debate and inspiration which we intend to extend and elaborate. They enabled us to bring together the contributors whose work this volume represents. We are grateful to those contributors for entrusting themselves to a new environment, where their skills and experience were not uniform but contiguous, and for helping us start define that new environment and put down some markers both for the students who will be the pioneers of future endeavour, and for the practitioners who are currently working in the field.

Working on the book has had its frustrations, precisely because of the crossover area it occupies, but it has been a hugely rewarding and fruitful collaborative process. Without the dedication, skill and patience of Drusilla Calvert (Society of Indexes), Elliott Dumville (Cambridge Architectural Research Ltd), Richard Green (University of Cambridge, Department of Engineering), Janet Owers (University of Cambridge, Martin Centre), Elizabeth Stocker (University of Cambridge, Department of Architecture) and Kira Zurawska (graduate, NFTS, Fiction Direction), who all took care of the nitty gritty of the transformation process from raw text to finished layout, there would be no book.

Introduction

In April 1995, a Symposium on Cinema and Architecture was held at Cambridge University, and this volume is the printed result. The less tangible but equally important and lasting result was bringing together a group of people from different disciplines who are all interested in carrying forward into the future the best traditions of the past, ensuring a solid foundation for emerging fields of enquiry.

Because we invited practitioners as well as academics to the symposium, the range of contributions presented is wide. Some were essentially extemporised talks accompanying the screening of clips and slides; while others were scholarly papers illustrated by examples. After much deliberation with our sympathetic and overworked editors at the BFI (Ed Buscombe, Rob White, Dawn King, to whom much thanks), we decided to try to retain the essence of both types of delivery. We have not attempted to alter the character of the less academic pieces by homogenising them into academic prose; nor have we tried to popularise those specialist articles which require precise academic argumentation and reference. However, all the contributions were originally designed to reach an audience of non-specialists as well as specialists, of students from both fields as well as experienced academics and practitioners.

Although much which is presented here is genuinely innovative, challenging received assumptions in the fields of Cinema and Architecture, or presenting new research, it is all couched in terms we hope readers from a wide range of disciplines and backgrounds will find accessible and exciting. The topics represented range from a careful scrutiny of early film with special architectural interest (**Early Images of the City**) through reflections on how the representation or creation of the city on the cinema screen feeds back into architectural practice and vice-versa (**The Modern City**), to the ways in which developments in computer science are bringing about new alliances between cinematic and architectural vision and practice (**The Virtual City**).

In itself, a symposium at Cambridge is no unusual occurrence. It is axiomatic that such an event is likely to attract the most creative and curious of the international academic community. But in this case, there was an innovation – the event was organised jointly by the Department of Architecture, Cambridge, and the National Film and Television School, the UK's post-graduate, post-experience centre for film and television arts and sciences. It celebrated the consummation of a relationship which had been being built between the two institutions since 1992.

In 1991 and 1992, seasons of films on the general theme 'Cinema and Architecture' were presented by the Cambridge University Department of Architecture, the French Cultural Delegation and the Arts Cinema. The Cambridge/NFTS 1995 symposium on the same topic was designed to provide an opportunity for interdisciplinary debate on the relationship between the worlds of Architecture and Film-making, exploring common area of interest in a historical progression over three days. A number of screenings of rarely seen films was arranged as part of the event, contributing to the celebration of the centenary of cinema:

Bâtir, Trois chantiers, Architectures d'aujourd'hui, P Chenal (1930–31)
Hintertreppe, L. Jessner (1921)
L'Inhumaine, M. L'Herbier (1924)
Les Mystères du château du Dé, Man Ray (1929)
New York, New York, F. Thompson (1957)
Die neue Wohnung, H. Richter (1930)
Paris qui dort, René Clair (1923)
Le Poème électronique, Le Corbusier (1958)
Rien que les heures, Cavalcanti (1926)
The Wonder Ring, S. Brakhage (1955).

The ambition of the symposium was to bring together the creative communities of Architecture and Film-making and review some of the achievements of their early association as a platform for future collaboration.

The two areas have much in common. Both are worlds where the artist has to cultivate flair alongside highly practised skill, and combine craft knowledge with originality in an immersive relationship with a cultural community. As Sir David Puttnam, film producer, wrote on the occasion of the symposium:

> When Architecture, the most public of all art forms, meets Cinema, the most popular of all art forms, something exciting is almost bound to happen. As Chairman of the National Film and Television School I know that the School's involvement with this Symposium represents a real commitment to the exploration of new relationships and new ideas, in the belief that they will have a profound impact on the creative and commercial future of the audio-visual industry.

The shared endeavour of the event, bringing together Cambridge University and the NFTS, demonstrates the convergence the rapid development of digital technology is facilitating.

Professor William Mitchell, himself at Cambridge in the 70s, now Professor of Architecture and Media Arts and Sciences at the Massachusetts Institute of Technology and doyen of the MIT Media Lab, writes in his book *City of Bits* (MIT Press, 1995):

> House of Microsoft mogul Bill Gates, Seattle. The interior wall panels are not what they seem. They turn out to be huge, flat video screens. In repose they simulate the surfaces of standard architectural materials, but activated they become electronic windows opening onto anything at all. Architectural solids and voids become fluidly interchangeable, and the visual relationship of interior to exterior space is twisted into jaw-dropping paradox (p. 33). ...Through superimposition of computed stereo displays onto actual scenes, the proscenium dividing the "real" world from the virtual can be made to disappear. You can find yourself on stage with the actors, trying to distinguish the scenery from the walls (p. 20).

Mitchell encapsulates the issues where architectural and filmic arts and sciences are intersecting and blending. Both deal with representing 3D space in a 2D medium. Until recently, in the main, Architecture created its visions in 2D and then projected the 2D rendering into 3D reality; while Cinema captured 3D reality and transformed it through the medium of film to a projection of moving images on the 2D screen. Now, both Architecture and Screen Arts use the medium of the computer to create simulated worlds directly in 3D Cyberspace. More and more, reciprocally, the skills of the one need to inform the practice of the other.

What Bill Gates has in his domestic environment today, we will all be able to have in our own homes the day after tomorrow, or the day after that. Our digital windows will be able to provide a screen version of the world offering anywhere, anytime, any reality, where once there was only the option of the immediate here and now or the fantasy world generated by our own imaginations. What once was created uniquely by film-makers, a screen environment where fact and fiction could be offered in all combinations as a continuum in time, is now becoming an everyday part of the creative realm of architecture. The areas of interest, the traditional skills, the arts and sciences of film and architecture, are reaching a symbiosis early practitioners could imagine, as the films screened during the symposium demonstrate, but few, mainly on account of practical limitations, could attain. Now, some of the dreams of those early visionaries can be approached at the flick of a few switches by an undergraduate at Cambridge or a student at the NFTS. We have found that the approach is more effective and productive when it is made by both kinds of student together. We hope that the present volume will contribute to laying a foundation for pursuing these topics for students in other places as well as for anyone generally interested in the areas under discussion.

It was via the convergence-potential of the digital domain that Cambridge University and the National Film and Television School first came together. The Martin Centre (Cambridge's Centre for Architectural Research) and the Cambridge Centre for Communications Systems Research (rooted in Computer Science) are both collaborating with the NFTS's digital arm, CREATEC (the Creative Media Arts and Technologies Centre) in research and teaching; while NFTS staff supervise students from the Cambridge Department of Architecture in the grammar of screen language they are beginning to negotiate, with a view to future developments. Architecture, Computer Science and Screen Production find themselves able at last to work together smoothly over distance, using electronic connectivity, and to reap the benefits of each other's insight and experience as we go forward into the emerging world of 3D synthetic imaging and digital creation.

As it is, we offer you voices from France, Germany, America and the UK; we offer the views of architects, of film-makers who are architects, of architects who are film-makers, and of production designers, the architects of film. We give you the thoughts on space, time and motion of some of the leading creative people exploring the new medium of 3D computer-generated moving images. Together with a review of the attainments and influence of pioneers in this area at the period when screen art was just beginning – though architecture was already venerable – we present the ideas of practitioners in both arenas who are moving forward into the new world of the digital domain.

It is our view that Cinema and Architecture have a great deal to offer one another. What follows is an indicator of the wealth of creative synergy waiting to be enjoyed and deployed.

PART ONE

Early Images of the City

Introduction

Nicholas Bullock

One of the most engaging characteristics of the avant-garde has been its lack of inhibition in claiming to speak for the spirit of the age. To those who attended the first meeting of Congrès International de l'Architecture Moderne (CIAM) at La Sarraz in 1928 it was only natural to assume responsibility for defining the architectural agenda for the modern age. Their film-making contemporaries seemed to have been equally willing to shoulder the burden of defining the way in which the 20th century was to see the world.

For the members of CICI (Congrès International du Cinéma Indépendant) the sense of a shared agenda between the architectural and cinematic avant-garde was strong. Meeting in La Sarraz, under the benign leadership of Madame de Manderot, only a year after the first meeting of CIAM, it seemed reasonable to believe that the 'universal language' for which Hans Richter was calling might soon be established. Film projects such as the series of films entitled *Wie wohnen wir gesund und wirtschaftlich?* (1927–28) seemed to present the buildings of the avant-garde architects such as Taut, Gropius and May in terms that exactly matched their designers' intentions. Richter's *Die neue Wohnung* (1930) was praised by *Die Form*, the Werkbund's magazine, as a masterly celebration of the Neues Bauen.

But other avant-gardes had different agendas. Man Ray's *Les Mystères du château du Dé* (1928), filmed in Mallet-Stevens's Villa de Noailles, might find favour with the members of CIAM and CICI as a cinematic rendering of the New Architecture but its elastic treatment of the surreal time and space of the Château du Dé was very different from the way in which the film-makers of CICI portrayed the combination of Utopian and pragmatic reforming ideals that underpin the vision of the Neues Bauen.

How does the avant-garde canon accommodate the variety of different approaches to the 'city film', another key dimension of film and architecture? Vertov's *The Man with the Movie Camera* (1929) and Ruttmann's *Berlin, Symphonie einer Großstadt* (1927) set out to record the city in *sachlich* terms that seem quite compatible with the claims of the Neues Bauen to be developing an architecture of objectivity. But are these films to be understood in the same terms as the films of different aspects of the city that were being made by English documentary film-makers like Grierson, Anstey or Jennings? Ruttmann's recording of the rhythms of Berlin are very different from the didactic and 'stagy' realism of films such as Anstey's *Housing Problems* (1935) where the real inhabitants of real slums speak their mind directly into the camera. This is no attempt to entertain the audience with a visual symphony of city life but the use of film to preach, to win the audience to the cause of social reform. How different again is Anstey's preaching from the affectionate and ironic observation of the comings and goings of Parisians in Cavalcanti's *Rien que les heures* (1926), or from the zany reordering of city life in René Clair's farce *Paris qui dort* (1924) where the Eiffel Tower is the only refuge of normality in a city put to sleep by the experiments of a mad scientist.

By the end of Part One, any lingering belief that there might merge some normative or preferred 'universal language' for rendering in film the qualities of architecture or the city would have been exploded by the variety of the different film-makers whose work is discussed and illustrated here. How refreshing that the vitality of successive avant-gardes should ensure that the programme of each for rendering the nature of architecture and the city should have been overtaken by claims of its successor. How attractive to find that even the avant-gardes' case for conformity and regulation had been routed by the forces of experiment and invention.

The City in Twilight

Charting the Genre of the 'City Film' 1900–1930

Helmut Weihsmann

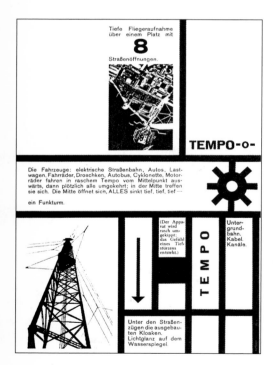

Script for *Dynamik der Großstadt* (1923) by
L.Moholy-Nagy (*Malerei-Fotografie-Film*, Bauhaus-
Books Vol.8/1926)

The City Street

This study is ostensibly about the (re)presentation of the 'metropolis' in the early history of cinematography, but its primary aim is to explore the points of reference and complex relations between the cinema and the city, between the concern of 'language' and meaning, specifically in regard to Kevin Lynch's notion of 'imageability' and their genealogical roots. Ever since the first film camera reproduced the cityscape, a hundred years ago, there has been a continuing relationship between the cinema and the city.

Certainly one of the major reasons why the pioneering film-makers were so fascinated by metropolitan motifs, motion and development was the fact that cinematography could depict urban reality scientifically as visual evidence. Early examples of film were received, like photography, as true-to-life documents and therefore as scientific proof. They showed without much attempt at rhetoric or aesthetics that the incorruptible camera-eye was a reliable tool that made the magical appear in the seemingly bland and banal of everyday places and situations. Their work thus emphasised primarily the (re)*presentation* and *perception* of space rather than special effects, fake or pseudo-realistic, surrealistic and magical elements as in Méliès's marvellous trick theatre. The particular manner in which the city with its famous landmarks, buildings and public spaces is presented in these early films seems to refer to the older medium of architectural imagery of the *tableau* map in its organisation of parts and geographical units. This is done specifically by means of cinematic and geographical manipulation of montage, camera, lighting, lens, and so on.

Cinematography was put to uses which were historically and functionally determined, which grew out of prevailing economics, visual and artistic strategies and ideologies operating during its inception. Each film, then, became a historic record of what cinema is or could be for visual expression. Thus the realm of cinematography was of documentary value, and 'reality' became a synonym for 'actuality'. The French, for example, initially termed all non-fiction films *actualités*. Tom Gunning once noted that from the moment of its birth, the cinema showed city crowds, street attractions and urban traffic: 'The first film shows were primarily "big city" affairs ... Nearly all early film documents present a *mise en abîme* of audiences filling vaudeville halls from busy city streets in order to see projected on the screen – busy city streets. The transfer to film allowed the city street to become another sort of spectacle, one mediated by an apparatus ... the street is filled with endless attraction.'[1]

Therefore it comes as no surprise to find that many early film documents reveal the relationship between reality and its representation as a 'picture'.[2] Vice versa, architectural form relates to the form of film as one text to another, in terms of a structure composed of so many patterns, or rather fragments of structure or language, organised in time and through space. Film becomes analogous to the modern perception of a city, continuous sequences of space frames perceived through time. In the pioneering days of cinematography when technical problems of lighting, shooting on location and other formal preoccupations prevailed over those of language or aesthetic codes and norms, the celluloid material had the quality of a mere record, or a silent witness of reality, rather than a work of art.

This documentary style developed steadily and was firmly established by pioneering cinematographers by the 1900s, when people like the Lumière brothers, Skladanowsky, Edison, Friese-Greene, and Notari produced both a relatively correct, accurate record and a very caricatured image of the current architecture and urban development. By wandering through the busy streets of city centres and promenades as *flâneurs,* as Walter Benjamin suggested in *Das Passagen-work*[3], they incidentally and selectively reproduced various views of different subjects and urban motifs. The cinema, stemming from theatrical and literary roots, logically continued this literary tradition of 'story telling' by spatial walks through the built environment and public spaces of cities. Like urban archaeologists, the Lumière brothers and their associates came closest to the 'reality' of urban chroniclers and photographers such as Atget by depicting the hidden yet omnipresent and commonplace character of everyday existence in public places (métro, bars, theatres, amusement parks and gardens).

After its documentary beginning, the next phase of the city's encounter with cinema was the pictorial *colportage*, spiced with sensation and often mingling newsreel facts with fiction in a super-naturalistic way. French and Nordic film-makers were famous for their naturalistic settings, often shot *en plein air* exclusively. Victor Sjöstrom and Urban Gad in particular integrated authenticity quite successfully within the framework of a plot by shooting under natural light and surroundings in cities, even without actually being on 'authentic' locations. In contrast to the illusionistic studio drops, the lyrical and charming *Fantomas* (1913) by Louis Feuillade and the semi-stylised, but still naturalistic works of Urban Gad such as *The Poor Jenny* (1912) show a mixture of documentary footage and narrative fiction in their attempt to integrate unstaged scenes with narrative methods.

In the noteworthy *The Poor Jenny*, the Danish-German director Urban Gad depicted the milieu of Berlin's drab working-class neighbourhood by using actual footage of districts and busy streets as the background for outdoor sequences. The camera shows the not always photogenic side of a fast-growing and ugly industrial city and urban society. During a short ride on an open-decked bus, one can see the fast-moving traffic of Berlin's famous boulevard, the Friedrichstrasse, already crowded with motor vehicles and tramways, as a perfect early example of cinéma vérité!

Although in such obviously undubbed scenes the film presented a powerful image of contemporary Berlin and a slice of reality, it avoided any deliberate social criticism and did not propose an alternative solution to the problems arising from capitalistic growth. Indeed some of the so-called proletarian 'milieu' studies based on Heinrich Sitte's sense of romantic *Verklärung* (a successful and popular figure of Berlin's low-life literature at the turn of the century in the Wilhelmische Reich) were nevertheless a realistic touch in cinema, but again did not focus on the burning issues affecting the unprivileged masses at that time: sociopolitical, health and housing problems.

Even the classic of this genre, Urban Gad's often cited comedy, *Vordertreppe–Hintertreppe/Frontstairs–Backstairs* of 1915, exposes (as the title suggests) the contrast in living conditions merely in its metaphor between the 'front' and 'back' of a dwelling. Even though Gad approaches the problem quite satirically, he nevertheless remains loyal to the status quo, and of course to the common, effective clichés of the 'rich' and the 'poor'. It had become somewhat progressive and even fashionable to demonstrate 'social interest' but also to romanticise 'how the other half lives' (Jacob Rijs). By expanding and exploiting this repertoire, pointing to the shady and often tragic side of humanity, the backstairs and backyards of the common people had become dignified enough for the sophisticated bourgeois film viewers. Looking at these films in this way also means tracing the cinema's economic development as a concept of textual social systems and urbanism, and developing a discourse of 'filmic' and 'architectural' reality through writing and reading. The films I will discuss can be defined as mirroring images of urban genealogical and social theory throughout the entire development of cinematography.

Of course my definition of 'metropolis' corresponds to the development of the cinema in this modernist tradition. When the city is the subject-matter of a film genre, one discovers a rather revealing psychological and social situation for the production of architectural theory and history. The cinema is certainly an exemplary product of urban modernity, but it is also a producer of urban culture and civilisation. The relationships that exist among phenomena such as 'metropolis', 'cinema' and 'modernity' are as complex as they are tentative in film writing. From its beginnings, film has been linked with the metropolis, and the motion-picture medium has featured the cityscape frequently and prominently. Every major capital of the world was soon catalogued on film. Presented in a factual, non-fiction framework, the city was the primary subject-matter of early avant-garde cinematography in the mid-1920s. A new genre was born: 'city film', or, better, 'city symphonies'.

To begin a detailed analysis of the tentative relationships between the avant-garde movement in film and architecture with the work of some pioneering protagonists is undoubtedly provocative, yet, to calm the sceptics, there exists an exceptional bias for the 'new city' prophesied by experimental designers and/or theoreticians and the efforts of the 'new cinema' which offers us a starting point for our thesis. It is significant that people such as Siegfried Kracauer, Walter Benjamin and, earlier, Georg Simmel or Charles Baudelaire insisted that the 'shock of the new' correlates to the history of montage in the different arts, especially among the precursors of the new film language, as exemplified in Sergei Eisenstein and Moholy-Nagy's draft for the screenplay *Dynamik der Großstadt* (Dynamic of the Big City). The 'montage of attractions', as Eisenstein said, is aimed solely at the nerves of the audience, to the extent of exploding his visual message. This pure nervous stimulation corresponds surprisingly to what Simmel had recognised in late nineteenth-century culture as the basis of the behaviour of the metropolitan man. For Simmel, the metropolitan individual is subjected to an acute *Nervenleben*, caused by the constant bombardment of contradictory images, floating in the flow of information, created by the capitalistic economy and the interests of *Reklame* (advertising).

It is therefore no coincidence that László Moholy-Nagy's graphic score for *Dynamik der Großstadt* (1923) tended to make of montage a technique directly inspired by a reading of the metropolitan universe, and it is perhaps no accident that a passage of his Bauhaus book of 1925, *Malerei, Photographie, Film,* is but a paraphrase of Simmel's famous text on the metropolis and nerve-racking urban life.

Given the controversies that shook German culture with the advent of socialism and contact with Soviet social experiments, it becomes evident that due to the crisis of bourgeois culture, intellectuals and artists alike either viewed urbanity as a sickness (as cultural pessimists such as Oskar Spengler did) only to be cured by a catharsis or by 'new' authoritarian leadership, or, at the opposite extreme, as a privileged site for experimental formalisation and cultural sophistication. Moholy-Nagy essentially picked up the demands already tackled by the abstract and futurist artists of the 'machine age'; ever since the metropolitan thematic that was present in contemporary culture from the beginning of the century touched upon aesthetic values, the phenomenon was fiercely debated. Just like Erich Mendelsohn's spectacular travel photographs taken a short time later in the metropolitan jungle of America with its electrographic neon-architecture, bare grain silos, modern skyscraper scaffolding and building technologies, the 'metropolis' of the future – Manhattan being its concrete manifestation – was either a nightmare or a chimera.

The vision of Fritz Lang's film *Metropolis* (1925–6) is immersed in an atmospheric framework switching from apocalyptic allusions to a city losing itself as a subject to a metaphorical 'new age' civilisation reminiscent of a biblical epoch. *Metropolis* is therefore a good example to describe the polemical role which 'urbanity' played in German cultural critique: whether that critique expressed conservative, reactionary beliefs like Alfred Rosenberg's *Mythus des 20. Jahrhunderts* or its fascination with a synthesis of past, present and future. Therefore the concept of the 'metropolis' became the epitome of the (over-civilised) mass society in one way or the other; in American culture it was seen simply as necessary for progress whereas in Russia it proclaimed the socialist victory over history. But German culture experienced this pragmatic or radical Utopianism as a trauma. The esotericism of Bruno Taut's *Stadtkrone* or Feininger's *Cathedral of Labour* for the Bauhaus community, conceived shortly before the reconstruction of the Tower of Babel in *Metropolis*, is literally the new leitmotiv for these mystical aspirations or exorcisms towards a greater society.

Another spectre of the myth of Babel can be seen in the mega-fantasies of Harvey Wiley Corbett and Hugh Ferriss in their famous renderings for New York's urban renewal plans of 1916–29. Whereas the aesthetics of realism and supernaturalism led film-makers of the avant-garde into the real world, whether in the wave of *Neue Sachlichkeit* or Futurism, the history of cinema is also full of numerous examples of just the opposite: the fantasy world of great Expressionistic set design. In this way, the German cinema demonstrates that the love-hate relationship with the 'big city' can be expressed as a collective nightmare, either 'visionary' or 'authentic', depending on its mood.

Metropolis

The Haunted Street

After 1918, the metropolis is no longer a place for the idler searching for amusement, excitement and diversion, but a horror-scenario for its frightened and threatened inhabitants. The present reality is neither idyllic nor prosperous, but rather a regressive/ aggressive infernal pandemonium. Expressionist art in particular drew attention to such issues as urban neurosis, decay and angst. This helped shape the bizarre and distorted screen architecture of the famous *Dr Caligari* (1919), which is primarily noted for its irrational elements and anti-natural treatment. Some German silent films in the wake of 'Caligarism' reflect this haunted, darkened atmosphere of apocalypse and unchained fear – so typical of this vulnerable era, with its intellectual escapism, pessimism, decline of morals and occult trends, and extremes. The films of the Weimar Republic portrayed contemporary urban life in transition according to these premises since they encouraged the audiences to perceive these demonic visions as the fantasies of the protagonists Dr Caligari, Golem, Nosferatu and Homunculus.

In the wave of populist contemporary literary and artistic criticism towards urbanisation (common since the industrial revolution of the 1800s but in successive, ever stronger waves), the cinema usurped this aversion to the metropolis quite spectacularly in both genres – the realistic 'city film' and in the monumental science-fiction epic *Metropolis* – and even used the same strong references and vocabulary, by depicting the metropolis as a diabolical *deus ex machina.*

In earlier examples of Expressionist cinema, metaphors frequently used for the characterisation of the city are the labyrinth and the jungle. Connections to latent Romantic art and symbolism are also evident as Lotte H. Eisner pointed out in *The Haunted Screen* (see note 7). In almost all of the early body of work, the city is represented as an evil, destructive and mystical Babylon. One can establish a quite unexpected link between the symbolic structure of these expressionist *Kinoarchitekturen* and their counterparts in existing cities like Manhattan and other Utopian skyscraper projects during this period in America as well as in Europe. In the aftermath of a vicious and senseless war, in the context of a catastrophic post-war economy and an upheaval of culture, the bourgeois class was in a state of permanent crisis and receptive to fantasies about violence and disaster.

The now classic yet ambivalent thesis of Kracauer's survey *From Caligari to Hitler* stated quite bravely that the Expressionist cinema reflected for the most part these strange phantasmagorias and authoritarian beliefs and projected them on the screen. Human and social catastrophes alike dominated the content and form of German Expressionist cinema – the logical consequences of this attitude is the 'fall' of the doomed metropolis such as in the futuristic film *Metropolis* or in the archaic, anti-modern ghetto of *Golem* (1920). The horror also reveals itself in the sheltered and protected *Biedermeier* village of Holstenwall as in *Dr Caligari*, or in the eerie appearance of an innocent-looking store-front window and shop sign as the sets of *Die Strasse* suggest, or in the turmoil of a mega-metropolis, where criminals, mass murderers and dangerous lunatics like Dr Caligari, Dr Mabuse, Jack the Ripper, Herr Orlac or 'M' (Peter Lorre!) are up to their evil and deadly tricks.

Siegfried Kracauer's interesting and valid thesis revealed important and until then hidden insights about the German soul and the psychological disposition that eventually nurtured National Socialism. For my own arguments of how the parasitic film industry supported or reinforced these authoritarian and inhuman ideologies, I want merely to state that the intact universe of the petit-bourgeois class and *civilitas* of society underwent a fundamental crisis and that the city order was shaken just as much as the crisis of culture by radical changes, and that the streets of German cities actually were the setting for terror and violence – both in real life and on the screen. It is therefore no coincidence that the German film industry exploited and utilised these latent and concrete fears just when the ill-fated democracy was threatened by political demagogues and economic and militant forces. Both the real and pretended dangers as well as the allure and forbidden attractions of the city street were given extensive coverage and meaning, but the 'street films' of this epoch could not accurately interpret the danger which already existed in the street in broad daylight.

Dark Expressionism

In the films discussed here, the political, economic and social reasons for such dramatic effects of capitalistic society upon the living and working conditions of individuals are seldom if ever properly recognised and analysed. A subjective and always mysterious situation remains unexplained, experienced mainly as unfathomable, impenetrable, and not as an objectively understood and interpreted reality according to Hegel and Marx. Strangely enough, even the great, legendary directors such as Fritz Lang and Friedrich Wilhelm Murnau reacted ambiguously towards these contemporary phenomena, lacking a clear standpoint on these issues.

Typical of the Expressionist cinema in its early stage is its deliberate escape from reality and the stylistic 'anti-naturalistic' treatment of its powerful *mise en scène* abilities, which includes a unique abstraction and in a sense a purification of the sets, which are no longer true replicas of existing objects and landscapes but instead a stripped-down version of reality, an archetypical 'dream-like' environment (*Umwelt*) which exaggerates fantasies of the studio imagination to perfection. It is striking how city-scapes and even nature were stylised to the extent that they became artificial and magical. Even the real buildings of Berlin, which were available just outside the studios, had to be reconstructed and created in the film sets as super-naturalistic, something which the critic Paul Rotha labelled appropriately as 'studio constructivism'.[4]

It is noteworthy how the 'street film' genre of 1923–5 shows broken souls and inhabitants of the dark quarters of life on 'skid row'. Frequently the main characters are cripples, underdogs, outcasts, criminals, lonesome creatures of the night and lunatics. The majority of these (anti)heroes with ill-fated destinies live on the shabby side of the city, behind the splendour of the grand city boulevards, where the sun apparently never shines. The rainy, dimly lit city defeats these street creatures. If one notices a horizon at all, one usually sees symbolic and grotesque silhouettes, graphically bold images, which project the protagonist's feelings and fears. The city of futuristic Berlin becomes, in Fritz Lang's dystopic vision of the future, literally a 'gravestone' for the working class.

A perfect example of a street film before its time is *Die Hintertreppe/Backstairs* (1921) by the director Leopold Jessner and the film designer Paul Leni. The film enriches the genre by its effective use of the famous theatrical 'Jessner stairs' and by the gloominess of city life for its basement dwellers. The celebrated scriptwriter Carl Mayer invented this 'true fable' about the activities of the dwellers which significantly has one locality that never changes: a miserable back staircase. The fable meticulously follows the doomed destinies of three inhabitants until their tragic endings. The back area of a typical *Zinskasnerne* (apartment block) and its twisting stairwell act as a metaphor for their fate, in which the distorted forms and angles of the architecture make allusions to the broken and deformed sets of *Dr Caligari* or *Raskolnikow* (1923) (although they are treated quite realistically). *Die Hintertreppe* is not necessarily an expressionist movie, but it is not possible without Expressionism.

However, despite the Expressionist tone and mood – featuring lighting effects, exposed acting and design features – the setting of Mayer's fable is indeed quite different from 'Caligarism', because it uses its fantastic resources for starkly realistic touches and technical purposes for broader acceptance, rather than adopting the elitist *l'art pour l'art* approach of the decorative style. Expressionism had turned shortly after the box-office success of *Dr Caligari* into a rather mannerist trend of applied arts and crafts. Seldom was it used as a vehicle for dramatic realism, but rather bluntly for fantastic, weird 'photogenic' effects (for example *Genuine*, *Algol*, *Schatten*, *Raskolnikow*). However *Die Hintertreppe* masterfully changed this and thereby created an abundance of possible uses of Expressionism in any genre, and realistic setting/coding, casting its shadow all the way to Hollywood and film noir, as we shall see later.

The atmosphere created here is claustrophobic and depressing; Paul Leni's shabby-looking and often eerie sets suggest melancholy and despair. Corresponding to the three allegorical figures of the play, the maid, her lover, and the crippled postman, who apparently don't bear names but rather are typecast from the shadow world, the set designs also have all too many allegorical and symbolic meanings. The basement quarters of the postman and the dark back stairwell, walls, courtyards and fences literally imprison the scenery. Even more threatening than the narrow, winding stairs and the drab rooms in which they live is the meeting place of the couple under a twisted street lantern. The street itself is identifiable only as irregular contours. A few brightly lit windows in awkward shapes and a sharp distinction of dark/lighting effects (*Hell-Dunkel* contrasts) suggest a nervous tension and a feeling of unease. The rain-wet asphalt creates irregular reflections of light and shadow.

Carl Mayer, the scriptwriter, stresses in his parable the social boundaries and differences between the manor house (*Herrenhaus)* and the servants' quarters in the backyard of the grounds. The gloomy backstairs are in stark contrast to the noble entrance of the manor house. The master and mistress are seen only once, as mysterious, strange-looking, but nevertheless omnipresent figures, as dancing shadows during a party, flickering on the grey walls of the maid's room and through an opaque glass door connecting the kitchen with the parlour. Carefully treated objects and a huge pile of dirty dishes suggest the line that divides the maid's world from her employer's.

These parallel worlds are deliberately separated in the film by shielding doors, windows, walls, curtains and railings indoors and by separate entrances and paths outdoors. Their obligatory contact remains discreet, almost symbolic. This is expressed vividly through an authoritarian signal of communication – a bell in the maid's room. A contemporary

Die Hintertreppe (1)

observer noticed the eloquence of the 'silent objects in this setting, giving them the status of allegorical meaning and commenting on their importance to understanding of the characters and their situation. One critic for the journal *Der Film* noticed how some objects actually play a silent role and how some literally speak out without being obtrusive: an alarm clock, a bell, a doorknob, and so on. Even the mundane and trivial daily routines of the maid in the kitchen become instructive and 'supportive icons' (the German word used is *Bildhelfer*). Jürgen Kasten accents Mayer's gift for small details and stresses his ambitions as a 'realist' before his time when he states:

> Realistic representation of the "milieu", the spaces, the figures, and the conflicts are in *Die Hintertreppe* no less programmatic staging attempts than in naturalistic theatre, since they are the invocation of a metaphysical conflict in an abstract sense. His imagery follows the narrative structure in its assumption to transport a psychological drama in a true proletarian "milieu" towards a general validity about the human condition and mankind in general.[5]

In spite of the extensive use of Expressionist rendering techniques by Paul Leni's wizardry with lighting and directing, Jessner's treatment of space and Mayer's staging and storytelling abilities, *Die Hintertreppe* makes way for a new genre in German silent cinema: the *Kammerspiel*-film with its chamber-like intimacy and extreme minimalism of treatment. The reference to contemporary topics and realistic surroundings can be seen in the treatment of characters, depicting ordinary people, selecting everyday settings instead of fantastic landscapes and futuristic architecture. In the film's prologue Mayer announces his concern for reality and a new interest for the factual rather than the fictional by releasing a programmatic statement:

> The majority of motion pictures today deal with people who belong to the ruling, privileged class of society. However, some of the most fascinating and interesting human characters never are shown and explored by the movie camera … We want now to be witness to what occurs in "everyday life" on the backstairs of life and not what's happening in the luxury parlours!

In a sense *Die Hintertreppe* is still a 'fiction' film to the extent that it makes up a story, using actors, but its intention is a deliberate break with the common practice of Expressionism and a departure from 'Caligarism' altogether. With its choice of an authentic setting in a contemporary workers' district of Berlin, the film finally breaks from the world of fantasy. The shabby settings convey the social conditions in which the majority of the people lived, opposed to the glamorous side of the Roaring Twenties in Berlin. It occurred to an early film critic for the *Film-Kurier* that these images are a lamentation of the servant's position: 'the narrow corridors and stairwells suppress the maid's feelings thoroughly and eventually drive her away to doom in the basement, where her fate fulfils itself so tragically.'[6] Mayer's skilful dramas are always executed with such tragic destiny and vigour, but instead of passivity towards the inevitable fate of the German soul he shows the mechanisms. Instead of the unexplained supernatural, mystical forces and

Die Hintertreppe (2)

tyrannic powers of ghosts or demons dictating one's livelihood, Mayer's characters here are the products of their will and passion, driven by their own ego in a realistic manner. The new genre he created attempted to portray contemporary life in Germany by the artistic use of everyday material and inspiration with reference to the heroic, theatrical and tragic as in grand opera. Films such as *Scherben* (1921) and *Sylvester* (1923) – also scenarios by this important screenwriter – encouraged cinematic techniques and styles suggesting authenticity.

But in a way *Die Hintertreppe* shows an even darker shade of the human condition, which could be perceived as an early form of 'black realism'. As much as the formal language remains largely expressionistically stylised, the intentions and meanings change. The set designer turned film director Paul Leni used all the tricks of the trade to increase the metaphysical aspects: the energetic, soul-inspired architectural renderings are actually decorated by lighting effects. Also the famous *sfumato* and *disegno* drawing effects and the quality of these extraordinarily large three-dimensional film decorations are mainly created by chiaroscuro lighting techniques, to illustrate the magical, unseen meaning of things.

For most of the film – no matter whether day or night – darkness dominates the screen. Only a few streaks of flickering light streaming from door cracks and tiny window openings split the nocturnal picture. This ability to create a film noir atmosphere before its time was one of the virtues of Paul Leni's craftsmanship. Also his ability to shape 'spatial' tableaux into haunting images was termed later by the critic Rudolf Kurtz a 'blueprint of the soul' (*Seelenabdruck der Seele*).[7] Much like a magnifying lens, the camera focuses on psychological details to create a remarkable mood of depression (*Stimmung*).[8] The glowing windows suggest 'eyes' in the darkened metropolis. Through the application of the picturesque, grotesque and sinister vocabulary as a standard studio style, Expressionist film noticeably degenerated in the years to come to a fashionable style of ornamentation, which could no longer stand up to the former quality and originality of these sets, which Kurtz referred to as the 'darkness of the human soul'.[9] After the first wave of German 'Caligarism', the Expressionist style became very successful in other countries, so that French, American and even Japanese independent film-makers plagiarised its sets, or invited some of the protagonists to work in the film industry.

Magic and Myth of the Street

In Expressionist cinema, the streets of the city become an obtrusive and obsessive theme – not always negatively as the cliché of horror but instead as the dream vehicle for the frustrated male. In search of 'something else' or 'something bigger' – for a German male this something must mean Destiny – he plunges into the turmoil of the street. The commercial strip with its glamour appears to him to be the goal of his desires. Paradoxically, with the emergence of a stronger critique of 'metropolis' or 'megalopolis', the film industry began to discover and idealise the potential of the street and the metropolis. Much like earlier French films and literary works, the street becomes the focus for the German film-makers. The street is not only an ugly, dirty, dangerous and/or chaotic place of crime, anarchy and turmoil but also a place of liberation, an impossible dream and desire for a Utopian, non-bourgeois existence. Expressionist and neo-realist fantasies have often been associated only with negative, apocalyptic ideas and visions, but there is the other side as well, which can be interpreted as a quasi-religious hope for a better, socialist future. By forecasting and depicting the street as a platform for the organisation of the masses, as later in the liberal and communist phase of German film production, the street and the anonymous city were naively stamped with a bright future.

In the film entitled *Die Strasse/The Street* (1923), the street and Plato's cave metaphor of the house as a womb are dialectically drawn together as the vivid activities outside break directly into the action. We first see how the flickering lights from outside cast luminous shadows of temptation into the sheltered parlour of a well-furnished middle-class home, which reveal the male's fantasy and his longing to leave. In a subjective way he envisions the erotic allurement of the city outside his home. At the same time his humble wife looks out of the window onto the street and notices nothing of his vision, observing only the realistic-looking studio set of a normal city street. Through the temptations of the play of light and shadow coming into his living room and printing a seductive lace-pattern on the ceiling, the sexually frustrated husband goes off into the street hoping to find adventure that will deliver him from the boredom of an uneventful family life.

His expectations of the street pull him out of his 'snailhouse' existence when, overwhelmed by the false illusions, he falls into the maelstrom of lust. Suddenly everything and everybody become hilarious demons. The fascination of German Romanticism for dead objects also comes into play: an optician's sign is cleverly transformed into the devil eyes of an enormous creature. A shop window is a mirage that reflects simultaneously an ocean liner voyage promising escape and the equally persuasive mirage of an enigmatic young lady. However, towards the end of his sojourn, the images gradually become naturalistic and normal again. In contrast to the chaotic structure of the early shots, the home is now the castle, a shelter for retreat. Gone are the flashes of neon advertisement and blinking signals on the walls and ceilings of his cave dwelling, replaced now by the contemplative, kitsch atmosphere of the bourgeois *horror vacui* interior.

The safe environment of his home is juxtaposed deliberately with the destructive and chaotic effect of the street. Once in the open street he becomes vulnerable to mischief, crooks and dangerous illusions; his vision vanishes quickly and leads, ultimately, to his surrender, so that he returns with an enormous hangover to his faithful mate and his arrival is also dependent on the protection of the police force. The adventure has a bitter ending. Freedom and social mobility have their high price. The 'metropolitan' experience – advocated by the leftist and futuristic groups – does not hold in *Die Strasse* the endless possibilities of freedom and positive connotations of the *Neue Sachlichkeit* films. Perhaps the reason why street films achieved such great popularity and had considerable commercial success lay in the ambiguous feelings most German artists and intellectuals had towards the metropolis to begin with. The street film genre shaped these doubts and hopes and it became a major issue for many opinion-makers at the time. The sociologist Siegfried Kracauer often described the streets of Berlin as gigantic warehouses full of false expectations, but also of silent creatures about to be awakened to destroy these false temples of capitalistic cities.

The street was also a major issue for the critic of the *Vossische Zeitung,* who wrote upon the opening of *Die Strasse*: 'The street rules … the street glows … the street begins to articulate itself … the street comes to life and finally is the main character !'[10] The street

Die Strasse

17

in all its facets and its multidimensional complexity remains an important *topos* of German silent and sound films, since *Die Strasse* gave birth to a very large number of significant films dealing with the metropolis in one way or another. *Die Strasse* not only marked the departure from the cliché of quaint villages and medieval settings from German fables towards a contemporary image of the city, it also featured a novel aspect of urban reality. Then editor of *Das Tagebuch,* Stefan Grossmann gives the director Karl Grune credit for developing from a Dickens to a Zola of film epics, and concludes with a final positive statement about the film: '*Die Großstadt.* Fantastic shots of the hectic and energetic hullabaloo of a street crossing. The city street in twilight, the street at dusk, the street at night, the streets of housing blocks, all this becomes a pure symphony of metropolitan lights. Images as a powerful, overwhelming rhythm, unforgettable variations of a theme: *Großstadtstrasse!*[11] Despite Karl Grune's profound attack upon the modern city, he seems to secretly admire it, because he celebrates the vibrancy of the crowded city rather than the depression.

City Poems

Two of the most famous, influential and nearly simultaneous examples of films that created literally their own genre in the history of film are Alberto Cavalcanti's *Rien que les heures* (1926) and *Berlin, the Symphony of a Great City* (1927), directed and edited by Walter Ruttmann and photographed by Karl Freund. Unlike the literary or narrative tradition discussed, both of these statements are much more lyrical and idiosyncratic. Although both filmic experiments attempt to express the pulse of modern life through a similar formal and rhythmic framework, they are quite different in attitude and execution. Also, their approach to the subject is different, which makes the 'reading' of each city portrayed – Paris for Cavalcanti, Berlin for Ruttmann – a very personal statement. Even though Ruttmann's material seems to be better organised, it lacks the vision Cavalcanti had for his city portrait.

Perhaps the appropriate method to define their style and inherent formal and structural differences is to make the fundamental distinction between 'epic' and 'symphonic'. In *Berlin*, the term 'symphony' in its title is significant to the film's content, character and purpose, because it represents visually the musical structure of its material and form perfectly, and it does so through the rhythm of the montage and patterns of its movements. The structure of the 'plot' is built around a cross-sectional reading of the city from dawn to dusk, randomly depicting hectic modern contemporary metropolitan life, loosely connected by vignettes and imaginary means of montage and collage. In contrast to Ruttmann's superficial vision, the rhythm of Cavalcanti's film is slowly paced, the sequences are more elliptical, having endings and beginnings, rather than the obsessive use of frantic and often tiresome editing and/or associative, but effective, 'stream of consciousness' thoughts. Being more episodic than thematic, Cavalcanti's vision of Montmartre, the oldest quarter of Paris, has more historical, lyrical and anecdotal episodes, more atmospheric vistas than the cold, matter-of-fact attitude and 'documentary' shots characteristic of Ruttmann's appraisal of Berlin. The historian Jay Chapman observed that Alberto Cavalcanti 'feels closest to the people of the city, while Ruttmann somewhat stands back in admiration of the rhythm of the city'.[12]

Under the influence of the French avant-garde, the Brazilian-born screen decorator, architect and documentary film-maker Alberto Cavalcanti completed his debut film as an impressionistic kaleidoscope of Paris during his stay in Montmartre. Historically and stylistically *Rien que les heures* represents an important step towards unmasked realism and marks the departure from pure impressionism. Not only was this pioneering film a genuine document within the French avant-garde cinema, it also marked the start of a new genre of 'city symphonies'. Even though Cavalcanti began his project after Ruttmann's *Berlin*, he released it before Ruttmann could finish his film. While these two films were being made, others, such as René Clair and Dziga Vertov, were working on similar subjects for films about Paris and Moscow (*Paris qui dort,* 1923; *Moskava,* 1925; and *The Man with the Movie Camera,* 1929). Both the German and the Soviet productions had greater funding and larger crowds than Cavalcanti's semi-amateur film ever achieved; nevertheless, his low-budget production became a classic.

Rien que les heures (1)

Although all of these films had the same theme – the big city as a living organism, symbol of industry and progress – they do differ considerably from each other. While the 'purist' documentary approach of Ruttmann and also of Vertov merely tries to 'abstract' and verify the material by montage and also by recoding it, Cavalcanti illustrates his tale of the city by using 'real characters', anecdotes and urban environments that speak for themselves. Cavalcanti shows his interest in people as individuals and places as locations as opposed to Ruttmann's impersonal, mechanical vision and concern for showing people as robot masses, and places as 'concepts' of juxtaposition and displacement of the spectator. By using certain melodramatic staged scenes and dramatic trick effects, Cavalcanti deliberately tries to break from abstraction and to create a sense of naturalism: life accords with chronological events and architectural history, and to some extent elements of oral history also come into play. Cavalcanti shows us vagabonds, prostitutes, a pest-ridden beggar, *flâneurs*, idlers and common folk. One can surely review his film as a pictorial homage to the underdogs of Paris.

Cavalcanti divides his story into a classic structure of Prologue, Main Theme and Variations, and then ends with an Epilogue. It is important to note the time-space framework of *Rien que les heures*. The flowing, repetitive pattern of his plot serves as a backdrop to reflect on time, since his film is mainly about the passage of time in places. He shows this quite explicitly by depicting a clock's rotating hand at the beginning and the end of the film. He stretches and compresses the intervals of movement by slow motion, freeze images and trick animation. The subjective human feeling of time dominates over the real physical schedule of events and places. Somehow this is a surrealist idea.

The camerawork is at times handled with great virtuosity and poetical moments; in contrast to Ruttmann's endless movements, *Rien que les heures* is often minimalistic and motionless. The frozen beauty of his images recalls the quietness of pictures from a camera obscura. There is often no action in the abandoned streets and romantic backyards of the decaying quarters around Montmatre. The stillness and often eerie emptiness of *Rien que les heures* is the exact opposite of the frantic montage sequences of Ruttmann's *Berlin*. Stray animals as well as sleeping or loafing *clochards* seem at times to be the only inhabitants and protagonists of the film.

Rien que les heures (2)

Today, it may seem either strange or irrelevant that *Rien que les heures* could provoke a scandal at its opening in Paris in 1926. thereby attracting the attention of the censors.

The international repercussions of the case also spurred Ruttmann and his scriptwriter Carl Mayer to visit Cavalcanti in Paris and review his film. Both were obviously so impressed by it that they considered changing parts of their own efforts while working on their *Berlin* project. It has been reported that they actually did re-shoot some episodes due to the influence of Cavalcanti's film. Because of its great success in ciné-clubs, Cavalcanti considered as late as 1945 producing a sequel with the slogan *Vingt ans après*, which unfortunately could never be realised due to funding problems.

So *Rien que les heures* remains a unique independent attempt to chart the city through characters as much as through locations. Cavalcanti was neither as radical as Ruttmann or Vertov nor as idiosyncratic as the artists of the pretentious group *Cinéma pur,* but he nevertheless remained loyal to the experimental phase of his origins in Impressionism and Surrealism. Furthermore, Cavalcanti can also claim to be the first film-maker to show the naked reality of a city by semi-documentary means, not just as a rapid kaleidoscope of random images. Even if his attempt is now an outdated and perhaps even banal version of 'Social Realism', the city itself is depicted by no means as inhumane, but as a constantly changing living cycle. The only virtue a city has is its tempo and its progress. *Rien que les heures* takes this important factor into consideration and treats it seriously.

In contrast to Cavalcanti's film, the rhythm of Ruttmann's *Berlin-Symphony* is orchestrated rather than paced, more thematic than episodic. Ruttmann pushed the formal aspects and potential of cinematography to an extreme – his creation being mainly a manifesto of movement. Concerned more about presenting as many facets of reality and activity in a city as possible, Ruttmann ignored the individual inhabitant. Much like an abstract film-essay, Ruttmann's 'camera poem' made no reference to actual people, places or events in history. Instead of pure and simple reporting, the feature-length picture tried to realise its subject-matter in terms of the potential of the film-making medium itself. Coming from a background of abstract graphic design and painting, and having earlier made pioneering abstract experimental shorts, Ruttmann created and manipulated factual material to express the 'feel' of his city through refined abstract patterns and design methods. The opening sequence of *Berlin* represents visually the musical structure of its material and form perfectly through the rhythm of its montage and patterns of images, as seen through the speed of a fast-moving commuter train towards the centre of Berlin. One can see only glimpses of blurred train tracks, train signals and the road sign 'Berlin', juxtaposed brilliantly with abstract design animations, producing an overwhelming futuristic introduction to a dynamic film.

Ruttmann's contrasting cross-sectional representation of modern Berlin does not seem to care much about a story or people's lives or about what they are actually doing in the picture. If any social aspects are suggested by rich/poor contrasts throughout the film, they are treated aesthetically and merely utilise these motifs as threads in the fabric of the film. Hunger as a social thematic feature, for example, did not interest Ruttmann very deeply. He attempted to show this aspect colourfully and perhaps ironically by injecting a lunchtime sequence with workers of various ranks eating their meals. In this sequence, 'we not only see them eating, but also horses, elephants, businessmen in pubs, ladies in restaurants, a lion, a baby, a camel, an outdoor café, the elegant banquet preparations in a hotel kitchen, a monkey, and, only then, the dishwashing machines of a large restaurant

Berlin, the Symphony of a Great City (1)

and the final end-product, garbage. All of these vignettes are rhythmically linked by editing. This lunchtime sequence is a complete sequence, opening with the workers and animals eating, and closing with them all resting.'[13] Ruttmann's strict but virtuoso rhythmic editing breaks down reality into small compartments, fragmenting a city's parts into a dynamic decomposition or recomposition, much like the Cubist method of collage.

Without a conventional script or score, Ruttmann's crew went out to grasp the 'feel' of a city, shooting as many facets of Berlin as possible, round the clock for a year, using a system of index-cards, which could be enlarged and altered upon demand. Ruttmann tried to portray a monumental panoramic vista of Berlin by editing his vast material into five orchestrated 'movements' – each reel being an act in itself – organised as a symphony and later complemented by a brilliant score by the composer Edmund Meisel. Ruttmann neither intended like so many faithful documentarists to reproduce merely an imitation of nature, nor wanted to be a political reporter or even a social commentator or critic (as did Carl Mayer, the original scriptwriter), but imagined an ultimate filmic presentation of the dynamic metropolis.

Perhaps reviewing this film now with contemporary eyes one can see better the collaboration of the director, his excellent cameramen and his composer as a unified effort of 'artistic expression' rather than the misunderstood 'documentary' effort many claimed it to be and to have failed. The film might seem to have no insight into the political and economic structure of Berlin, but its emotional power is overwhelming.

It is true that Ruttmann's image of Berlin is shaped by the hectic pace of machines and rushing traffic. A catalogue of moving parts and images unfolds; Ruttmann's vision of the city is revealed by various montage principles which were developed from the collage techniques and sophisticated movie posters by Umbo, which advertised the film's premiere and are not actually the frame enlargements for which they have often been mistaken. How much of an influence Moholy-Nagy's graphic design and his early but never realised film project *Dynamik der Großstadt* played on the shaping of Ruttmann's *Berlin* is uncertain, but nevertheless the same ideas were current at that time.

Ruttmann's fascination with endless motion and mechanics transforms the city into a machine devoid of human content. This film about the power and pace of the city provides a poetic dawn-to-dusk progression and visual impact unparalleled for its time. In fact, the film is, as its title implies, a visual 'symphony': Ruttmann – certainly inspired by the contemporary matter-of-fact photo- and cinematography of Russian and German constructivists – ventured out into the busy streets of Berlin to shoot a movie about the real life-force of a city, advocating a 'new' untouched reality outside the sheltering walls of the studio set. It is no coincidence that exactly the same people who conceived the realistic *Kammerspiel*-film were eventually frustrated with the hermetically sealed studio atmosphere and finally left the seclusion of the studio film to open the door to the exterior. Thus even the claustrophobic German silent movie had the possibility of emerging from the studio into the streets.

Another influential city poem of that era was Dziga Vertov's *The Man with the Movie Camera* (1929). 'Life caught unaware' was one of the slogans that Vertov claimed to have invented for his seemingly unrehearsed newsreel series *Kinoglaz*. Therefore the protagonist in this film is no longer any particular person but the cameraman himself or the 'camera eye' (*Kinoglaz*) itself, as it observes the streets and events of Moscow as

Berlin, the Symphony of a Great City (2)

filmic truth. However, the film-maker transforms these impressions into an emotional collage, in which diverse fragments of daily existence are mingled to achieve a new 'filmic' expression and representation of reality. All the unlimited possibilities of the cinematic apparatus and its technology are allowed to interfere, construct and change this 'picture'. Such features as reversing and/or expanding time, superimpositions, trick shots, jump-cutting and parallel montage sequences are some of the new possibilities for documentary footage for Vertov's intention, which is to influence the making of reality itself – similar to the ideas of Russian Futurists and Contructivists – not only to express his claim of 'life caught unaware', but also to reconstruct reality with technical and optical means in a new manner. 'Vertov's fame', writes Richard M. Barsam, 'was not as an editor, but as a theorist and developer of the approach to film-making that is similar in many ways to today's "cinéma vérité", or "direct cinema". Vertov called his theory Kino-Eye" … externally, the "Kino-Eye" method has much in common with the newsreel, but it is a powerful form of factual film, for its aesthetic intent is to separate and to preserve the more permanent aspects of everyday life from the transient stuff that makes up newsreels.'[14]

Besides being an essay on film truth, the film reflects on the mechanical procedure of film production; the viewer is constantly reminded that it is a film projection he is (re)viewing, and therefore the relationship between the viewer and the object becomes a playful one as well. 'We see the making of a film and at the same time the film that is being made … We get a through-the-camera view of a passer-by; see him reacting to the camera; then we see the camera as seen by him, with his own reflection in the lens. The film incessantly reminds us that it is a film.'[15] In a very imaginative way the city of Moscow is described with typographical hieroglyphics. In one characteristic superimposition we can see the camera on a tripod, seemingly the size of the Eiffel Tower, with the giant cameraman recording a vast crowd of tiny people. Vertov uses all the grammar of avant-garde cinematography to catch and construct the eventful reality and even impossibilities. We can see the cameraman in action, travelling in cars through the traffic, climbing bridge spans, smokestacks, lying on the tracks for views of trains passing overhead, constantly in action, demonstrating the importance of the reporter as documentalist. We even witness the resurrection of buildings and landscapes by means of camera tricks and freeze-frame.

Ruttmann's *Berlin* was also perceived as a non-topical 'documentary' film, attempting to create a film-object with neither a conventional plot nor the participation of actors, sets, costumes and screenplay. Ruttmann's team planned their factual film as a complex 'symphonic' structure which also included a scenario of contemplative scenes and staged sequences. A camouflaged camera in a box unnoticed by the pedestrians passing by was wheeled up and down the boulevard cafés in search of candid sensations. However there were obvious restrictions and limitations on what one could actually catch 'unaware' in front of a candid camera, so that the operating crew not only had to 'steal' their scenes from reality, but also had to cheat. Unlike honest film documentary methods, Ruttmann uses a few staged moments and occasionally scenes for 'dramatic' effect. An episode with a woman committing suicide by jumping from a bridge into the river was played by an amateur actress, and two quarrelling men on the crowded street were in fact hired provocateurs. The scene was filmed with a hidden camera, thus catching 'action' unseen,

Berlin, the Symphony of a Great City (3)

until a bogus policeman appeared. If someone became aware of the camera's presence, the film unit would stop shooting immediately. Needless to say, the sequences were assembled according to the perceived dramatic needs and arranged for the camera, and not as they might have occurred in real time. Much of the film's virtuoso moments were created in the editing room and not during actual shooting, proving the picture to be a lively demonstration of Berlin as a 'real' montage. Ruttmann's masterpiece celebrates city life just as much as he celebrates the function of the eye and the versatility/flexibility of the apparatus, the 'camera eye' being one's own lens of perception.

Berlin was a lively work which called the viewer's attention to the exquisitely controlled rhythm of editing, as well as the ebb and flow of visual rhythms within individual sequences. For Ruttmann, the essence of a city is its rhythmic spatial organisation and time structure, changing by the hour, provoking not only the viewer's perception of its diverse patterns, but also through the 'camera eye' and his own sense of perception of his environment. *Berlin* inaugurated a wave of so-called 'cross-section' or 'city symphony' films. In the wake of an emerging city tourism industry, a series of one-reel shorts appeared as travelogues, depicting postcard clichés. Being by nature mainly modest low-budget productions by independent or avant-garde film-makers, this category of factual film actually used either 'found footage' sequences or episodes extracted from newsreel prints, creating a sort of patchwork.

Ruttmann's *Berlin* succeeded in producing such an intoxicating emotional impact that it became a reference for both kinds of film genre, but nevertheless one should not overlook the fact that the same techniques were used equally skilfully by the Nazi propaganda machine. Ruttmann's new perception of reality and of a city as a religious metaphor for modernity would essentially characterise his further projects under Nazi rule up to the films he later produced on Düsseldorf, Stuttgart and Hamburg while in the Third Reich. This sort of factual persuasive documentary with a so-called detached, neutral position played a strategic role in the Nazi propaganda agenda. The Nazi leaders knew all too well how to use propaganda aids efficiently for their own purposes, and to integrate the avant-garde's once legitimate belief and enthusiasm for the technical machine age into their dictatorial apparatus. Like Lang's epic *Metropolis*, the non-fiction *Berlin* demonstrates a blind and fatal attraction to the energy, mechanics and industrial artefacts that eventually killed millions of people in war, in bombing raids, in death camps or on the killing fields of Nazi barbarism. Both Fritz Lang and Walter Ruttmann describe with childlike charm the rhythm and dynamism of modern existence, alienation and self-destruction of man in an industrial age without much morality.

City Symphonies

The preoccupation of the European avant-garde with relative abstraction took either an impressionistic or a constructivist approach.

An example of the impressionistic approach was the neat and uncritical pictorial reportage *Berlin von unten* (1928) by Alex Strasser, featuring unusual low-angle shots of hurrying feet, car tires and traffic movement from 'below' everywhere in Berlin. *Mit der Pferdedroschke durch Berlin* (1929), by Carl Fröhlich, is a sentimental observation, no more, no less. Another, perhaps even better known example, *Markt am Wittenbergplatz* (1929), by Wilfried Basse reported life on a market street through an assemblage of vignettes and picture postcards. Shortly afterwards, *Hoogstraat* (1929), by Andor von Barsy, *Images d'Oostende* (1930), by Henri Storck and, of course, Jean Vigo's celebrated *A propos de Nice* (1930) appeared. The latter along with Joris Ivens's early film shorts *De Brug/The Bridge* (1928) and *Regen/Rain* (1929) not only belong to the leading representatives of experimental cinema but also formed the vanguard of the non-fiction 'city films'. If Ruttmann's *Berlin* was a monumental 'symphony', then these later examples were definitely powerful 'movements' or a lyrical 'sonatina'. The aim of *Regen* was to show the changing face of a city, Amsterdam, during a rain shower. What appears to be a short ephemeral moment in film-making, beautifully depicting the stages of a passing shower, actually took four months to shoot. Subtitled a 'ciné poem', this little finger exercise of a master of cinematography is a lyrical, almost impressionistic picture of city life before, during and after a rainstorm. Weather, light and rain had become an obsession with its creator, as Ivens later noted:

> 'I had decided upon several places in the city I wanted to film and I organised a system of rain watchers, friends who would telephone me from certain sections of town when the rain effects I wanted appeared. I never moved without my camera – it was with me in the office, laboratory, street, train … To achieve the effect of the beginning of the shower as you now see it in the film, I had to photograph at least ten beginnings and out of these ten make the one film beginning.'[15]

With extraordinary poetic beauty and careful observation, Ivens caught the most thrilling moments of a shower over a city. The diffuse but moody lighting effects in stark black and white on the dark surfaces of the Gracht houses along the canals of Amsterdam produce striking images. Through descriptive montage of water ripples in puddles, raindrops falling from window eaves, water rushing down full gutters, pedestrians and cyclists frantically looking for cover, wet asphalt streets, umbrella spokes, dark clouds, billowing clothing on a line and glistening reflections of raindrops running down a window pane, the smallest details create a surreal, supernatural atmosphere. We are viewing Amsterdam entirely through the lenses of a rain-maker. *Rain* is less a commentary on and observation of a city than the film-maker's poetic diary of a thunderstorm in a city.

Deliberately destroying the normative character of reality and presenting a city as a syntagmatic system can be said to be part of the 'surreal' method of deconstruction practised by the French film-maker René Clair. His poetic farce *Paris qui dort* (1924) deliberately breaks with the agreed convention of time and space in the representational arts. In this grotesque adventure of a group of individuals brought together by pure chance against the backdrop of Paris and its famous landmarks, the city stands motionless as in a still-life. Clair manipulates his 'everyday' material by freezing all common human activities with the help of a few original camera tricks. Understanding not only how to manipulate reality, but also what dramatic necessity to impose on that manipulation, is the major achievement of Clair's contribution. This demonstration of how to construct out of so-called unrehearsed observed material a text which exhibits all the characteristics of drama is the fascinating aspect of *Paris qui dort*. Here the movements of life, traffic and progress – so common for a city – have come to a complete and final halt. History ends. As a result of the fact that only a few privileged people in this science fiction tale

Paris qui dort (1)

are allowed to run free in the lifeless streets, not only does this film seem absurd, but one is also surprised to note how much our perception of a cityscape is dependent on motion, speed and action.

A significant characteristic of the film is the way Clair treats his observation with lightly surrealistic touches. Clair uses these techniques to create an unreal and constructed representation of Paris for the purposes of telling of an unlikely event. The tangible reality of Paris becomes a tenuous dream-scape. It is interesting to note what a prominent role the Eiffel Tower plays in this scheme, being not only *the* most important icon of Paris, but also a symbol of modernity. The structure acts as the last remaining refuge, a 'tall tree' for the city's threatened inhabitants to retreat to in the mad jungle of urbanism, threatened of course by a mad scientist who wants to control the world with his extraordinary experiments with rays which can paralyse the planet. His ray attacks can make time stand still, much to the benefit of his criminal mind.

Logically, Clair constructs his camera sojourn through contemporary Paris out of bits which by no means necessarily go together in this particular way. Paris is seen as a collage of fragments, of diverse parts to become a series of actions of both aesthetic and personal quality. Paris is not on display, but suggests an idyllic stone desert, noteworthy for its frozen, representational, yet deadly, architecture. Shortly afterwards, René Clair completed another short film solely on the most famous landmark in Paris. This elegiac three-part study *La Tour/The Tower* (1928) is a hymn to the machine age and its steel monument.

With smaller ambitions, yet in the same mode as *La Tour*, were the sober, more newsreel-documentary efforts, like the 'lecture film' and *Kulturfilm* prototypes, which linked information with education, or summarised factual footage into a narrative framework for theatrical cinema. Customised later with sound, music or symphonic score and narration, this type of film short was extremely popular among government propaganda offices and city councils. Many of these 'lecture films' or ciné-shorts on modern architecture, housing problems and urban development were shown for congresses, schools and training programmes as well as in ciné-clubs or theatres. This sort of work was usually, however, standard industrial cinematography.

Slice of Life

No listing would be complete without reference to the film *Menschen am Sonntag/People on Sunday* (1930). This semi-documentary report marks the film debut of Robert Siodmak and Billy Wilder. Several other distinguished film authors and technicians worked on this independent production as well: Eugen Schüfftan and Fred Zinnemann on camera; Edgar G. Ulmer as a co-director. Moritz Seeler and Béla Balázs were also involved in scriptwriting, but the final draft was based on the treatment by Robert Siodmak's younger brother, Curt Siodmak. This important collective effort was much influenced by the 'matter-of-fact' tendency of German constructivist art, but *Menschen am Sonntag* heightens the banality of New Realism by sublime photography. The film depicts authentic scenes with ordinary people. No professional actors were required or wanted; the film owes its freshness and immediacy, even so many years after its release, to this unique situation.

More about actual places and people in Berlin than about the industrial pulse of a city, this is, nevertheless, the ultimate *colportage* of Berlin. This remarkable effort differs from any other similar film of its period (for example, *Emil und die Detektive,* 1931) due

Paris qui dort (2)

Menschen am Sonntag

to its imaginative observation and avoidance of clichés. The film is never a pretentious 'art' or educational didactic effort (like the increasingly pedantic *Aufklärungsfilme* of the period), nor is it a superficial pictorial reportage of the tourist perspective, nor an uneventful 'diary film' or travelogue like so many in this genre.

The picture shows a group of working-class young people in their spare time on Sunday. At the weekend, they leave their jobs, apartments and quarters for one of the surrounding lakes and woods near Berlin to camp, cook-out and picnic with their friends and neighbours. In supernatural sequences they are shown relaxing, sunbathing, swimming, playing games, and loafing about on the white sandy beaches of some modern establishments in Wannsee, flirting with their friends and joking with their elders. The film crew obviously sympathises with these like-minded young people. There is no generation gap to be felt. The film captures the spirit of a young generation's revolution, somewhat like the classic film of the 1960s, *Woodstock*.

This is about all that occurs in the film. There is no plot, no character development, no highlights or animating scenes, no beginning and no ending to this tale of an unspectacular day in the city. But it is, however, significant that the loosely knit story still tells us more about life than the usual 'fanaticism for facts' – as the Marxist critic Béla Balázs labelled the films of the New Reality – inasmuch as the record of people relaxing during the weekend expresses the attitude of these inhabitants towards city life in general and modern lifestyles in particular: the so-called 'unchained living'.

Although *Menschen am Sonntag* may have certain formal analogies with Dziga Vertov's 'camera eye' principles, it proves to be as noncommittal as the other 'cross-section' reportage films of the genre. There are no explicit or hidden political messages or rhetorical statements, nor even an ideological reference. Neither dogmatic nor political, its spirit and insight reflected only the 1920s 'new philosophy' of freedom in arts and living. In complete contrast to any ideological film that preceded it, *Menschen am Sonntag*'s contribution lay in its pure aesthetic vision. Only gradually did leftist and liberal film-makers emphasise and promulgate their ideas and propaganda into factual, heavily ideologised statements in the manner of contemporary Soviet film-makers and co-operatives. The early films of many left-wing or left-wing-associated groups are carefully researched and intensive case studies of all kinds of local phenomena and social issues, including poor housing conditions, health care, welfare, pollution, industry and town planning, which are of such important pragmatic value that their artistic quality is secondary.

Notes

1. Tom Gunning, 'Images of the City in Early Cinema', unpublished paper presented at the Getty Center 'Cine-City' conference, Santa Monica, California, 28 March 1994.
2. The flat projection plane used within a film or video camera works on a similar optical principle to that of Renaissance perspective rendering. I wish to thank Dr Earl Mark for this suggestion and his insight on the problems of visual representation.

3. Walter Benjamin's unfinished study 'Das Passagen-werk', in the original edition *Das Passegen-werk*, Rolf Tiedemann (ed), (Frankfurt am Main: Suhrkamp Verlag, 1983). See also Walter Benjamin, 'Paris: Capital of the Nineteenth Century' (1935) and 'Paris of the Second Empire in Baudelaire' (1938), in Edmund Jephcott (trans), *Reflections* (New York: Harcourt, Brace & Jovanovich, 1979).

4. Paul Rotha, 'Rise and Fall of the German Films', *Cinema*, April 1930, p. 24.

5. Jürgen Kasten, *Carl Mayer – Filmpoet, ein Drehbuchautor schreibt Filmgeschichte* (Berlin: Vistas Verlag, 1994), p. 135.

6. *Film-Kurier*, No. 289, 12 December 1921.

7. Cf. an early study by Rudolf Kurtz, *Expressionismus und Film* (Berlin: Verlag der Lichtbühne, 1926; reprinted Zürich: Verlag Hans Rohr, 1965), p. 84.

8. Cf. Lotte H. Eisner, *The Haunted Screen, Expressionism in German Cinema* (London/Berkeley: University of California Press, 1969), pp. 199–206.

9. Kurtz, *Expressionismus und Film*, p. 65.

10. *Vossische Zeitung,* 30 December 1923.

11. Stefan Grossmann, *Das Tagebuch,* 15 December 1923.

12. Jay Chapman, 'Two Aspects of the City: Cavalcanti and Ruttmann', in Lewis Jacobs (ed.), *The Documentary Tradition* (New York: Hopkinson & Blake, 1971), p. 42.

13. Richard M. Barsam, *Nonfiction Film, A Critical History* (New York: E. P. Dutton & Co., 1973), p. 31.

14. Ibid., p. 24.

15. Erik Barnouw, *Documentary, A History of the Non-Fiction Film* (Oxford/New York: Oxford University Press, revised edition, 1983), p. 63.

16. Joris Ivens, 'The Making of Rain', in *The Camera & I (1969)*, cited in Jacobs (ed.), *The Documentary Tradition*, p. 61.

Robert Mallet-Stevens

Architecture, Cinema and Poetics

Odile Vaillant

Robert Mallet-Stevens remains the pre-eminent architect of the 1930s who achieved the synthesis of architecture and cinema. He began to design film sets just after the war in 1920 and produced his two masterpieces, the film *L'Inhumaine* and his first building, the Villa Noailles, on the Riviera, both in 1924. This castle looked so much like a film set that Man Ray was asked by the owner, the Vicomte de Noailles, to film a cinematographic poem of his dwelling, *Les Mystères du château du Dé* (1928). What is, if any, the interaction between architecture and cinema in these two works?

Influences: 1886–1923

Born in Paris in March 1886, Robert Mallet-Stevens spent his childhood in Maisons-Laffitte near Paris where a mansion built by Mansart in the middle of the 17th century made a strong impression on him.[1] In his childhood, he was influenced by both his paternal grandfather, who was living in Brussels and had a fantastic Impressionist collection, and by his father, who was a famous art expert in Paris.

When he had to choose a profession, he decided to study architecture at the École Spéciale in Paris where the director, Émile Trélat, proposed a new training method based on Viollet-le-Duc's rationalist thinking and on an in-depth knowledge of the techniques which were then put into practice and into words: 'Form is at the intersection between light and matter.'[2]

While he was studying, he wrote a book entitled *Guérande* (a small town in Brittany), in which he analyses the evolution of ideas concerning the arts up to his time. 'Whoever creates an architectural pattern tries to reproduce beautiful forms to meet this ideal. When a city has an expressive cohesion, it becomes a magnificent work. Guérande is able to awaken these feelings by the interaction of its forms.'[3] Out of this first book emerge all the main principles of the spirit of the artist: ratio, expression, formal discoveries extracted from the world of geometry.

At the same time, Mallet-Stevens's uncle asked the architect Josef Hoffmann to build his house: the Palais Stoclet in Brussels.[4] There Robert Mallet-Stevens met Josef Hoffmann, who was Otto Wagner's student. Otto Wagner was famous for his research bringing together all forms of art. Hoffmann applied this to the Palais Stoclet. He built the house, designed the furniture and Mrs Stoclet's dresses and jewels: she even had to

Robert Mallet-Stevens by Man Ray (Circa, 1928)

wear these in a special room at a precise hour of the day, either in the daylight or electric light: this was 'total art'.

When the Palais Stoclet was built, Robert Mallet-Stevens had already acquired some practical experience and gained his diploma, having been a brilliant student. He began his career by participating in exhibitions and salons in France, other countries in Europe and the USA.

During the war, he served in the Air Force and learned a great deal about the rationalism of the machine. The war over, Robert Mallet-Stevens returned to his own research and work. Because of his inflexibility towards his clients, he failed to build, but he was well known as an interior designer and designed interiors for Mrs Paquin, Jacques Doucet and Paul Poiret.

Back from the war, his friend Léon Moussinac wrote about him: 'Mallet-Stevens made rationalism his own, a monster as a machine, a monster as a practice of death. Back to its first vocation, rationalism makes it possible to release art from the prejudices of education, these vulgar ornaments that reduce the mind of the architect to slavery. The purity of the lines of an aeroplane, the economy of the machine, the mathematical resistance of a concrete beam became a way of life for the young architect during this tragic war.'[5] In those days French artists were convinced that they had to work together with other European artists and artistic movements – De Stijl and the Bauhaus, for instance.

In 1920, Robert Mallet-Stevens was thirty-four and, because he met film-makers such as Raymond Bernard, Henri Diamant-Berger and Marcel L'Herbier, he began to design film sets. His meeting with Ricciotto Canudo was a crucial one.[6] Robert Mallet-Stevens was so enthusiastic that he was caught up in the development of cinema as well as his own architectural research. He helped Canudo who founded the *Club des amis du 7ième art* and *La Gazette des 7 arts,* which was published throughout Europe, and he presented his argument in a manifesto in 1924.

Palais Stoclet in Brussels

Marcel L'Herbier's *L'Inhumaine*

The cinema was already considered to be a huge industry and Hollywood was seen as a fantastic workshop. The film-maker Marcel L'Herbier, a member of the *Club des amis du 7ième art,* thought that the strength of French cinema resided in its culture: the fight with Hollywood was on. Marcel L'Herbier proposed bringing together all available artistic skills necessary to make a film.[7] He then managed to obtain the necessary finances to start his manifesto film *L'Inhumaine* in 1924.

Robert Mallet-Stevens was asked to be the art director. For him, a studio was like a factory where all human artistic activities were gathered. He saw it as a unique opportunity to analyse the various activities surrounding film sets. His thoughts were expressed in an article entitled 'Le Décor'[8] and can be summarised as follows:

He argued that a film is composed of two elements: the scenery, which is static, and the actors, who are dynamic. The art director must direct the actor and the scenery, then light them both.

How did he characterise the scenery? It is both the interior and exterior settings; it is also the furniture, the architecture, the gardens.

The Engineer's house by Robert Mallet-Stevens (*L'Inhumaine*)

First of all, it is necessary to establish the relationship between cinema and theatre. In fact, the theatre always had special sets; the early cinema had none. Cinema art directors used some very unusual interior design. If they needed a bank, a sitting-room, a bedroom, a hall, then the stage would be set up, made with a painted sheet of paper or cardboard and one or several pieces of furniture in the style of Henri II or Louis XV. Attempts to look 'modern' were worse, due to the lack of any established style.

Whatever part the film set played, realistic or expressionist, modern or antique, it had to work and be obvious before the actor entered the stage. Each period had its own special set: harmony resulted from a total intermingling.

To support his argument, Robert Mallet-Stevens explained some concepts about techniques:

1. While a stage set is designed like a painting, a film set is designed like a working drawing (*épure*). For the theatre, only a few vertical and horizontal lines are enough to evoke columns, but in films, to be more realistic, you have to consider the third dimension, which will oblige the architect to reconsider his work compared with the theatre's two dimensions. Finally, on the theatre stage the scenery is brightly coloured; on the screen it is black and white; the shapes therefore have to take the place of colour.

2. Film needs to overemphasise an object's real volume. Photography flattens an object and its several levels are restored on one vertical plan: the screen. In fact, the three dimensions are changed into two dimensions because of the perspective effect which gives the impression that the volumes disappear. We have the same difference between reality and projection and between stereoscopic photographs and ordinary ones.

3. Lighting is a real issue. If in the studios artificial light is coming from every direction, then everything will come out rather flat. However, playing with the contrast, shadow and light will help to define the volumes. For instance, a container lit up on one side gives the correct impression of a cube because of the difference between shadow and light on the other three sides. If the container is lit up on all its sides, all the faces are white and flat! Robert Mallet-Stevens proposed the following three possibilities to exaggerate the relief of a volume:

a) Paint with a dark colour the volume's shadow as it is projected onto a real element of the scenery using lateral lighting. The side of the volume in the shade will also be painted with a dark colour. However, it is impossible to change the direction of the light during shooting because the shadow is painted. If the shadow is painted in, the actors should not go into the shaded (painted) area.

b) The second way of emphasising a volume is to cut the object's shape out of the floor and then, through the use of high-angle shots, the shape will seem to appear on the floor.

c) Another way of showing depth is to locate an object in the foreground on which the eye can focus, to give the impression that the background is further away. This is a common technique used by painters and photographers (depth of field).

«qu'il soit d'abord bien établi que le modernisme de "caligari" et celui de "l'inhumaine" sont absolument différents. pour marcel l'herbier -le cubisme n'est pas le rêve d'un fou c'est le résultat d'une pensée bien nette -ce meilleur en scène a établi dans- "l'inhumaine" des images qui vous enlèvent la respiration—

c'est une chanson éclatante sur la grandeur de la technique moderne. toute cette réalisation visuelle tend vers la musique et le cri de- Tristan devient vrai 'j'entends- la lumière' -les dernières images de- "l'inhumaine" dépasse l'imagination. en sortant de la voir on a l'impression d'avoir vécu l'heure de la naissance d'un nouvel art adolf loos —

Lithograph, Jean Burkhalter (*L'Inhumaine*)

4. The film screen is rectangular and a ratio of 3:4 is standard, so any tall element of the setting is likely to be truncated. Therefore it is better to keep such elements shorter and place them lower down in the frame.

5. Because of an exaggerated perspective on the screen the furniture in the background will appear tiny while the objects in the foreground will appear rather large. All the objects, therefore, have to be positioned near to the camera. This process amplifies the impression of distance.

6. The film is black and white so it is best to paint the set with a grey colour in order to be sure you differentiate between tonal values on screen. For example, should you paint a door red and the walls green, don't be surprised if, on the black and white film, the door blends into the walls!

7. If you use masterpieces in the scenery, take care where you hang them and locate them correctly otherwise they could detract from the action! Also be warned that they will lose their colours and shapes on the screen. A less famous abstract piece might be a better solution to reconcile human life with art.

8. Finally, straight and direct lines allow for easier acting.

Besides these technical considerations, how did Robert Mallet-Stevens analyse the composition? For him, it made no difference whether the style was modern or historical. There were only two kinds of setting: a realistic one, such as a historical re-creation or a more expressionist one, and the evocation of an atmosphere. In order to respect the scenario, the actor's part and the setting's part had to be of equal importance. But the distortion of the image does not necessarily give the right sensation. Though an expressionist set gives a feeling of quietness because of its background, its lines and its colours, the effects of extravagance, novelty and freedom are given by the scenario.

Finally, it is best to act in front of a sheet of squared 'graph' paper which allows one to perceive the value of the space, even if the background is as far as possible from the actor.

You should not forget that in nature, vertical, horizontal, orthogonal lines, geometrical curves do not join; it is a clear sign of opposition, an antithesis of shapes. Therefore, the background will be designed with the characters in mind, because they are the 'ornaments', a part of the scenery. For example, a crowd, hands up, before a plain wall is a very architectural scene and shows up the composition of the scenery: geometrical lines, flat colours and contrasts. The film-maker has simply to adjust the light and the duo 'actor/ setting'. Historical scenery is not necessarily realistic, but 'The truth can sometimes be unlikely'. A camera's eye, a standard film, a lack of volume may reflect more truth than truth itself. The art director is a good observer, the camera a good recorder of details, and the film-maker can play with both. The result of his work might be better than a copy, because we know historical periods through their artistic works. 'On stage, as in life, it is necessary to consider the appearance', the appearance of truth. The actor must be the total character: cardboard might be true, china never.

La Gazette des 7 Arts (first issue, Dec. 1922)

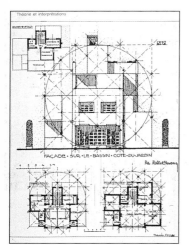

Standard layout *La Villa de 1924*
Robert Mallet-Stevens

Model, Villa Noailles, Hyères

Villa Noailles, Hyères

Finally, you must consider the public. The cinema aims at educating its public. The cinema audience witnesses its progress and asks for more and more, which is a powerful opportunity for the cinema to advance and progress.

The Villa d'Hyères and *Les Mystères du château du Dé.*

Mallet-Stevens was not interested in social architecture. In fact, he built for the upper middle class who were keen on the arts.[9]

As a set designer he discovered framed space: models and cinema sets helped him to develop his own ideas about real life. As an architect, he gave the cinema its artistic dimension: architecture was acting as much as the scenery.

Thanks to its clean lines without ornament and with its clear contrasts between light and shade, he made modern architecture become a photogenic architecture. The architect could begin to be an essential collaborator with the film-maker and, in so doing, the art director and models became necessary in theatre scenery.

Did the cinema in turn influence his architecture? His buildings were built like a film set conceived to allow camera movement.

The artists of the time were curious to see how their ideas were taken up and some tried to apply these ideas to reality. However, Mallet-Stevens thought it was wrong. For him, paradoxically, the more ornamental the details were, the more a building would appear formal and solid. Going out of the studio, Mallet-Stevens noticed immediately that artificial light does not suit a real building because then the shadows are improbable. In fact, our visual field applied to nature is much larger than when applied to film which is limited by its frame. For Mallet-Stevens, the cinema needs an architecture without ornament and the use of concrete helps this characteristic of simplicity.

After the war, the economic crisis, the domination of the machine and the birth of a modern style converged to introduce a simpler and more sober architecture. It also explains the architectural unity found in the double concept: architecture/cinema and everyday life/habitat.

But what were his ideas about architecture? First he wanted to design in a modern way and to live in his own period. The forms had to be harmonious; he meant by this true forms where everything was in the right place. His sculptural ideas invoked ratios and expressive lines. First, in 1923–4, he elaborated a polyvalent model, so that he could materialise the theoretical approach that he applied in the cinema. Because he was known as an architect who made drawings and cardboard models, he imagined a kind of prototype that he could experiment with on an adjustable layout.

What was the prototype like? He would fit a façade into a square and draw circles. He constructed a network made of vertical and horizontal lines joined by a geometrical relationship. Subsequently, a harmony emerged between solids and voids, leaving the geometrical structure in its right place. This polyhedric cube that he imagined gave his architecture an elegant and monumental aspect at the same time.

In that sense, the construction of the Villa Noailles in 1924 was the opportunity to express his ideas. He imagined a unity between interior and exterior architecture, a relationship which would organise the continuity of the design, and to obtain it he used walls, openings and terraces: 'What I mean is that a terrace with its details and ornaments would pick up the light and give it a depth of field.'

Meanwhile, he was working on Marcel L'Herbier's *L'Inhumaine* and was designing both the Prima Donna's and the Engineer's houses.

Charles de Noailles was very fond of the cinema and modern art and he wanted a house where all the arts would be represented and which would reflect a new way of life. His house completed, Charles de Noailles, in 1928, decided to commission a documentary entitled *Les Mystères du château du Dé* and asked Man Ray to film the cubist villa that Robert Mallet-Stevens had conceived. He had to film not only the architecture, the interior design, the modern art, but also the new way of life. He proposed to his friends an essentially sporting and cultural life. In fact, 'total art' became the reality of life.[10]

Man Ray made this film in its natural setting and he thus showed Robert Mallet-Stevens's architectural merits as a cinema designer and as an architect. He made a film where each image was a painting which together developed into a single large movement. By the use of the camera, 'a scientific machine', Man Ray could show the movement of the human body while still controlling it.[11]

Robert Mallet-Stevens was considered a humanist, an aesthete, an artist, a man of his time, a user of concrete, a sophisticated spirit who loved to live in a comfortable house whose volumes had a symbolic function, in opposition to Le Corbusier's 'machine à habiter'.

Les Mystères du château du Dé by Man Ray

Notes

1. Michel Louis, *Robert Mallet-Stevens, architecte* (Brussels: Éditions des Archives d'Architecture Moderne, 1980).
2. *Robert Mallet-Stevens: architecture, mobilier, décoration*, ed. Jean-François Pinchon (Paris: Action Artistique de la Ville de Paris, Philippe Sers, 1986).
3. Robert Mallet-Stevens, *Guérande* (Paris: Henri Jouve, 1904).
4. Vienne-Bruxelles ou la Fortune du Palais Stoclet', in *Archives d'architecture moderne*, 1987, no. 35,36, hors série.
5. Léon Moussinac, *Mallet-Stevens* (Geneva: Editions G. Grès, 1951).
6. Ricciotto Canudo, *L'Usine aux images,* with a preface by Fernand Divoire (Geneva: Office Central d'Édition, 1927).
7. Marcel L'Herbier, 'Le Cinématographe et l'espace: Chronique financière (1)', in *L'Art cinématographique* (Paris: Librairie Félix Alcan, 1927), no. 4, pp. 1-22, planche.
8. Mallet-Stevens, 'Le Décor', in *L'Art cinématographique* (Paris: Librairie Félix Alcan, 1929), no. 6, pp. 1-23, planche.
9. Mallet-Stevens, *Le Décor moderne au cinéma* (Paris: Charles Massin, 1928).
10. Mallet-Stevens, 'Le Cinéma et les arts: L'architecture, *Les Cahiers du mois*, 1925, no. 16,17, pp. 95-8.
11. Man Ray, *Autoportrait* (Robert Laffont, 1964).

'Only Film Can Make The New Architecture Intelligible!'

Hans Richter's *Die neue Wohnung* and the Early Documentary Film on Modern Architecture

Andres Janser

Hannes Meyer: The Standard and The Film as part of the 'new world' (1)

Introduction

Films on building, architecture and urbanism were produced in several countries from the mid-1920s on. These joint ventures of architecture and film-making had mainly propaganda or educational purposes. And they were often based on a mutually affirmative, even euphoric interest. 'Still photography does not capture them clearly. One would have to accompany the eye as it moves: only film can make the new architecture intelligible!'[1] With these words the architectural theorist Sigfried Giedion in 1928 commented on the houses in Pessac by Le Corbusier and Pierre Jeanneret. The comment illustrates the regard for film as the medium in which conceptually modern architecture as an idea can be realised. The architects thus adapted to the expanded spectrum of the media.

In most cases fiction films have been the main issue of research and debates on 'architecture and film'. I will argue that these debates need to be broadened in order to include the field of the documentary or non-fiction film which has been underestimated so far. Today it is important to acknowledge and analyse these works as original documents relevant for both the history of architecture and film, especially in the German context in which the notion *Kulturfilm* in most cases applies: the research presented here analyses industrial, advertising and propaganda films and film essays from the time of the 'International Style'. The films in question were made between the early 20s and the early 30s.

In this essay I will first comment on the New Architecture and the New Vision as well as on films on architecture in general. I will propose a classification for films on architecture. In the second part I will – as a case study – examine *Die neue Wohnung* (1930), a little known film by the German film-maker Hans Richter, and relate it to *Architectures d'aujourd'hui* (1930–31) by Pierre Chenal. Characteristically, these two films, although starting from firm common ground, reveal fundamental differences concerning their filmic strategies.

Part 1: The New Architecture and the New Vision

After the First World War a constantly growing public attended the cinema. At the end of the decade Berlin had 180,000 cinema seats and an equal number of people went to the cinema each day. The public not only grew bigger, it also changed since the middle and upper classes increasingly accepted the film as *the* new mass medium. At the same time, and partially on the same cultural basis, a film avant-garde tried to establish itself, especially in Germany and France.

This atmosphere inspired architectural magazines with a broad cultural spectrum such as *Die Form* or *Das neue Frankfurt* to publish articles on film. Like many others, the Swiss architect Hannes Meyer dealt with specific relations between the New Architecture and the New Vision. Meyer – who was to become director of the Bauhaus in Dessau from 1928 until 1930 – wanted 'to demonstrate the interrelationships of this new cultural structure'[2] and its links to the New Architecture in an issue of the architectural magazine *Das Werk*, entitled 'Die neue Welt':

> Neon signs flash, loudspeakers shriek, klaxons rattle, posters advertise, shop windows glitter: the simultaneity of the events immeasurably widens our concept of 'time and space', it enriches our lives. The constantly growing perfection of the graphic, the photographic and cinematographic processes renders possible an ever more precise reproduction of the real world. The visual image of the landscape of today is more multiform than ever: the hangars and the dynamo halls are the domes of the zeitgeist.[3]

Among his collectivist ideal of the necessities of life in the contemporary 'new world' Meyer related pictures to keywords such as The High-Rise Building, Material, International, The Stage, Photography and Propaganda. He ended the series with The Standard and, finally and significantly, The Film. This last page presented a naturalistic film, a symbolic film by Lotte Reiniger and an 'art' film by Viking Eggeling, characterised as 'spatial- temporal-rhythmic-abstract' and standing for the widened 'concept of "time and space"', whereas film in general was considered to contribute to the multiform visual imagery and to the 'ever more precise reproduction of the real world.'[4]

The new interest of many architects in the cinema paralleled the growing importance of small- and large-scale cinemas as design problems. And it paralleled the growing interest of many architects in set decoration. Finally it paralleled debates about structural analogies and differences between the film industry on one hand and the building industry and the changing professional position of the architect in that field on the other hand.

Cross-cutting: CIAM and CICI

An analogous mutual interest between the 'space art' architecture and the 'time art' film led to the fact that in November 1930 the meetings of two avant-garde movements were held at the same place and time, namely in Brussels: the third meeting of CIAM (Congrès International de l'Architecture Moderne) and the second meeting of CICI (Congrès International du Cinéma Indépendant). Both movements had been founded at La Sarraz in Switzerland. The art historian Georg Schmidt commented sharply on this parallel: '1928 the architects – 1929 the film people! Madame de Manderot, the owner of the château La Sarraz, knows where life is! The film people – of course again the avant-garde.'[5]

The architect Victor Bourgeois, a member of the Brussels group Sept Arts and vice-president of CIAM, probably initiated this convergence of architecture and film. There were no debates scheduled on the interrelationship of the two media but the film programme organised by CICI was part of the official CIAM activities. Films on architecture had

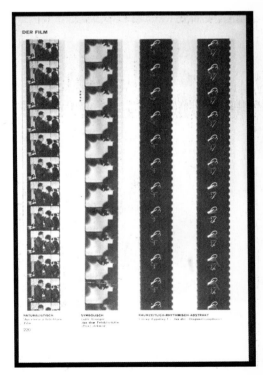

Hannes Meyer: The Standard and The Film as part of the 'new world' (2)

The members of CIAM at La Sarraz, 1928. Among others: Mart Stam, Max Ernst Haefeli, Rudolf Steiger, Hans Schmidt (back row, from left to right), Le Corbusier (in the middle), Sigfried Giedion (third from right) ...

... and the members of CICI at the same place, 1929. Among others: Hans Richter, M. Tsuya, Sergei Eisenstein, Béla Balazs, Walter Ruttmann, Léon Moussinac (second row, from right to left)

already been screened at the second CIAM congress in Frankfurt in 1929. Four years later László Moholy-Nagy shot *Diary: Architects' Congress*, the film on the fourth CIAM congress on the boat from Marseilles to Athens and back. In 1930 Mannus Franken, the Dutch delegate of CICI, made *Nederlandsche Architectuur*. This short film was the first to be produced by the Amsterdam avant-garde cinema De Uitkijk. It presented a survey on the state of modern architecture in the Netherlands since Hendrik Petrus Berlage.

The meeting of architects and film-makers in Brussels in 1930 was to be the first and the last, primarily because CICI ceased to exist. The reasons for its failure were political but also programmatic ones, casting light on the different attitudes of the avant-garde in film and in architecture towards the industry. Whereas the members of CIAM were determined to go on a 'long march through the institutions' in order to strengthen their influence on the decision-making bodies of politics and the economy, for the members of CICI such a strategy was out of the question. Under the characteristic motto of independence, the autonomy of the artist/film-maker was a clarion-call to them. A minority of CICI, including Sergei Eisenstein, Hans Richter, Léon Moussinac and Georg Schmidt, considered the situation to be more complex. However, they also regarded working for the film industry as problematic, because they were convinced that the intellectual content of the avant-garde and the industry were fundamentally different and incompatible. In the light of this view the failure of the CIAM and CICI joint venture was foreseeable within the historical situation.

Nevertheless, interest in the cinema as a mass medium cannot be separated from the debates on the aesthetics of film: films on architecture must be seen as manifestations of attitudes towards architectural as well as filmic modernity. For many protagonists, like some of the members of CIAM and CICI, the avant-garde attempt to establish a 'universal language' – a notion chosen by Hans Richter in the early 20s – seemed to bring results.

Films on Architecture: A Typology

The research presented here is focused on German and Swiss films, dealing with about sixty titles dating from the time of the Weimar Republic and twenty titles from Switzerland. Moreover, it includes selected titles from the Netherlands, France and other countries. The German films are part of the promotion of the educational film and the *Kulturfilm* in the Weimar Republic: a collection of essays on the phenomenon of these films published in 1924 presented seventy-five contributions and in 1926 a specialised catalogue of educational films and *Kulturfilme* listed 6,000 titles, all made after 1918.[6]

Whereas the first proposals for films on architecture were made around 1915, only ten years later a protagonist could write from the point of view of 'Neues Bauen': 'The growing knowledge about the importance of film as an efficient means of advertising has led to the fact that in the field of building, as well as housing too, a long series of films either are planned, begun or already carried out.'[7] On one hand, such an optimistic formulation reveals that architects believed that film was a new and useful means for propaganda purposes. On the other hand it reveals that architects were inspired by an (already) existing filmic practice.

I propose to classify the wide and heterogeneous range of films on architecture according to the way they were commissioned, a criterion which can be related to the communicative function of the films, being communication media in a specialised context. The commission certainly had a strong influence on both form and content, as well as on the way the film was to be screened.[8] Thus, the following categories can be distinguished:

1. Films for interest groups (1a) within architecture: films for architects or planners, propagating specific contents; (1b) within film: films for *film-ligues* or film-clubs, often focusing on formal or aesthetic aspects. Combining (1a) and (1b), *Wo wohnen alte Leute?* by Elisabeth Bergmann-Michel (1931) was initiated by the Dutch architect Mart Stam and produced by the Arbeitsgruppe Neuer Film. The carefully shot and edited film shows the Henry and Emma Budge Home for the Aged in Frankfurt, designed by Stam, Werner Moser and Ferdinand Kramer and built in 1929–30. (1c) Films for interest groups outside both architecture and film, such as political parties or workers' unions, often dealing with housing problems.

2. Clients had films made on either the construction of, or about the completed buildings which they had commissioned, namely (2a) institutional clients, but occasionally also (2b) private clients who could afford it. The best known film on a single (private) building is certainly the one on the Villa de Noailles in Hyères in the south of France, designed by Robert Mallet-Stevens. Man Ray was totally free to direct what became the film-poem *Les Mystères du château du Dé* in 1928.

3. Films for industry. (3a) Industrial films were commissioned by the building industry and the furniture industry, in order to document and propagate the efficiency of the companies or new building techniques. The Swiss company Losinger & Co. did so with *Der Bau der Lorrainebrücke in Bern* (1928-30) by Paul Schmid, presenting in great detail the construction of a bridge in concrete and steel designed by the Swiss engineer Robert Maillart. (3b) Advertising films, for the furniture industry and gas or electricity companies as well as for specialised exhibitions, such as *Bauen und Wohnen* in Berlin (1928) or *Woba* in Basle (1930).

4. Newsreel shots with basically informational or representational functions, as opposed to the promotional function of (most) films in (1) to (3). Newsreels occasionally presented recently finished buildings, such as the Salvation Army building in Paris (1929–33) designed by Le Corbusier and Pierre Jeanneret.

5. In addition to these commissioned films (1) to (4), there were occasional independent productions. (5a) Home movies were often made on amateur formats like the 16mm or the 9.5mm film introduced in the early 20s. Julian Stein, probably in 1928, took shots of his own villa in Garches, designed by Le Corbusier and Pierre Jeanneret. (5b) Occasionally, architects filmed the construction of buildings they themselves had designed. (5c) Independent productions for commercial release were shown in cinemas as supporting films. Such an attempt was made by the French film-maker Pierre Chenal with his architectural trilogy in 1930–31, including *Architectures d'aujourd'hui*, *Bâtir* and *Trois chantiers*.

The *Mise en Scène* of Architecture

As implied by this classification, the modes of production and distribution of films on architecture differed considerably from those of fiction films. The films, mainly short ones, were not usually produced by the film industry, being in most cases non-theatrical: they were screened at specialised exhibitions and congresses, in film-clubs and at private occasions. Only exceptionally was a film integrated into the programme of a commercial cinema.

The aim of the research is to investigate the strategies of interpretation of existing buildings and sites by means of film. In other words, the aim is to analyse the specific use and the limits of the means of film known so far for the mise en scène of architecture, as opposed to the mise en scène of set decorations designed in order to produce specific forms of expression within fiction films. Occasionally advanced techniques, such as montage and montage-tricks, superimposition, simulation with models and cartoon-like animation, were used, as in the three examples of films commissioned by interest groups that will briefly be examined.

Neues Bauen in Frankfurt-on-Main (1927–28)

A motion study (*Die Frankfurter Küche*)

In 1927 the city of Frankfurt as an institutional client commissioned a series of films on the achievements of the housing reform initiated by Ernst May. This resulted in three short films by the Frankfurt film-maker and photographer Dr Paul Wolff: *Die Häuserfabrik der Stadt Frankfurt-am-Main*, *Die Frankfurter Kleinstwohnung* and *Die Frankfurter Küche*.[9] The didactic character of these shorts is close to the *Kulturfilme*, and especially to scientific and industrial films of the period. However, avant-gardists such as Hans Schmidt showed a strong interest in scientific films which presented photogenic and 'ever more precise' reproductions of the world.

The sequences on the use of the minimal multifunctional spaces in the flats as well as the animated cartoons explaining the plans in *Die Frankfurter Kleinstwohnung* and especially in *Die Frankfurter Küche* are reminiscent of the motion studies in Frank B. Gilbreth's book *Primer of Scientific Management*. In 1917 it had been published in German as *Das ABC der wissenschaftlichen Betriebsführung*. The architect Margarete Schütte-Lihotzky was inspired by this book when designing the Frankfurter Küche. Whereas Gilbreth recommended the use of films to *improve* the efficiency of industrial production, here the film was used to *prove* the efficiency of the kitchen that had already been improved according to the 'principles of scientific management' and 'scientific management in the home', which had been put forward by Frederick W. Taylor and Christine Frederick, respectively[10]

Wie wohnen wir gesund und wirtschaftlich? (1927–28)

The series *Wie wohnen wir gesund und wirtschaftlich?/*How to Live in a Healthy and Economical Way was an ambitious project, produced by the small company Humboldt-Film in Berlin. It was supported by the Filmausschuss für Bau- und Siedlungswesen, a Berlin-based organisation founded in 1926 whose declared aim was 'to inform with educational and fiction films about the reform of housing as well as the renewal of our building methods and the spirit of building (Baugeist)'.[11] Among the members of the

Filmausschuss who were named were Adolf Behne, Walter Gropius, Ernst May, Leberecht Migge and Bruno Taut.[12]

The series, directed by Ernest Jahn, was made between 1926 and 1928. The young architect Richard Paulick, who would later work in the office of Walter Gropius, was involved in the shooting and wrote an accompanying booklet with the same title, *Wie wohnen wir gesund und wirtschaftlich?*[13] The film was a heterogeneous compilation in nine thematic parts, integrating previously existing material from different sources into the film.

Walter Gropius used frame enlargements from the films made in Dessau, especially the one shot in his own house entitled '*Neues Wohnen*'. On facing pages of his book *bauhausbauten dessau* he repeatedly combined two different kinds of visual surrogates: on the left-hand page a photograph – mostly by Lucia Moholy-Nagy – of movable as well as built-in furniture and on the right, a series of three frame enlargements of the same furniture.[14] Whereas the photographs are precisely composed and uninhabited overall views, the series of frame enlargements are presented as Gilbreth-like motion studies, showing architecture and furniture in use and in the process of being changed, adapting to different functions in the course of time in an analogous way to Paul Wolff in his film *Die Frankfurter Küche*.

Die Stadt von morgen (1929–30)

Die Stadt von morgen – Ein Film vom Städtebau, made in 1929, was probably the first film on problems of urban planning.[15] It was initiated and co-directed by the planners Maximilian von Goldbeck and Erich Kotzer, together with a group of architects and planners. It was financed by several planning departments and the Prussian Ministry of Public Welfare, thus gaining a quasi-official status.

Like the series *Wie wohnen wir gesund und wirtschaftlich?*— the first part of which was entitled *Wohnungsnot – Die Stadt von morgen* begins with the dangers and the unhealthy conditions of urban life. Soon the film turns out to be a plea for town and country planning in general. Its argument for a better future is visualised by means of elaborate animated cartoons designed by Svend Noldan, a skilled animation professional. The uncontrolled growth of an ideal town is contrasted with a planning scheme, proposing a limited growth and a series of new towns located at a distance from the (now) central town and connected by a transportation system. The film also proposes the separation of working and living areas. The town is consequently shown from a 'military' birds-eye view, using different focal lengths and alternately using an oblique and a vertical perspective. Also existing in a Dutch, an English and an American version, *Die Stadt von morgen* was frequently shown in Germany and in other countries.

Part 2: Die neue Wohnung

Die neue Wohnung, directed by Hans Richter, was commissioned by the Schweizerischer Werkbund (SWB), in order to be screened at the Woba, 1. Schweizerische Wohnungsausstellung (First Swiss Exhibition on Housing and Living), which took place from August to September 1930 in Basle. The film was initiated in November 1929 by the architect Hans Hofmann, who 'due to the experiences he had in Barcelona and Lüttich,

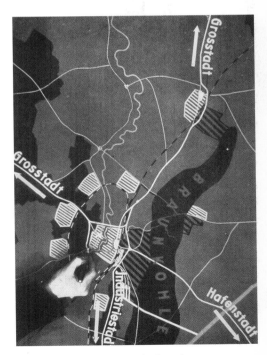

The planner's hand controls the urban development (*Die Stadt von morgen – Ein Film vom Städtebau*)

knew that the public at an exhibition is especially grateful for the opportunity to sit down, and is very receptive to instruction'.[16] A comfortable film show was believed to give easy access to a tired public! It was part of the strategy to get hold of the public where it was most easily met.

The SWB did not agree with the general idea of the Woba exhibition but wanted to be present there nevertheless. It therefore concentrated on the erection of the modern Werkbund-Siedlung Eglisee near the exhibition halls as well as on the production of a film to be shown in the halls. This film, *Die neue Wohnung*, thematically reflects the SWB's views on the debates on housing and furnishings. Formally it is clearly a work of the avant-gardist Hans Richter, who made the film together with the cameraman Emil Berna and members of the SWB. This teamwork of film-makers and architects reflects the idea of a synthesis of film and architecture.

Hans Richter: Film Expert for Architecture
It is not surprising that Hans Richter was chosen as film-maker, being the Werkbund's 'film expert' and having proved his affinity to architecture on several occasions. In architectural circles he was appreciated for his art films and for the avant-garde magazine *G,* which he edited together with Werner Graeff and El Lissitzky between 1923 and 1926. In spring 1927 Kasimir Malewitsch contacted Richter in order to discuss with him the project for an art film about his concept of a supremacist architecture. Malewitsch had drawn up a detailed coloured treatment for a film in sixteen parts with the title *Painting and the Problems of Architecture*. In this he confirmed his conviction that cubism had reached a degree of maturity 'in which the painter turns to the construction of his visual conception in space'.[17] But Malewitsch soon returned to Leningrad and Richter gave up making abstract films and turned to the poetic montage of shots taken from real life, and the project of a propaganda film on supremacist architecture was not carried out.
Working for the publicity film company Epoche, Richter made a two-minute commercial for the exhibition Bauen und Wohnen in Berlin-Zehlendorf in 1928. After the housing estate Im Fischtalgrund was completed, the furnished apartments could be visited. The buildings, designed by a group of architects considered to be traditionalistic such as Hans Poelzig and Paul Schmitthenner under the direction of Heinrich Tessenow, triggered the so-called 'Zehlendorfer Dächerkrieg' (the flat-roof versus peak-roof controversy). Right next to the Im Fischtalgrund housing with sloping roofs the first section of the flat-roofed housing, *Onkel Toms Hütte,* had been completed one year earlier, designed by Bruno Taut, Hugo Häring and Otto Rudolf Salvisberg.

Richter's commercial – made in collaboration with the cameraman Otto Tober and probably commissioned by GAGFAH, the owner of the houses[18] – may have been a reaction to the controversy aroused by the housing. On the other hand it may have been commissioned by AHAG, the building company owned by Adolf Sommerfeld, who erected the houses and commissioned temporary exhibition pavilions, designed by Walter Gropius, László Moholy-Nagy and Marcel Breuer. The commercial is probably lost. But the frame enlargement of a superimposition which Hans Richter published together with a similar frame enlargement from Dziga Vertov's film *The Man with the Movie Camera* (1929) in his book *Filmgegner von heute, Filmfreunde von morgen*[19] reveals his interest in an aesthetic experimentally developed out of the technical possibilities of film. It may be numbered among the commissions he later commented on as: 'In each of these films I tried to develop a new cinematographic element.'[20] Such an avant-gardist conception contrasts with the declared traditionalism which characterises the Im Fischtalgrund housing. However, a formalindependence between a commercial and the product it advertised was not unusual in the works of artistic directors in the 1920s.

The Making of Two Movies
In summer 1929 Hans Richter organised the programme of avant-garde films for the Werkbund exhibition Film & Foto, dedicated to the New Vision in both film and photography. After Stuttgart, the exhibition was shown in Zurich and in early 1930 Hans Richter went on a lecture tour through several Swiss towns organised by the SWB. On the occasion of these talks on 'Der Film als künstlerische Sprache' the idea of a Richter-Werkbund film must have been developed. Shooting for *Die neue Wohnung* started after the end of April and the film was first screened on 24 August. The architect Hans Schmidt had written a script, but this was only partly used. However, there are two different versions of *Die neue Wohnung*, which were made at around the same time. One version, in which SWB appears twice in the credits and Richter once, is closer to the ideas of the SWB and the situation in Switzerland. This version was probably screened at the exhibition. The other version, giving the name of Hans Richter twice without mentioning that of the SWB in the credits, is closer to Richter's more radical view and takes into account the housing problem in Germany, which was more serious.

Tabula Rasa
Both versions offer a contrasting montage of example and counter-example. The film criticises heavy and impractical furniture, unhygienic living in the kitchen, and reserving the living room only for visitors on Sunday. In a turbulent sequence the living room, or *gute Stube,* crammed full of furniture and kitsch objects such as figures of William Tell (!) and Richard Wagner, is put an end to. In its place the film makes a plea for bright and suitable living spaces: movable or built-in furniture with clear lines, practical curtains and a compact laboratory-kitchen. Healthy living in relation to nature is praised; quiet forms are recommended as a counter-measure against the hectic pace of modern life. During the whole film, dark 'old' pictures contrast visually with bright 'new' pictures.

The *tabula rasa* approach corresponds to the radical attitudes of progressive circles in the late 1920s. One reason for the clarity of *Die neue Wohnung* was certainly the effort to mark a clear counterpoint at the Woba exhibition, which was thought to be too traditionalistic. Similar reasons motivated the presence of the international examples, especially the ones from Frankfurt, which complement the Swiss buildings in the film: its internationalist tenor was meant to contrast with the nationalistic attitude present at the exhibition, due to the economic crisis.

In Search of the Standard for Furniture and Film
Die neue Wohnung is a film about principles, that is to say the good and the bad. The search for standardised furniture, developed out of the materials, had a formative influence on the activities of the Werkbund. It was also committed to the principle. The problem of industrial standardisation – the standard being one of the fundamental notions reconsidered

The living room or *gute Stube (Die neue Wohnung)*

41

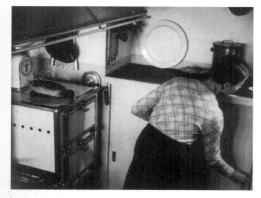

Details (1) from the Rotach-Häuser, Zürich, architect: Max Ernst Haefeli (*Die neue Wohnung*)

by Hannes Meyer – was discussed in the field of the film at the same time. Siegfried Kracauer, one of the most prominent theorists of realism in film, insisted on the fact that not the standard but the fundamental attitude behind it was important. His statements could actually stem from a Werkbund debate: 'It is not the standardisation which is to blame in film. On the contrary: instead of experimenting indiscriminately it is better to vary specific models. And besides that even the biggest corporation could not supply new and original patterns week by week. What is to blame is the "attitude" of the films.'[21]

At the end of the 20s Hans Richter tried to give the notion of the 'type' a positive connotation. To him it was a means to intensify the expression. This interest in the 'typical' was a strong connection between the Werkbund and Hans Richter. He wrote in the SWB magazine *Das Werk* in September 1929: 'Instead of simply photographing the natural motion we raise its expression beyond the natural event, by means of superimposition or optical prisms. We heighten the single event to the typical by suppression of the particular, we make "screaming people", excitement in itself, out of the material.'[22] This principle of generalisation was a principle of anonymity subordinating the technical premises of creation to a social responsibility. It was equally valid for *Die neue Wohnung*. On the one hand the designers and manufacturers of the proposed solutions remain unnamed: the ideas are not personalised. With the same attitude the Swiss architects had participated before in the 1927 Werkbund exhibition Die Wohnung in Stuttgart-Weissenhof: the flats they had furnished in the Mies van der Rohe building were attributed to a collective group, not to individuals.

On the other hand, up to seven details of specific buildings can be seen in *Die neue Wohnung*. But the connections of the parts with the buildings they belong to remain undeclared. This can be exemplified by one of the important buildings of modern architecture in Switzerland: the Rotach-Häuser designed by Max Ernst Haefeli, built in 1928 on the bank of the River Limmat in Zurich. A view from inside of one of the living rooms looking out onto the river was used in 1929 by Sigfried Giedion for the cover of his booklet *Befreites Wohnen*.[23] Henry-Russell Hitchcock Jr and Philip Johnson published the plans and the side and back elevation of the Rotach-Häuser in *The International Style: Architecture since 1922*.[24] However, exterior views cannot be seen in the film.

The details that can be seen, in the order in which they appear in the film are: the open hall beneath the house; the window looking onto the river; the small laboratory-kitchen; the serving hatch between the kitchen and the dining room; the dining room with the built-in cupboard; and the living room. This filmic deconstruction of buildings serves the presentation of themes, as opposed to the presentation of specific houses. Sigfried Giedion formulated and practised in his *Befreites Wohnen* a similar journalistic strategy: 'We do not want to impart the knowledge about single buildings but the CONCEPTION [*Anschauung*] of today. Therefore it was necessary to tear the buildings into details and assemble them where it seemed feasible.'[25]

A Different Attitude: *Architectures d'aujourd'hui* (1930–31)
A comparison of *Die neue Wohnung* and the film *Architectures d'aujourd'hui* by the independent film-maker Pierre Chenal shows clearly that starting from firm common ground substantial differences were eventually developed. *Architectures d'aujourd'hui*

was part of the architectural trilogy initiated by Chenal. The trilogy also included *Bâtir* and *Trois Chantiers*.[26] *Bâtir* shows in great detail the construction of a large building in steel and reinforced concrete and denounces the tradition of 'decorating' the façades, contrasting them with modern examples such as the Citroën garage in the rue Marbeuf and ending with Le Corbusier presenting the model of the Salvation Army building, then under construction. *Trois Chantiers* focuses on construction sites of dams and bridges like the Pont de Plougastel, designed by the engineer Eugène Freyssinet.

Architectures d' aujourd' hui was made in collaboration with Le Corbusier, a member of CIAM. At that time the SWB comprised the Swiss members of CIAM: namely Rudolf Steiger, Werner Moser and Siegfried Giedion. The collaboration of film-makers and architects took place at a moment when the two avant-garde movements they were all part of unsuccessfully tried to establish a joint venture. Pierre Chenal was the only protagonist who was not part of these movements. Both films were independent productions made at about the same time in the summer of 1930. Subsequently they were screened together in Paris, at a soirée organised by the architectural review *L'Architecture d'aujourd'hui* and attended by 3,000 people. A second 'meeting' in Frankfurt was planned but in the end *Architectures d'aujourd'hui* was not screened.

In both films, the use of cinema as an instrument for internationalist propaganda was concerned with the issue of housing – housing problems, the single house and housing projects on an urban scale. For that purpose they both establish a filmic interpretation of a series of well-known buildings, designed by several architects, but some being dominant in each case: Haefeli and Steiger in the Swiss film, Le Corbusier and Pierre Jeanneret in the French one. Finally, they both use narrative elements, without being narrative in a strict sense.

In order to compare the interpretation of the architectural space in *Die neue Wohnung* and *Architectures d'aujourd'hui*, two notions by Maureen Turim seem to be helpful: referential space and conceptual space.[27] A referential (filmic) space is structured in analogy to the given structure of an existing space but also according to the representational apparatus, mainly perspective, reference and symbolism. A conceptual space is based on the original method of film, subordinating one or more existing spaces to an intellectual concept, comparable to what Hans Richter called *Ideenassoziation* (intellectual association).

In *Architectures d'aujourd'hui* both the chronology of time and the relation of spaces remain untouched, referring to the real world according to the perspectival centring of the viewing subject on which filmic spaces are usually constructed. Identified buildings are set in motion by an organic montage, focusing on the experience through use. Processes – rather than objects – are documented, as for instance the slightly stretched *promenade architecturale* on the ramp of the Villa Savoye. A house is a house – or rather a 'villa' – and the personalisation is made explicit through the declared presence of Le Corbusier. A series of iconic images that encode single buildings as emotive objects is carried out with the photographic logic of stills. Compared to the development of the documentary film at the end of the silent era, which Hans Richter stood for, the films of Pierre Chenal remain restrained. On the other hand, he worked with light in an interesting way, interrelating architectural light and filmic light.

Details (2) from the Rotach-Häuser, Zürich, architect: Max Ernst Haefeli (*Die neue Wohnung*; credit: Schweizerischer Werkbund/Institut für Geschichte und Theorie der Architektur, ETH Zürich)

Villa Savoye, Poissy, architects: Le Corbusier &
Pierre Jeanneret *(Architectures d'aujourd'hui)*

In contrast to *Architectures d'aujourd'hui* most of the buildings in *Die neue Wohnung* can hardly be identified: the film does not present spatial sequences of entire houses, so their villa-character (which would have been inappropriate for the middle-class public at the exhibition) is dissolved. The camera captures only fragments of space and the thematic montage mixes fragments of different buildings. Both decisions serve the concept of the 'type': *the* living room, *the* chair, *the* window. In addition to that, none of the (amateur) actors can be seen throughout the film, thus keeping the public from identifying itself with a single face or person. Through this interest in the typical, *Die neue Wohnung* differs from most of the films on architecture made around 1930.

In *Die neue Wohnung* the houses are neither named nor located. Only insiders were able to identify the fragments of the architectural objects. By means of fragmentation and filmic montage a miraculous augmentation of the few buildings considered to be good was achieved. In the case of the living room, even a single space is manipulated: the shot of the people dancing in the living room is cut into short pieces, every second piece turned round and respliced. Through this simple montage the impression of a more complex, at any rate a bigger space, is achieved.

With the help of Le Corbusier, and clinging to film impressionism, Chenal transforms identified and personalised architecture into referential spaces. Richter transforms 'anonymous' architecture – recognisable only to a professional public – into conceptual spaces, dominated by fragmentation. He uses his experience with montage and film tricks to support a thematic argument for the type and the standard, in accordance with the architects' interest in industrialisation and the *Typenmöbel*. Thus the juxtaposition of architectural and filmic concepts led to specific solutions reflecting different debates on modernity and modernisation going on in France, Switzerland and Germany.

Conclusion

General conclusions are difficult, since many of the films on architecture from the 1920s and early 30s are presumably lost. Fortunately some of the films on modern architecture are preserved, which is no coincidence, given the avant-garde impetus behind them. However, it will remain difficult to say whether these films are typical in relation to the whole production of films on architecture of the period.

However, the wish for films to be instruments of mediation for the New Architecture – as expressed by Sigfried Giedion and others – was only partially fulfilled. On one hand film did not replace photography as the major medium of visual representation of architecture. This was mainly for structural reasons, such as the considerable financing required for the production of films and the complications involved in screening them. But there was to be, in fact, promotion of the *Städtebaufilm* (films on questions of urban planning) during the reconstruction period after the Second World War. On the other hand, when Giedion expressed his wish at the end of the 20s, it had already become clear that not only modern but all architecture could successfully be turned into film.

Nevertheless, it would be wrong to expect that a film on avant-garde architecture necessarily turned out to be an avant-garde film. First, because the notion of avant-garde is problematic in itself, it would be wrong to underestimate the achievements of the 'ordinary' *Kulturfilme* on architecture as a means to propagate specific contents to a general public. Second, the two media have their own respective logic and inner structure.

In the long run the differences remained stronger than the similarities. Nevertheless, the mutual interest between architecture and film based on these similarities led to the production of important films around 1930.

Notes

1. 'Sigfried Giedion, *Bauen in Frankreich – Bauen in Eisen – Bauen in Eisenbeton* (Leipzig/Berlin: Klinkhardt & Biermann, 1928), p. 92.
2. Hannes Meyer, 'Autobiographische Skizze', *Daidalos* no. 52, June 1994, p. 110.
3. Hannes Meyer, 'Die neue Welt', *Das Werk,* vol. 13 no. 7, 1926, pp. 205, 221.
4. Ibid., p. 220.
5. Georg Schmidt, 'Der Internationale Kongress für den Unabhängigen Film in La Sarraz', *Das neue Frankfurt* vol. 3 no. 10, October 1929, p. 207.
6. Definitions of the notion *Kulturfilm* differed. For instance, advertising films in most (but not all) cases were not included. Cf. Walter Uricchio, 'The "Kulturfilm": A Brief History of an Early Discursive Practice', in Paolo Cherchi Usai, and Lorenzo Codelli (eds.), *Before Caligari – German Cinema 1895–1920* (Pordenone: Le Giornate del Cinema Muto, 1990), pp. 356–78.
7. Richard Paulick, *Wie wohnen wir gesund und wirtschaftlich?* (Berlin: Filmausschuss für Bau-und Siedlungswesen, 1927), p. 32.
8. Starting with this functional criterion, additional criteria – such as the number of buildings presented, the building types, specific buildings and/or architects, the time-structure or the chosen means of film in general – are of course useful. [Hahn, Fachkommunikation:] These parameters consist of the public a film is addressed to, the distance of communication, the message transmitted ('Handlung').
9. Cf. Kristin Vincke, 'Kleine Stadt, ganz gross – Frankfurt im Dokumentarfilm zwischen 1920 und 1960', in Hilmar Hoffmann and Walter Schobert (eds.), *Lebende Bilder einer Stadt - Kino und Film in Frankfurt am Main* (Frankfurt: Deutsches Filmmuseum, 1995), pp. 132–41.
10. Cf. Nicholas Bullock, 'First the Kitchen – then the Façade', *AA Files* no. 6, 1984, pp. 58–67.
11. Filmausschuss für Bau-und Siedlungswesen', *Deutsche Bauzeitung* vol. 60 no. 71, 1926, p. 584 (unsigned).
12. Paulick, *Wie wohnen wir?* (1927), p. 34. The actual activities of these protagonists within the Filmausschuss are not yet clear.
13. Ibid.
14. Walter Gropius, *Bauhausbauten Dessau* (Munich: Langen, 1930)
15. Only ten years later, in 1939, two films on urban planning entitled *The City* were made in the USA and in Great Britain.
16. Peter Meyer, 'Werkbundfilm', *Das Werk* vol. 19 no. 1, January 1931, p. 29. In 1929 Hans Hofmann had designed the Swiss section at the International Exhibition in Barcelona. It included a small movie-theatre where films selected by the Swiss Chamber of Commerce were shown. In the 30s a cinema became standard practice in the Swiss pavillions.

17. French translation and facsimile of the treatment in Christophe Czwiklitzer, *Lettres autographes de peintres et sculpteurs* (Éditions art-c.c., 1976), pp. 487f.

18. GAGFAH = Gemeinnützige Aktien– gesellschaft für Angestelltenheimstätten.

19. Hans Richter, *Filmgegner von heute, Filmfreunde von morgen* (Berlin: Hermann Reckendorf, 1929), p. 12.

20. Hans Richter, *Der Kampf um den Film* (Munich and Vienna: Carl Hanser, 1976), p. 169.

21. Siegfried Kracauer, 'Der heutige Film und sein Publikum', *Frankfurter Zeitung,* 30 Nov. and 1 Dec. 1928. Reprinted as 'Film 1928', in Siegfried Kracauer, *Das Ornament der Masse* (Frankfurt: Suhrkamp, 1977), p. 296.

22. Hans Richter, 'Film von morgen', *Das Werk* vol. 16. no. 9, September 1929, p. 281.

23. Sigfried Giedion, *Befreites Wohnen* (Zurich/Leipzig: Orell Füssli, 1929).

24. Henry-Russell Hitchcock Jr and Philip Johnson, *The International Style: Architecture since 1922*, (New York: Norton, 1932), pp. 148f.

25. 'Giedion, *Befreites Wohnen*, p. 4.

26. See Andres Janser, 'Le Corbusier und die filmische Propaganda für moderne Architektur', *Archithese* vol. 22 no. 5, September/October 1992, pp. 56–60.

27. See Maureen Turim, 'The Displacement of Architecture in Avant-Garde Films', *Cinéma & Architecture = iris* no. 12, Paris 1991, pp. 25–38.

PART TWO

The Modern City I

London/Paris/New York/Rome

Introduction

Gavin Hogben

The Mitterand era brought the world not only the *Grands Projets* but also the spectacular last-minute hijack of the GATT trade talks over the protection of French films. Less publicised but equally revealing of Mitterand's cultural agenda was a raft of Petits Projets: neighbourhood renewals devised with architects and film-makers working together as urban pathologists. In New York, the Mayor's Office of Film bids against rival cities and studio lots to bring location work to its streets. In Paris and New York, the answer to the questions how and on what grounds architecture should meet film evidently must be the city itself, or at least homage to, or propaganda of the same. But are architecture and film simply the representational servants of a prior reality of city? And further, as the novel was said to eclipse architecture as the primary vehicle of civic representation in the early 19th century, does film now doubly leave architecture in the shadows, perhaps as no more than a scenic backdrop for the actions by which film captures the city in flux? Or is it more likely that far from a prior reality the city itself is a construct of the parallel projected hard and soft fictions of architecture and film?

With cinema we step through a chink in time and space to visit our favourite cities, here London, Paris, New York and Rome. We know their situations, their personalities, their eccentricities, even their pathologies so well, and yet, even when we come to visit one or other of them, we may never venture beyond the envelope of our fictive experience. Widely as we may be travelled, it is astonishing how many cities we are content to know in this way, as projected fictions (even propaganda). But these half-truths serve us more than a truth. They are measured not by faithfulness to the spatial, social, political actualities but by the degree to which individually and as a set they define all the possible histories and geographies not our own – the plurality that is definitively not home. In this sense, even the movies that are about our home city depict a strange place not of our actuality, but, all the same, contributive to the horizon points that mark its limit.

The articles which follow range across many of the horizons, territories and propositions which bind architecture, film and the modern city, and we are introduced to the multiple spurious geographies of Rome, the two non-intersecting New Yorks of Scorsese and Allen, the new London which would efface the old, and Tati's wry observations on architectural transplants and cultural immunities.

With the close-up encounters of New York streets, rooms, skylines in the films of Scorsese and Allen, the architecture emerges from the shadowy role of backdrop or scrim to take on a narrative part. Design and place act alongside the cast.

However, with Tati, it is as if the architecture frame passes beyond the simple plot advancement role of 'fifth business', even beyond the part of protagonist, to become the master storyteller/director. The architecture establishes the choreography, the rhythmic structure of action and dénouement (indeed radically easing the grip of narrative), and most importantly sets the self-mocking tone. Surprisingly, Tati's character Hulot is perhaps the straight man to this architectural comic force. Here the comedy is not played out in front of the architecture, but that architecture is itself the opportunity and provocation for an action/humour that is self-characterising.

The most valuable aspect of Tati's treatment of architecture within *Playtime* is his meditation on corporatism as a social and architectural force characterising the modern city. It is corporatism's international style that *Playtime* lampoons, and functionalism that is the point of Tati's attack. Hulot/Tati's problems are with function – whenever there is a purpose expressed as a form, Hulot misconstrues, misapplies, mistimes.

Hulot and swing doors – no, they slide. Hulot and motor cars – his very body is a tall misfit and affront to the functional norms of the car. And yet, Hulot is triumphant – his tennis method, his humour, prevail. Tati's crusade is against the monovalent detached object of modern functionalism, and is for the idea that things and place have multiple attributes and meanings which are in a constant state of mutual exchange with the neighbours that make their context. In Tati's analysis, architecture's nineteenth and twentieth century obsessions with function are the precise cause of its eclipse by literature, or, later, film. To compete with the dynamic of the nineteenth century locomotive, architecture ignored all but its constructional *raison d'être*, process and purpose. Similarly, challenged by twentieth century film it now apes that medium's characteristics of action, reflexivity, and ephemerality by a display of mobile, even intelligent, elements and an attenuated, flimsy materiality – buildings rushing towards interactive, sub-robotic self-parody. Tati's lesson here is that a building is not a programmed box of tricks like a microwave oven or a gameboy, that indeed its great merit lies in resistance to changefulness, in a temporality that is synchronic (in contrast to film's tendency towards diachronic expansion of a static instant). Architecture's proper state is the impassive countenance of an Olympian detachment. Only as this impassivity is recognised can architecture (as Tati coaxes it to do) revert from the pursuit of isolated functional icons towards upkeep of the continuity of architectural settings which in their entirety constitute urban tissue.

In this scenario, architecture and film emerge as complementary in their processes. Film supplies the action that puts architecture into motion, but equally architecture, by its particular emptiness, spurs the motive, not as subject or object of an action but as opportunity and potential. As architecture apes film, film can say less and less, and is pushed into territories of the historic or the futuristic, where that sustaining glimpse of what we call the city, dependent as it is upon the mutual provocation of film and architecture, is dangerously narrowed.

Imagining the Post-War World

Architecture, Reconstruction and the British Documentary Film Movement

Nicholas Bullock

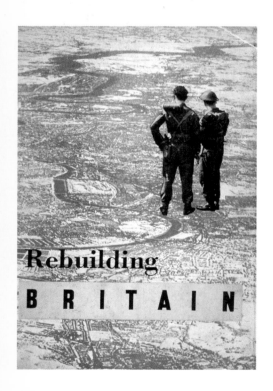

Rebuilding Britain Exhibition 1943

The leaders of the British documentary film movement, John Grierson and Paul Rotha, regarded education and social reform as central to the work of the documentary film movement Grierson stated that his ambition as a film-maker was 'to command, and cumulatively to command, the mind of a generation'.[1] This sense of proselytising, this concern to change the world is evident in the nature of the films and in the public pronouncements of those involved in making them. Paul Rotha places the same emphasis on this view of documentary film: 'Briefly, I look upon cinema as a powerful, if not the most powerful instrument for social influence today; and I regard the documentary method as the first real attempt to use cinema for purposes more important than entertainment.'[2]

It was the ability of film to present a particular point of view that constituted one of its principal attractions as government sought to rally the nation at the beginning of the Second World War. What better means could be found of telling people what they were fighting for and why it was necessary to make the sacrifices that they were being called upon to make. As wartime government conscripted the documentary film movement to present its case to the people, it was only doing in 1940 what business and government sponsors had done in the 1930s.

In the early days, it was Grierson's ability to translate what he understood of the American practice of public relations into film that had prompted Stephen Tallents to hire him in 1926 to make films for the Empire Marketing Board. Film-makers and film-making did not always fit easily into government or commercial organisations. But, despite Grierson's battles with the Treasury and the civil service hierarchy at the GPO, there was unanimity on this value of film as a way of championing a particular set of values in its most accessible form. All were agreed that film made it uniquely easy for the audience to absorb the mesage.

This quality was as attractive to all who wanted to put across a point of view: business, politicians, government, all those in the business of selling ideas.[3] The use of film to present the case for business and to advertise this or that product is well established. So too is the use of film by different political parties: if the Conservative Party was the first into the field in using mobile projector vans to get across the party message, Labour was soon just as enthusiastic about exploring the new medium. But, for the leaders of the documentary film movement, the use of film for partisan propaganda of this form was less important than the possibilities of using documentary film to educate and to change people's attitudes to broad social issues.

Early on, the advantages of film were recognised by those in Britain keen to challenge the complacency of government about social questions.[4] During the 1920s a number of local authorities had started using film not for political purposes but to educate and inform those for whom they were responsible. In Bermondsey, for example, cinema vans travelled around the borough preaching the benefits of cleanliness with films like *Where There's Soap, There's Life*, and films vaunting the services of the borough's fumigating and delousing facilities. Using this kind of approach, street-corner audiences of children and others could be told of the reforming programmes promised by the borough council and the plans of Dr Salter.[5]

By the 1930s film was being used to reinforce the case being made for government action on key issues like slum clearance, health and unemployment. The films made by the Gas, Light and Coke Company may not have been aggressive in overtly political terms – they were a product of commercial sponsorship, albeit by an organisation with a liberal nonconformist ethos – but films like *Housing Problems* (1935), *The Nutrition Film: Enough to Eat* (1936), *The Smoke Menace* (1937) and *Children at School* (1937) did much to dramatise the plight of the less fortunate members of British society in the 1930s, and the indifference of the official eye to social problems of this kind.

Housing Problems represents one of the best examples of the pre-war documentary social campaigning films to address questions of architecture and housing. It demonstrated to those pressing for change and the modernisation of the city the advantages of film as a way of winning a large non-theatrical audience to these causes. The film treats with apparent detachment the families who address the camera directly in what pass as their own words in order to provide the direct documentary evidence on the slums. Despite the size of the cameras and the equipment necessary for sound, Anstey and Elton were able to shoot on the spot, encouraging the slum-dwellers to 'simply talk for themselves, make their own film'.[6] The deadpan quality of Anstey and Alton's presentation of the subject was praised by Graham Greene for being 'superbly untroubled by the aesthetic craving'.[7] It is this very quality that conveys the sense of impartiality and of factual authenticity. Perhaps to modern audiences, rendered infinitely more knowing than audiences of the 30s by exposure to television and an all-pervading film culture, the techniques of the film look dated. But for contemporaries film like this was a powerful spur to reform.

The War-time Debate on Reconstruction

The war created entirely new opportunities for documentary film. Given the identification of the documentary movement with social reforming causes and the recognition by government of the value of film for propaganda, it was not surprising that governments on both sides should have enlisted the documentary film-makers immediately when war broke out. Government-sponsored film-makers such as the GPO film-unit as well as those working on documentaries for commercial sponsors were brought together under the wing of the Ministry of Information (MOI) to make films as part of the war effort. This history, together with the establishment of the Films Division of MOI, the setting up of the Crown Film Unit, and the key roles played by figures like Jack Beddington has been

A Bermondsey Cinema Van

The Southwark slums (*Housing Problems*)

Model of Kensal House (*Housing Problems*)

Fires Were Started

Army Bureau of Current Affairs poster

extensively documented elsewhere.[8] Much too has been written about the value of the films to the war effort, particularly to the task of maintaining morale both in the services and in the civilian population, but less has been said of the value of film in shaping the debate on reconstruction.[9] Government wanted films to tell people not only how it was fighting the war but how it hoped to set about the tasks of reconstruction when the war had been won.

The kind of skills that the Crown Film Unit was using to present the achievements of the services in films like *Target for Tonight* (1942), *Coastal Command* (1942), *Close Quarters* (1943), *Fires were Started* (1943), were already being deployed long before the end of the war to explain to the vast mass of the population how the war that they were fighting would lead to a new and better Britain. To the bomber crews stood down because of the weather or to the troops preparing for D-Day, documentary films shown along with full-length feature films in mobile cinemas were intended to provide a way of making vivid and believable the message about government policy that the Army Bureau for Current Affairs and the Army Education Corps were struggling to get across in their 'briefings' and publications like *The British Way and Purpose*.[10]

Nowhere was the task of lifting morale and explaining government plans more important than in discussions about reconstruction on the home front. Mass Observation, along with other bodies who were monitoring public opinion and civilian morale, recorded the strength of feeling in the forces and amongst civilians alike on this subject.[11] All were united in wishing to believe that the post-war world really would be better than the pre-war world with its inequality and unemployment. If a job was the first priority, a reminder of the bitter unemployment of the 30s, the second priority for both men and women was for a home. People wanted to feel they were fighting to give something better to their children. More, they wanted their cities to be rebuilt to provide better housing, new schools, more green space.

This discussion about reconstruction was being encouraged by government from Dunkirk onwards and gathered pace with the beginning of the Blitz in September 1940.[12] Within less than a fortnight of the start of the first heavy raids on the East End, the BBC Third Programme had launched a series of talks by architects and planners on the rebuilding of London which was to run over the next eighteen months.[13] Lewis Mumford, author of *Culture of Cities* and historian of the American city, and Clough William Ellis, author of *England and the Octopus* and tireless campaigner against suburban sprawl, were asked to present their views on the future of the city. John Summerson talked of the way that Le Corbusier had envisaged rebuilding the entire centre of Paris. Young architects like Leslie Martin and Richard Llewelyn Davies talked optimistically of the way in which standardisation and prefabrication would transform the task of rebuilding housing.

By the end of 1942, a critical year for the debate on reconstruction, the government could point to a host of initiatives.[14] Committees had been established to look at new forms of construction, to examine new standards for housing and for schools; plans were being commissioned up and down the country: even the LCC had called for a plan for the County of London, and, beyond that, for the greater London region. Looking back on the wartime plans that government was making for reconstruction, Richard Titmus, an acute observer of social processes in wartime, stressed the critical importance for morale of persuading people that government was indeed making just these kind of plans:

'There existed, so to speak, an implied contract between Government and People; the People refused none of the sacrifices that the Government demanded from them for the winning of the war; in return, they expected that the Government should show imagination and seriousness in preparing for the restoration and improvement of the nation's well-being when the war had been won.'[15]

But how could government convey the qualities of the plans it was making? The radio was a natural medium of verbal communication but rather an abstract way of encouraging discussion of what the new post-war Britain should actually look like. The quality newspapers took seriously the task of leading the debate and illustrated magazines such as *Picture Post* did much to publicise the kind of plans that government was making, but too often this kind of publication failed to reach the vast mass of the population whose morale was central to the war effort. Yet it was for these people – the factory worker, the miner, the agricultural labourer, the soldier, the merchant seaman – that the New Britain was to be built. How could they be encouraged to start thinking what it might be like?

Documentary film provided one of the most immediate means of reaching out to these people. Shown to non-theatrical audiences in the forces, in factory canteens and, under the arrangements contracted between the Ministry of Information and the Cinematograph Exhibitors Association, in commercial cinemas along with mainstream feature films, the films made by the Ministry of Information were capable of reaching a wide audience. It is difficult to gauge their effect.[16] The evidence is fragmented and contradictory: *Kine Weekly* records examples of MOI shorts being shown to empty houses in the morning, or being run when audiences were changing their seats between features; on the other hand, MOI films, for example *Target for Tonight*, enjoyed considerable commercial success. The size of audiences for MOI films generally, and films on the physical form of reconstruction in particular, remains the subject of partisan debate. But the ability of documentary film to present these issues is clear: Pronay lists fifty-four films that dealt with reconstruction and Britain's peace aims and were produced or bought and distributed by MOI between 1940 and 1945.[17] Taken together these films are a remarkable testament to the vitality of the discussion and the hopes for reconstruction.

The challenge for the documentary film movement was to show how this new post-war Britain might look. In the absence of finished designs the film-makers had to convey the unprecedented scale of the opportunities for rebuilding and replanning Britain's cities. In films like *New Towns for Old* (1942), *When We Build Again* (1942), *A City Reborn* (1945), *New Builders* (1945), *The Plan and the People* (1945) and *Proud City* (1945), the documentary movement set about encouraging people to think about how new housing, schools and neighbourhoods would look after the war.

Imagining a Post-War Britain

The task was daunting: how were the film-makers to convey the scale and the diversity of the opportunities? Would they seek to create the illusion of a future Britain, using the kind of sets that had been created by Moholy-Nagy for *The Shape of Things to Come* to suggest a modernist Utopia? Would they favour a particular style of architecture? The relationship between architectural style and social policy or political conviction has always been vague, but by the end of the 1930s a loose linkage had been established between the

Army Bureau of Current Affairs: briefing session

Patrick Abercrombie (*Proud City*)

Explaining the County of London plan
(*Proud City*)

Model of the Stepney Reconstruction Area
(*Proud City*)

new architecture and social reform. Of course there were exceptions: the LCC, controlled by Labour since 1934, continued to build suburban cottages in the arts and crafts style or tenements in the stripped classical manner that had been used by the council under moderate control since 1919. But widely publicised examples like the Finsbury Health Centre built for the Labour-run Borough of Finsbury by Tecton, or Kensal House built by a collective of young architects (and the housing expert Elizabeth Denby) for the London Coal and Coke Company could be used to illustrate the strength of the connection between the architectural avant-garde and social reform. This connection had also been exploited in film, particularly in the documentary films of the 30s. In the last section of *Housing Problems*, for example, Anstey uses shots of a model of Tecton's winning entry for a competition for working-class flats and film of the model of Kensal House to show what modern housing could be like if the slum campaign were to succeed. Footage of families enjoying their leisure time at the Peckham Health Centre designed by Owen Williams reinforced the link between the promise of social reform and the New Architecture before the war.

But this kind of association, straightforward in the 30s, no longer seemed so clear-cut nor so obvious in wartime. The war demanded new values, new priorities: the equivalence between modern architecture and progressive social policy is barely detectable in the run of films made by the documentary movement on questions of reconstruction. In films like *New Towns for Old*, *When We Build Again*, *The Plan and the People* and *Proud City*, all of which treated questions of rebuilding and planning, modern buildings may be shown but their significance as the face of a future Britain is no longer emphasised.

How then was film to convey how post-war Britain would actually look? Certainly the vision that was being presented in these wartime films was the very opposite of futuristic. In *Proud City*, which describes the way in which Abercrombie and Forshaw were setting about the planning of London and the London region, or in *When We Build Again*, which explores the way in which Birmingham was to be rebuilt after the war, the emphasis is on the familiar and on humanising the plans that are being made. Thus in *Proud City* Abercrombie is presented (as indeed he was) as a benign if slightly eccentric figure with his monocle and his tweed suit who leads the viewer in friendly fashion through his plans for London. He stabs at images and diagrams with the stem of his pipe, explaining the central ideas of the County of London Plan and the Greater London Plan in terms that would have been readily understood by all. The planning principles that he expounds, the control of suburban sprawl, the consolidation of density within the Green Belt, the opening up of more open space, are all set out as being the product of good sense and well-tried practice. The radical nature of his proposals is glossed over and the plans are presented as being free from polemical or ideological taint of any kind. Indeed, there is little real attempt to show what post-war London might actually look like. In *The Plan and the People*, for example, in a set of shots devoted to a model of a rebuilt section of the city, the ability of film to create a sense of the future is played down; instead the camera focuses on the crowds looking at the model as if to emphasise public approval of the designs. The images of architecture in so far as they are emphasised at all are variously of stripped classicism, the arts and crafts, and views of what the pre-war architectural avant-garde had unflatteringly called 'soft modernism'. There is no highlighting of the role to be played by the modern architecture of the avant-garde.

This lack of interest in exploring the architectural challenges of reconstruction might be explained in a number of ways. Beyond the different issues addressed by individual films, there are a number of general considerations to bear in mind. First, it is important to remember that the general case for reconstruction was a case that still needed to be made, and made against the prevailing attitudes of the pre-war years. Moreover, there was strong opposition within government, not least from Churchill himself, to expending too much time or effort on discussion of post-war plans before the war had actually been won. Government might have established the key committees to prepare for post-war reconstruction, but it remained generally unwilling to commit itself publicly to the plans that these committees were preparing. Nowhere was this more true than with housing, one of the central programmes of post-war reconstruction and an issue of keen interest to the public at large. Churchill was persuaded to say something about post-war housing in the spring of 1944, but it was not until March 1945 that the White Paper on housing was published, and even then it provided only a summary statement of the government's intentions.[18]

In this situation what was needed in film was a broad-brush statement of the case rather than a detailed investigation of the issues, many of which might be contentious. As the flow of debate in films like Rotha's *Land of Promise* (1945) suggests, the issue was less how post-war housing should look than mounting the argument that government should avoid the mistakes it had made after the First World War, clear the slums and launch a major housing programme using the resources and skills that had been used so successfully in war. It was natural that films should concentrate on social priorities, the need for government action and the need for planning. The simplifying message of film was to concentrate on showing what was being planned for housing, health and education. The niceties of architecture could be left until the war was over.

Second, it is important to remember the audience at which these films were aimed. The MOI films were intended to make the case to the mass of the population; they were to be shown in factory canteens, in hostels, in the recreation centres used by the services. The message they conveyed was to be as accessible as possible. What was needed was a view of the future that could be shared by all, not a modernist (not conservative) Utopia. There was no veto on images of modern architecture, but the old association between modern architecture and social reform received no special emphasis. Instead, the post-war future was presented in the most reassuring terms as the best of pre-war practice but shorn of the failings of the pre-war years. In housing, for example, garden city developments such as Letchworth, Hampstead Garden Suburb or Welwyn and Wythenshawe were favourite examples: *When We Build Again* takes Bournville as the model for the post-war ideal.

Finally, it is important to remember the paradox that lay at the heart of reconstruction. Reconstruction was not simply an opportunity to sweep away the old, and to replace it with a new post-war Britain. Rebuilding and reconstruction was to remake the pre-war world, keeping it largely the same but improving it. The failures of the 30s were to be swept away to be replaced by something new, but something that would still be familiar.

The characters in the Pub (*Land of Promise*)

Turning out tanks by the thousands
(*Land of Promise*)

Producing Housing (*Land of Promise*)

G. D. H. Cole tried to convey this conflicting response to the promise of a new post-war world in the following terms:

> Even if people have in them the spark of idealism and are ready to play their part in making the world a better place than it used to be … they are still apt to keep their private and their public aspirations in separate compartments, so as to speak to you one minute about the new world they hope to see, and the next about how nice it will be to get back to their old jobs, and their old homes, or to something as like them as can be managed.'[19]

Images of a modern post-war architecture might be acceptable but they would need to be complemented by images of an affectionately remembered past. Along with hopes for a new future, people still wanted somewhere where you could recover again the pre-war memories of Christmas lunches, children's parties, and the jollity of family life before the black-out.

Reconstruction on Film: *Land of Promise* and *Neighbourhood 15*

Some impression of the treatment of reconstruction on film can be gleaned from two very different examples. Typical of the MOI films which address the issues of physical reconstruction is *Land of Promise* (1945) by Paul Rotha.[20] Made at a time when the documentary film movement seemed at the peak of its achievement and singled out as one of Rotha's most successful campaigning films, *Land of Promise* shows how the documentary film could be used to make the case for a radical programme of post-war housing.

The film concentrates on the actuality of housing in the past and the present, but the structure of the film is constructed in a highly artificial fashion around a discussion group in a pub. This discussion is animated by a number of participants: the voice of reaction 'Mr Know-All', the voice of 'History', the 'Housewife', the pub landlord 'Observer', and 'The Voice of the People', all played by professional actors, with John Mills as The Voice of the People. Framed by the discussion in the pub, the film follows the development of housing conditions in Britain since the industrial revolution with the lessons of 'Past' and 'Present', summarised by the voice of History and authenticated by the voice of 'Hansard' and a series of statistical diagrams by the Isotype Institute. The message, spelt out simply in the script and reinforced by images, is that by using the ability to plan and mobilise the resources of Britain in war the country has created the means to overcome the problems of peace: 'We have learned how to turn out planes by the thousand and tanks, guns, shells, rifles, torpedoes, ships and the machinery for making them. We have an equal capacity to turn out goods for a better way of living. If you could produce planes you can produce houses. That's logical.'[21] By juxtaposing shots of the factory assembly of airplanes and munitions with film of the building of housing, and by contrasting these sequences of assembly and building with the squalid conditions of pre-war slum housing, Rotha drives home the argument that is spoken by the characters in the pub. The effect of the combination of images and words together with the rhythm of the whole is highly stylised but compelling. To contemporaries like Wright this use of film had an almost relentless quality: ' … a very, very difficult and dangerous way of film-making because documentary movemen, Rotha bludgeons the audience into agreement, creating propaganda of the most effective kind. The means he brings to achieving this are remote from a mere rendering of actuality. The film contains, it is true, newsreel footage of munitions production and housing construction but this is orchestrated around the discussion group in the pub who appear to engage directly with the cinema audience. Rotha's Land of Promise answers to Grierson's characterisation of documentary films as 'the creative treatment of actuality' but does so by emphasising creativity and treatment at the expense of actuality.

In contrast to the artificiality and sophistication of Rotha's work there remained another essentially unselfconscious tradition of films about reconstruction which emphasises 'actuality' and the reporting not the propaganda value of documentary film. This is represented by *Neighbourhood 15*, a film made by West Ham to describe the plans for rebuilding one of the most heavily damaged areas of the Borough [23]. Produced three years after *Land of Promise* when the task of rebuilding was already in hand, the purpose of *Neighbourhood 15* is not so much to preach about what should be done as to reassure those in West Ham that something was actually being done. But beyond these differences of intention, the contrast between the style of the two films is striking. *Neighbourhood 15* has none of the rhetorical quality of *Land of Promise*. The mood of the film is sober and worthy, a continuation of a tradition of local authority films made to publicise the work and the achievements of boroughs such as Hackney or Bermondsey. There are no actors; the officials play themselves. At certain points in the film, as in a meeting ostensibly held to report on the progress of reconstruction, there is a quality of awkwardness and self-conscious woodenness in the acting that looks back to the tradition of direct filming reminiscent of films like *Housing Problems*. The simple narrative structure of the film introduces the present conditions and the history of the borough as seen through the eyes of a local teenager, John. In place of the different voices of Rotha's actors, *Neighbourhood 15* uses the voices of the mayor, the school teacher, or the borough's planning officer. The unhurried pace of the film and the simplicity and directness of the script invite the viewer to identify with the way in which his or her neighbourhood is being rebuilt. The documentary style of reportage with its apparent absence of artifice does much to reassure, to offer visible evidence of the progress of reconstruction. To the relatively unsophisticated audience of West Ham it patiently, if slowly, sells a set of ideas that are new and complex. It explains the central elements of the County of London Plan and their relevance to West Ham, offering the plan to the community. It demystifies Abercrombie's and Forshaw's proposals, making them common-sense and approachable, offering them for the approval of the community. Remote from the artifice and the excitement of the avant-garde, *Neighbourhood 15* seeks to achieve its desired effect by very different means from *Land of Promise*.

Conclusion

Neighbourhood 15 goes further than most films to explain what was actually being done in the name of reconstruction. Generally, the documentary film-makers could show little of what, say, post-war London, Liverpool or Leicester might look like. The films necessarily lack architectural substance; at best they are suggestive. They may offer

John amongst the war damage in West Ham (*Neighbourhood 15*)

The meeting on reconstruction (*Neighbourhood 15*)

John and his friend discuss the reconstruction of the borough (*Neighbourhood 15*)

impressions of leafy low-density housing, they may give glimpses of the modern flats, health centres and schools to come, but they could do little more.

So, how effective were films like this in winning the case for reconstruction, either during the war or immediately after? Looking back through the Mass Observation archive, the most comprehensive source of information on public attitudes for this period, Tom Harrisson, one of the founders of Mass Observation, had reservations about their value, arguing that films like most 'deliberate' propaganda had little or no measurable effect on morale. He allowed that film used for specialist training or education might be very useful but that the impact of the general films made by organisations like MOI was difficult to detect. But this was not to deny the value of these films in creating a general sense of expectation of the benefits that reconstruction would bring. Harrisson concluded his assessment by arguing that film had done much to shape the way in which the nation thought about itself and to form the imagination of its future.[24] Above all documentary film had helped to create a climate of positive opinion in support of reconstruction. In doing so, films like *Land of Promise* and *Neighbourhood 15* had come close to achieving that quality of influence to which Grierson aspired; documentary film might indeed 'command the mind of a generation'.

Notes

1. F. Hardy (ed.), *Grierson on Documentary,* (London: pub., 1979), p. 48 I have relied heavily on the accounts of the British documentary film movement offered by E. Sussex, *The Rise and Fall of British Documentary* (Berkeley, Calif.: pub., 1975); P. Swann, *The British Documentary Film Movement 1926–1946* (Cambridge: pub., 1989); and B. Winston, *Claiming the Real, Documentary Film Revisited* (London: BFI, 1995).
2. P. Rotha, *Documentary Film* (London: pub., 1952), p. 25.
3. See especially N. Pronay and D. W. Spring (eds), *Propaganda, Politics and Film, 1918–45* (London: pub., 1982).
4. Swann, *British Documentary Film Movement,* chapter 5; and I. Aitken, *Film and Reform*, chapter 7
5. E. Lebas, 'Every Street Was a Cinema: The Film Activities of Bermondsey M.B.C., 1923–1954, *History Workshop Journal,* vol. 5, 1995.
6. Sussex, *British Documentary*, p. 62.
7. Quoted by Rotha, *Documentary Film*, p. 123.
8. I. Dalrymple, 'The Crown Film Unit', in Pronay and Spring, *Propaganda, Politics and Film*, pp. 209–20; Swann, *British Documentary Film Movement*, chapter 7.
9. But see N. Pronay, 'The Land of Promise: the Projection of Peace Aims in Britain', in K. R. M. Short, *Film and Radio Propaganda in World War II* (London: pub., 1983), pp. 51–77.
10. *The British Way and Purpose*, The Directorate of Army Education, 1944; for a general discussion of the presentation of peace aims in the services see P. Addison, *The Road to 1945* (London: pub., 1975), chapter 5.

11. T. Harrisson, 'Films and the Home Front – the Evaluation of their Effectiveness by Mass-Observation', in Pronay and Spring, *Propaganda, Politics and Film*, pp. 234–48.
12. For a general discussion of the debate on reconstruction, see P. Addison, *The Road to 1945*, chapters 4–6.
13. 24 October 1940: 'How Shall We Rebuild: Le Corbusier City of Tomorrow'; 7 November 1940: 'London Restored or Remodelled?' *(The Listener)*.
14. N. Bullock, 'Plans for Post-War Housing in the UK', in *Planning Perspectives*, vol. 2, pp. 71–98.
15. W. K. Hancock and M. M. Gowing, *The British War Economy*, p. 541.
16. H. Forman, 'The Non-Theatrical Distribution of Films by the Ministry of Information', in Pronay and Spring, *Propaganda, Politics and Film*, pp. 221–33; see also Swann, *British Documentary Film Movement*, chapter 7.
17. Pronay,'Land of Promise', pp. 73–4.
18. P. Addison, *Now the War Is Over* (London: pub., 1985), pp. 55–85.
19. G. D. H. Cole, *Plan for Britain* (London: pub., 1943), pp. 1–2.
20. *Land of Promise*, Films of Fact, directed by Paul Rotha (Great Britain, 1945).
21. Pronay, 'Land of Promise', pp 67–8.
22. Sussex, *British Documentary*, p. 138.
23. *Neighbourhood 15, West Ham,* Look & Learn Film Unit (Great Britain, 1945).
24. Harrisson, 'Films and the Home Front', p. 244.

Architecture in the Films of Jacques Tati

François Penz

L'École des facteurs

François at the fair (*Jour de fête*)

Background

The French mime and music-hall artist turned film-maker Jacques Tati,[1] made six films from 1949 to 1973. He is interesting firstly as a chronicler (a witness) of the architecture of the post-war period, secondly as a critic of it, but no less importantly as a humorous observer of its effect on the culture and on the individual.

Each film can be seen as a chapter of an on-going story with a series of themes which Tati develops and elaborates as he progresses. Central to his preoccupation is his suspicion of modern technology in general and more particularly of modern architecture. It is on this aspect which I shall concentrate here by looking at his first four feature films[2] with a particular emphasis on the last two: *Jour de fête*, (1949); *Les Vacances de Monsieur Hulot*, (1953); *Mon Oncle*, (1958); *and Playtime*, (1967).

Tati's suspicion of modern technology became apparent in *Jour de fête*. Although it is a film which celebrates rural France and in that sense has an almost timeless documentary-like quality about it, we are reminded that it is the post-war period through the projection of two American films[3] in the market square. One in particular is a pseudo-documentary concerning technological advancement in mail distribution in the USA. When François (Tati), the postman, tries this out the next day, it creates a whole series of hilarious mishaps.

In fact, if we step back a couple of years, in 1947 Tati had already tackled this theme of the 'human robot' in *L'École des facteurs*. In this film we can already discern a number of the characteristics of a Tati film, such as the use of the long shot/long take, the simplified narrative structure and the use of Tati himself as the main character and as a source of humorous slapstick effects.

Jour de fête received numerous awards and was compared (Fischer, 1983) by Marcel L'Herbier (Director of *L'Inhumaine,* 1924) to Vittorio De Sica's *Bicycle Thieves* (released the same year, 1949) because of its comparable film realism and the use of the bicycle as a central prop.[4]

In his next film, *Les Vacances de Monsieur Hulot*, Tati develops the accident-prone character, out of step with the routinely organised world. Mr Hulot's antics are a classic example of the Bergsonian idea of the comic arising when 'something mechanical is superimposed on the living'. With the creation of the character of Mr Hulot (named after an architect whom the family knew), Tati had finally found the vehicle for his comic genius to represent the individual in the face of modernism.

In his article entitled 'Monsieur Hulot and Time' (*Cahiers du Cinéma*, 1953), André Bazin called *Les Vacances de Monsieur Hulot* the 'most important comic work of the international cinema since the Marx Brothers and W. C. Fields and an event in the history of the sound cinema'. André Bazin gave Tati the intellectual credentials he needed; Tati was not just a clown any more but somebody who had to be taken seriously, which was of course important if you were an independent film-maker.

In the same article André Bazin highlighted four major points concerning this film, but which are valid for all of Tati's films:

1. The unachieved quality of the Hulot persona;
2. The extraordinary temporality of the film and its lack of traditional narrative structure;
3. The film's innovative soundtrack which caricatures sound;
4. The observational style of Tati's comedy.

Les Vacances de Monsieur Hulot established Tati as a major film-maker who rapidly gained an international reputation. It is also worth mentioning that, although Tati is not usually thought of as a New Wave director, he certainly was seen by many, includingTruffaut and Godard, as somebody breaking new ground in several areas. His lack of narrative structure in particular has attracted comparisons with directors such as Robbe-Grillet and Godard himself.

Mon Oncle

In 1958 Tati finished *Mon Oncle* and said that he wanted to show us who Hulot is 'where he lives, where he works, his family and friends'. On one hand we have Hulot living in the old quarter of Paris while his sister and brother-in-law and nephew lived in a modern house in a new part of town. The story revolves round the clash of those two worlds, the old and the new, or Hulot versus Arpel, with Gérard, the little boy (Tati's nephew) providing the link.

In this film Tati makes explicit his growing suspicion of modern architecture. If the 50s can be seen as the triumph of modernism, he certainly expresses some strong reservations, in particular regarding the type of built environment developing everywhere at the time. The post-war reconstruction boom was in full swing in the 50s and a large housing programme was in progress. It was the era of the 'HLM' (high-rise council housing) .

In an interview in 1958 for *Cahiers du Cinéma* Tati deplores the 'blandness and uniformity of the new cities' as well as the demolition of some old quarters of Paris. For *Mon Oncle*, he idealised the old quarters, shot in St Maur, a suburb of Paris. This is where Hulot, *Mon Oncle,* lives. Hulot's house was built specially for the film and was exactly tailored to Tati's height and bulk in order for the audience to follow intermittently his progression up and down the stairs. Through this tailor-made architecture, Tati is able to show his idea of architecture on a human scale both in a literal and a metaphorical sense.

Les Vacances de Monsieur Hulot

50's suburban development around Paris

The 'old' St Maur
(*Mon Oncle*)

Hulot's house
(*Mon Oncle*)

The 'threshold' (*Mon Oncle*)

The Modern house (*Mon Oncle*)

Quite crucial to Tati is the in-between or interface between old and new, which is very symbolically interpreted by the crumbling old wall in the foreground and the new city (in this case Créteil) in the background. The Villa Arpel in the new quarter symbolises the brave new world. It was built in the Victorines studio in Nice and designed by Tati and his long-time colleague, Jacques Lagrange, a painter. Tati has here gone out of his way to make it visually ridiculous. It was originally designed and assembled by Tati and Lagrange[5] as a collage from images of architectural reviews of the time.

In an article published by the *Journal des Monuments Historiques* (Sichère, 1985) Tati describes the design process: 'We had all sorts of architectural reviews and journals which we had gathered. We also had some scissors and glue. So I did a montage. I cut some features, a round window here, a ridiculous looking pergola there, some garden with a tortuous path to give the impression to be bigger than it really was etc., in effect it's an architectural "pot-pourri".'

The resulting villa is a strong statement by Tati posing here as a critic of modern architecture. The garden is virtually a desert, sprinkled with pink gravel. The house is in fact turned into an exhibition space for a string of visitors and loses all intimate and poetic quality, which Tati no doubt saw in the old quarter.

But it is not only the architecture which is in question, it is a whole way of life; in the old quarter Tati portrays the colourful market and the crowded café with immense affection and gives us a timeless view of what France may represent in its most convivial sense. By contrast, the sharp lines of the Arpel villa seem to have an effect, as if by osmosis, on their occupants and visitors alike, who, in terms of body language, have all the rigidity and severity of the surrounding concrete. Tati also takes the opportunity to unleash his humour on all the gadgets in the house, with Mr Hulot, the dog and the little boy playing havoc with them, reinforcing further the point made earlier about the Bergsonian ideal of 'something mechanical superimposed on the living'. Not surprisingly, this particular vision has spurred critics to compare *Mon Oncle* to Chaplin's *Modern Times* (1936) and to René Clair's *A nous la liberté* (1931).

He also gets the sounds and noises to reinforce his point. Tati was indeed a master in the composition of post-production sound effects which so often replace meaningful dialogues. In fact for the Villa Arpel he was trying to invent new types of sounds, such as the 'strangled fountain' and the 'aggressive-sounding cooker and cupboard', all to great comical effect. He realised that if he was to describe and propose to us a 'new architecture', it was not only a matter of how it looked but also very much about how it sounded.

Overall Tati expresses strong views on the architecture of his time through *Mon Oncle* (Tati the critic), taking housing as its central theme, which was of course the main post-war preoccupation (Tati the chronicler). By contrast, *Playtime* concentrates on the world of office buildings, skyscrapers and the like, which is of course very central to the 60s.

Playtime

In 1964, for *Playtime*, Jacques Tati built with the help of his architect/art-director, Eugène Roman,[6] an extraordinary setting which, in Tati's own words, was the 'real star of the film'. It was on a vast scale, built in the outskirts of Paris near Vincennes.[7] It was gigantic and became known as 'Tativille', possibly after Godard's *Alphaville* (1965),[8] which had just been completed. But, of course, it wasn't just any city; it was the city Jacques Tati needed to continue to explore his idea of the modern city, and, in order to get the shot that he required, the office blocks were in fact on wheels and tracks and could be moved at will. No 'real city' could have given him that flexibility. It was a gigantic enterprise[9] which was adding to a distinguished list of sets in the history of French cinema such as Meerson's sets for René Clair's *Sous les toits de Paris* (1930) and *A nous la liberté* (1930) or Trauner's design for Carné's *Les Enfants du Paradis* (1945).

The primary inspiration of the office buildings was the Esso building, which was built in 1963. In turn the Esso building was probably inspired by Lever House from SOM, built in 1952. The Esso building was the first office building erected at *La Défense* and Tativille is in effect a mock-up of how *La Défense* might ultimately look.

After a year's work on site, Tati started shooting in 1965. The plot is in typical Tati style reduced to the minimum. In his own words he summarises it as follows:

Lever House from SOM

> A group of foreign tourists arrive to visit Paris. On landing at Orly they find themselves pretty much in the same airport as those which they had left in Munich, London or Chicago. They ride in the same buses that they had used in Rome or Hamburg and arrive at a highway bordered by street lamps and buildings identical to those in their own capital (*Cahiers du Cinéma*, 1958).

Clearly in *Playtime* Tati becomes more radical than in any of his previous films by keeping the narrative structure to the bare minimum.

In this film, for the first time he shoots in 70mm wide-screen format, which he combines to great effect with his love for the long shot/long take. The main reason for this is to give him enough space on the screen for the eyes to wander. What Tati was doing with long shots is opening up a large window onto the world with actions taking place in more than one spot in order to let the spectator's eyes track across the whole screen very much as in real life. The long shot also allows him to lose Hulot, who is no longer the centre of attention (in fact in the opening sequence Tati does not appear for a while), and put non-professional extras at the centre of attention. He said 'I want to make people participate a little more, to let them change gear themselves; not to do their work for them.' This is in a sense a new concept, which the American critic Jonathan Rosenbaum called 'Tati's democracy'.

The Esso building *La Défense*

Wide-screen 70mm is a perfect format for embracing a large panoramic view of architectural spaces. Moreover, Tati practically never changes the lens throughout the film in order not to confuse the audience about the scale of the objects (he did the same with *Mon Oncle*). 'If I start on a long shot in a scene which has a table and a chair with a 40mm lens and then move closer and change to a 28mm lens, then it's not the same chair because the overall surface of the back of the chair would have increased proportionally' (*Cahiers du Cinéma*, 1958). This concern for scale and sense of perspective in space in relation to the technicalities of cinematography make him a particularly fascinating film-maker for architects.[10]

Movable sets (*Playtime*)

Office space (*Playtime*)

The ambiguous space (*Playtime*)

Hulot experiencing the sound of the
furniture (*Playtime*)

I will now highlight four elements which are closely related to his views on architecture: spatial ambiguity, sound, colours, and glass.

Spatial Ambiguity

In an interview with Bazin and Truffaut (*Cahiers du Cinéma*, 1958), Tati declared: 'I found uniformity unpleasant. I always feel nowadays that I am sitting on the same chair. While sitting in a brasserie in the Champs-Elysées, one feels as though one is in an airport, one never knows whether we are in a grocery shop or at the chemist. When I was little I used to go to the charcutier with my grandmother, there were tiles on the floor and sawdust and at the grocery shop it smelled of pepper and oak'.

Years later in *Playtime* Tati had the opportunity to vent his feelings about the uniformity of space in the modern world. In the opening sequence in the airport, Tati cultivates the spatial ambiguity of the international style and leaves us in doubt as to the function of the space. In fact he tricks us and makes us believe that we could be in a hospital. A couple wait anxiously in a corner, a nurse briskly passes by, people pace up and down a spotlessly clean and shiny corridor – and it is only when the tannoy sound resonates calling for various destinations and the tail of an airplane becomes visible, that we clearly understand that we are in an airport. In fact the same area will be used later on, but this time disguised as an office building.

But perhaps the best example of what he meant by uniformity and confusion of spaces is in one of the last scenes at the drugstore. There the guests, having left the Royal Garden in the early hours of the morning, assemble for a cup of coffee and a snack. But the space is part pharmacy, part café-bar, and even the food acquires a greenish tint more suited to clinical spaces than to a snack-bar.

Sound

The use of sound or the caricature of sound is extremely important in Tati as I have said above with regard to *Mon Oncle*. In *Playtime*, he records and post-synchronises the sound on five stereophonic tracks[11] (by contrast with the 'natural sounds' of the New Wave films). The sound here reinforces the echoes, the metallic resonance, and ultimately it is an added way for Tati to define a space, and in this case it is another attribute to make the spectator feel that the space we are in is not comfortable, slightly hostile, not just visually but acoustically. Two examples come to mind when thinking of Tati's 'architecture of sound'. One is when Giffard comes along the corridor to meet the awaiting Mr Hulot for the first time; here the infinitely long glassed corridor is made even longer by the painful punctuating and increasingly loud tapping of Giffard's shoes on the resonant surface acting as the invisible clock of 'time/space' wrapped together in the stillness of this long shot/long take. The other example is when sound gives life to furniture in the next scene, which has Tati alternately sitting down and standing up, experiencing the musical 'deflating and re-flating tunes of the modern-style fake-leather' chair, to great comical effect. Tati had understood not only that sound can say something about the nature of the space (a large space with hard surfaces may sound resonant, for example) but also that with sound he could tell us something about materials and their texture to complement the visual information on the screen.

Colour

While preparing to shoot *Playtime* Tati conducted an experiment. He asked a number of people very familiar with Orly airport to colour (from memory) black-and-white photographs of the inside of the airport, trying to match the reality (*Cahiers du Cinéma*, 1968). Not only did nobody get it right but Tati was struck by the diversity of the colour schemes proposed. It simply reinforced his feeling that 'colour in space' is not a fact of life, not something that we all universally remember and agree on. Except for a few 'primary examples', such as that London buses are red and a no-entry street sign is white on red, he saw colour as subjective, and in Tati's mind it was therefore to be manipulated to best effect.

In *Playtime* it is worth noticing the colours or the lack of them. Everything is vaguely blue/grey, not only to make a point about the blandness of the architecture, but also to focus one's attention on a particular detail or person by suddenly introducing a garish colour. For example, in the scene of the waiting-room where Hulot experiments with the seating (see the comments on sound, above), the only obvious colour present in the room is in the portraits of corporate executives, where an obviously garish red decoration is pinned on the chest of those proud and sinister-looking men. He uses colour in that way to draw our attention to a particular detail or character and otherwise he is happy to let our eyes wander in the 'grey modern world', concentrating on movements, actions, expressions and comical situations without further distraction from 'Technicolor fireworks'.

Glass

Tati uses glass as the ultimate symbol of modernism which contributes further to spatial ambiguity. He uses glass in many different situations and in many different ways.

In one scene in particular Tati uses to great effect the theme of glass and reflection: we see Hulot trying to find Mr Giffard and they both get confused by the glass reflections. He also uses glass to give us glimpses of the 'real Paris', which appears only as reflected in glass doors opening and closing. Glass is high on his agenda as it became such a symbol of the office building right up to very recently.

In another scene the camera is outside the flat of an old army friend, adjacent to Mr Giffard's flat.[12] The scene is mute and the sound is the street noise. We are in the position of a voyeur observing a domestic scene. People undress, pick their noses, behave very much as if they were behind closed doors but they are visible to everybody in the street. Surprisingly, no passers-by seem interested and it's only us the audience who are watching.

Most architects would surely see this set as a pure sectional perspective with the characters providing a sense of scale. It also reminds us of Tati's background as a mime artist. It is again an excellent example of the long shot/long take potential, framing perfectly the world of architecture. Tati, the critic, here also pursues the theme of glass invading the housing sector, giving us no sense of privacy.

In conclusion, I would say that Tati's *Playtime* and his elaborate sets and his use of the wide screen represent his ultimate vision of the cinema, namely to provide a large window onto the world in order to allow the spectator to observe individuals functioning in a modern world where accidentally and sporadically comical situations arise. There is a

Sectional perspective *(Tout va bien)*

...Sectional perspective *(Playtime)*

Discovering Paris *(Playtime)*

The 'real' Paris (*Playtime*)

clear progression in his work right from *Jour de fête*, filmed entirely on location with a very voluble main character, François the postman, right up to *Playtime*, with a near mute and self-effacing Mr Hulot meandering, ducking and weaving a tortuous path in sharp contrast to the straight lines of the international style. In other words, the less he talked, the more important the sets and the architecture became. When asked about architecture and architects, Tati always denied that he hated modern architecture, saying he was merely offering a comment, a way out. In the case of the Villa Arpel, he acknowledges the caricature but also blames the snobbish Arpels for turning their 'machine for living' into a showcase for neighbours and work colleagues. In the case of *Playtime*, he offers the vision of individuals gradually reappropriating for themselves bland and uniform spaces – the little old lady at the street corner, or the scene in the drugstore, which he felt ultimately one could not mistake for a drugstore anywhere in the world other than France. Finally, I would say that Tati as a chronicler, a critic of modern architecture and a humorous observer of his time offered us a good example of an architectural vision reinterpreted through the eyes of a film-maker, in which the film acts as a mirror for architects who can see buildings and cities reinvented on the screen. Although in many cases they might not like it.

Notes

1. Tati was indeed an accomplished mime artist who had performed in music halls throughout Europe for fifteen years before making his first feature. Many critics have likened him to Max Linder, Charlie Chaplin, Buster Keaton and others, pointing out their common years in the music hall before taking up working in films.
2. Tati acted in and scripted a number of shorts prior to his first feature, in particular *On demande une brute* (1932), *Soigne ton gauche* (1936), *Retour à la terre* (1938) and *L'École des facteurs* (1947). *Soigne ton Gauche* was directed by René Clement.
3. L. Fischer (see bibliography) argues that on one level *Jour de fête* can be read as a criticism of the 'invasion' of American films in France, which would have been particularly resonant in the French film world of the time and which also reminds us of current debates about quotas to improve European cinema.
4. *Jour de fête* was shot in colour and black-and-white. However, due to technical difficulties, the Thompson colour process was never processed until recently. *Jour de fête* currently enjoys a second career with the release in January 1995 of its long-awaited colour print.
5. Jacques Lagrange is a painter who comes from a family of architects. He has worked on most of Tati's films, turning Tati's ideas into drawings (private communication).
6. Eugène Roman is an architect turned art director at the end of the war when the Studio Victorines in his native Nice was heavily used by the film industry. He worked with Tati on *Mon Oncle* supervising the building of the Villa Arpel in Nice. After finishing *Playtime* he went back to Nice and worked for the rest of his career building and refurbishing casinos (private communication).
7. Sadly the entire set was demolished shortly after the film was completed. Tati had always wanted it to be a sound stage for film schools and young directors. The site was used instead for a gigantic motorway roundabout.

8. Paradoxically, Godard's *Alphaville,* which is describing a nightmarish sort of futuristic world, was shot on location, whereas Tati's supposedly realistic vision of newly built post-war world was entirely fabricated.

9. In 1961 in *The Ladies' Man* Jerry Lewis built the most enormous and spectacular set and one can only speculate that Tati might have been influenced by his approach. It would hardly be surprising given the   extraordinary respect and fame that Jerry Lewis has always enjoyed in France.

10. See Zbig Rybczynski's article about issues of scale and perspective in films.

11. The work on the sound was so considerable that Tati had to spend many months in post-production on this aspect alone. Combined with mounting production costs and delayed release, it all contributed to Tati going bankrupt after *Playtime.*

12. Godard seemed to have used the same idea with *Tout va bien* (1972), where we often have shots of the interior of the factory as a sectional perspective.

References

Chion, M., *Jacques Tati* (Paris: Cahiers du Cinéma, Coll. Auteurs, 1987).

Dondey, M., *Tati* (Paris: Ramsay, 1989).

Ede, F., *Jour de fête ou la couleur retrouvée* (Paris, Cahiers du Cinéma, Coll. 1er Siècle du Cinéma, 1995).

Fischer, L., *Jacques Tati: A Guide to References and Resources,* (Boston, Mass.: G. K. Hall, 1983).

Gilliatt, P., *Jacques Tati* (London: Woburn Press, 1976).

Harding, J., *Jacques Tati: frame by frame* (London: Secker & Warburg, 1984).

Kahn, A., *Playtime with Architects* (Design Book Review, Berkeley, Calif.: 1992).

Kermabon, J., 'Tati architecte: la transparence, le reflet et l'éphémère', *Cinémaction,* no. 75, 1995.

Maddock, B., *The Films of Jacques Tati* (Metuchen, 1977).

Sichère, M. A., *Jacques Tati: Où-est l'architecture?* (Monuments Historiques 'La dernière séance', 1985).

Cahiers du Cinéma
Three main articles have been published in the *Cahiers du Cinéma* concerning Tati:
1953, 'Mr Hulot et le temps', by André Bazin; 1958, 'Entretien avec Jacques Tati', by Bazin and Truffaut; and 1968, 'Le Champ large', an interview of Tati, by J. A. Fieschi and J. Narboni.

The Color of New York

Places and Spaces in the Films of Martin Scorsese and Woody Allen

Patricia Kruth

Martin Scorsese as the wedding photographer
(*The Age of Innocence*)

Woody Allen as Mickey, Central Park (*Hannah and Her Sisters*)

In an article entitled: 'Ville-Ciné et Télé-Banlieue', we find a provocative statement by the late Serge Daney: '... the cinema belongs to the city, ... it did not precede it, nor will it survive it. More than a form of solidarity – a common fate.'[1] This common fate binding the city and the cinema cannot find a better embodiment than in the works of Martin Scorsese and Woody Allen.

The place of life and the work of these two New Yorkaholics are forever sealed together. New York is their town and it always will be. Since the beginning of silent films, New York has certainly been the city that has most inspired film-makers, from King Vidor to Luc Besson, including Alfred Hitchcock, John Schlesinger, Sidney Lumet and Spike Lee. However, only Martin Scorsese and Woody Allen come out as the auteurs of a real New York work. Out of the nineteen films shot by Scorsese until now, eleven are New York films in which the city plays a predominant role. Woody Allen has directed twenty-five films; eleven are New York films, and another seven use the city as a backdrop.

I shall first focus on the two film-makers' relationship to urban space, then examine the role of editing, light and sound in the building of a screen city, and finally bring out some major aspects of the image of the city.

Location Shooting and Urban Geography
Chapter One. 'You don't make up for your sins in church. You do it in the street.'[2] Shooting on location is no doubt for Scorsese one way to expiate his relentless love for New York; Woody Allen also proves quite addicted to this method. However, the two film-makers' relationship to the geography they love is very different, as exemplified by the table at the end of this paper showing which neighborhoods and boroughs of New York appear in a given film.

Squares represent a straightforward relationship to space, a black square in the case of several sequences, a white square for one or a few shots. In Woody Allen's films what you see on the screen is usually unaltered reality. This accounts for the great number of squares on his side of the table whereas we find only some of them for Scorsese (*Taxi Driver,* 1976; *Who's That Knocking at My Door?*, 1969; *The King of Comedy,* 1983). Woody Allen of course shoots outdoor sequences on location in the City; yet he also uses New York interiors instead of resorting to studio sets. For example, the scenes in *Manhattan*

(1979), where characters meet inside the Whitney or in Soho galleries, were shot on location; to depict Alice's wealthy surroundings in *Alice* (1990) Woody Allen used an existing Park Avenue apartment at number 1125.

Scorsese's case is quite different. His relationship to space is much more intricate, as evinced by the number of circles, triangles and triangles within squares. Triangles and circles mean the location of the shooting is different from the location in the fiction. *New York, New York* (1977) for example, was shot entirely in studios, MGM for the interiors and the Fox studios for the exteriors. Triangles within squares correspond to the most complex cases – composite spaces which do not exist as such. For instance, the Bronx of *Raging Bull* (1980) is a mixture of Bronx and midtown Manhattan locations; *GoodFellas* (1990), which depicts the life of the Italian-American community of East New York in Brooklyn, was shot mainly in a reconstructed Astoria, in the north of Queens. Scorsese's construction of a screen metropolis owes no doubt a great debt to Kuleshov's 'creative geography'. What Scorsese aims at is to capture not the letter but the spirit of a place; this is done through meticulous and increasingly obsessive attention to details like hallways (*Mean Streets,* 1973), fire escapes (*Raging Bull*),[3] cars (*GoodFellas*) or pieces of clothing (*The Age of Innocence,* 1993). Whereas Woody Allen's New York can be taken at face value, Scorsese's city is a movie town. But, as we all know from reading *Moby Dick*: 'true places never are ... in any map'.[4]

Martin Scorsese is often known as the film-maker of Little Italy, and Michael Powell has described him as the 'Goya of 10th Street'. He was born in Corona, Queens, in 1942; when he was seven, his parents returned to Elizabeth Street in Little Italy, a poor and violent neighborhood where, according to the director, only gangsters and priests were respected. In fact only three of his feature films deal with Little Italy. *Italianamerican* (1974) was shot entirely indoors in his parents' apartment. *Mean Streets* gives a more than true to life picture of the neighborhood, and yet, for financial reasons, it was shot mainly in California. Indeed most interiors, as well as some exteriors, like the final massacre scene supposedly taking place in Brooklyn, were shot in Los Angeles. Which leaves us with only one feature film – *Who's That Knocking at My Door?* – actually shot on location in Little Italy.

Scorsese's camera explores all five boroughs: Manhattan, from Harlem (*New York, New York*) to Soho (*Life Lessons,* 1989; *After Hours,* 1985), as well as the Bronx (*Raging Bull*), Queens (*GoodFellas*), Brooklyn (*Taxi Driver, GoodFellas*) and Staten Island (*Who's That Knocking At My Door?*), with a predilection for Midtown and the Times Square area. Woody Allen's fantasy world is more focused on the island of Manhattan, especially Central Park, one of his all-time favorite locations. Allan Stuart Konigsberg was born in 1935, not actually under the roller-coaster in Coney Island, but close by, in Midwood, a middle-class neighborhood of Flatbush in Brooklyn. Therefore his autobiographical lens sometimes ventures into Brooklyn; it becomes idealized and partly a figment of his imagination (Coney Island in *Annie Hall,* 1977; *Radio Days,* 1987). In fact, Woody Allen's New York is a very idiosyncratic *Carte du Tendre*. It retains the flavor of the fairy-tale town that dazzled the six-year-old boy in 1941 as, when coming out of the subway, he first discovered Times Square. His world is centered on Midtown and the Upper East and West Side. Elaine's, Zabar's, Mia Farrow's apartment are – or were – all personal landmarks

Diane Keaton as Mary and Woody Allen as Ike, the Whitney (*Manhattan*)

The Midtown Manhattan Bronx' (*Raging Bull*)

Elizabeth Street shot from Scorsese's window (*Who's That Knocking at My Door?*)

71

Robert De Niro as Travis Bickle (*Taxi Driver*)

New York as a 24-hour life-size movie
(*Taxi Driver*)

Woody Allen as Mickey, Mount Sinai Hospital
(*Hannah and Her Sisters*)

of his everyday life which Woody Allen has turned, along with the Russian Tea Room, the Carnegie Deli, Dean and De Luca's – not to forget Bloomingdale's, – into his usual movie set.

Contrasting Styles and Urban Integration
Chapter Two. How to build a screen city with editing, light and sound.

A lonely character undergoing a crisis is a common situation in both cinemas. Let us compare two such scenes in *Taxi Driver* and *Hannah and Her Sisters* (1986).

Second sequence of *Taxi Driver*. Through a circular pan we discover Travis's shabby place – the rope substituting for his wardrobe, the cracked paint, a naked lightbulb, the bed littered with porno magazines, junk food here and there. The circular camera movement contributes to close up the space around him. The bars on his window which appear twice – once in the mirror, a favorite Scorsese visual motif – corroborate the image of New York as a prison cell or a cage. In the street, Travis is trapped too, a prisoner in the glass cage of his taxi. He is shown in medium close-up from all angles, front, sides, back; the fragmented editing and the staight cuts construct a cubist-like portrait which reflects his split personality. From behind his windshield the cabdriver is watching New York unreel like a 24-hour life-size color movie. A combination of horizontal and perpendicular tracking shots together with a circular pan create an impression of random movement and restlessness. There is no sense of direction or purpose. In American cinema, power is synonymous with knowledge and mastery of space. By producing visual chaos, Scorsese shows that Travis has no control over his destiny. New York is a human jungle, a venal zoo inhabited by strange night creatures who, seen through Travis's windshield, appear to be doomed to permanent wandering. One very brief shot of Times Square through the back window of the cab lets us know for sure where we are. It is, however, quite discreet. Woody Allen's New York, on the other hand, reads like an open map covered with signs and landmarks.

In the scene from *Hannah and Her Sisters*, in which Mickey comes out of the hospital where he has undergone a series of tests, it is impossible to miss the inscription: 'Guggenheim Pavilion – Mount Sinai Hospital' written twice on the marquee. Whatever his predicament, Woody Allen's protagonist – generally played by the Jewish film-maker himself – is never lost. By contrast, Scorsese's characters are often outcasts or misfits who are strangers in their own city, like the bunch in *Mean Streets* not knowing their way in Brooklyn or even Greenwich Village. New York is for Woody Allen's protagonists a shelter and a cocoon. This is made obvious here by the voice-over: 'Nothing's gonna happen to you. You're in the middle of New York City. This is your town. You're surrounded by people and traffic and restaurants.' It is also stated by the camera movements: a tracking shot backwards, and then a horizontal tracking shot. Tracking shots centered on the walking protagonist were – at least up to *Husbands and Wives* (1992) – part and parcel of Woody Allen's invisible *mise en scène*; they convey the protagonist's perfect integration in his urban universe. The second part of the excerpt is a static shot which seems to deny Mickey's hysterical reaction and be out of tune with the story line. And yet it confirms that, however distressing the situation, the stability of the relationship between the Woody Allen protagonist and his familiar surroundings is never at stake; the city is his.[5]

Light and the City

Among the great film-makers of architectural places are Fellini, Antonioni, Resnais and Greenaway. Peter Greenaway writes: 'Passion for architectural space cannot be dissociated from passions for light.'[6] And it is the lights of the city at night which perhaps best reveal the architecture of New York. Night and the city. The city that never sleeps becomes itself. For Scorsese's 'night hawks' artificial light is synonymous with nightmare (*Taxi Driver*, *Mean Streets*, *After Hours*) and Scorsese's empty city is very reminiscent of Edward Hopper's urban void. Even though *Manhattan Murder Mystery* (1993) or *Crimes and Misdemeanors* (1989) contain night scenes in the American film noir tradition, night is for Woody Allen the privileged time when the town belongs to couples and New York is turned into a romantic wonderland – lovers kissing on roofs (*Manhattan*; *Oedipus Wrecks*, 1989), riding a horsedrawn carriage in Central Park (*Manhattan*), or flying over an enchanted city in *Alice*.

Night and rain often go hand in hand. Scorsese's New York is flooded by a seemingly endlessly pouring rain, obsessively trying to wash the city clean from its sins and corruption. 'One day', says Travis, 'a real rain'll come and wash all the scum off the streets.' Rain for both film-makers can also be an aphrodisiac. The scene from *New York, New York* where Jimmy passionately kisses his soaked sweetheart could be found in a Woody Allen movie; it belongs to the great Frank Capra tradition (*Rain or Shine*, 1930; *Mr Deeds Goes to Town*, 1936; *It's a Wonderful Life*, 1946). Woody Allen uses rain, night, or black-and-white emulsion as filters to bring out the ever-changing beauty of his city. His New York is a town pulsating to the rhythms of the seasons. It is a place in which nature, epitomized by Central Park, is harmoniously integrated within the heart of American civilization. He thereby proves a descendant of a great photographer of nature and seasons in New York – Alfred Stieglitz.

Scorsese's New York, on the other hand, is a far cry from an urban pastoral. Central Park never appears; nature is reduced to a graveyard in *Mean Streets* or, at the end of *Taxi Driver*, to some trees blowing in the wind in front of Betsy's apartment and ruthlessly left behind by a swish pan. The Scorsese protagonist thrives in a city which, up till now, is the negation of nature.

Space and Sound

Let us now study the use of sound in relation to space in the beginning of two films, the pre-credit scene of *Mean Streets* and the prologue of *Manhattan*.

The sound in the opening of *Mean Streets* is made up of voice (Charlie's voice-over), noise (street noise, horns, a siren), and music (the song 'Be My Baby'). The existence of an urban world off-screen is established by the opening sentence heard over a blank screen. As Charlie wakes up in a start, the noises of the city invade the space around him. In *La Toile trouée*, Michel Chion notes that, since the beginning of talking pictures, a honking horn is *the* sound that, in all films, signifies and epitomizes *the city*.[7] He writes:

New York City a la Edward Hopper (*After Hours*)

Rain as an aphrodisiac (*New York, New York*)

Celebrating nature (*Hannah and Her Sisters*)

'You don't make up for your sins in church.'
(*Mean Streets*)

'Chapter One. He adored New York City.'
(*Manhattan*)

'... a town that existed in black and white...'
(*Manhattan*)

'a horn or a siren has the power to awaken space'.[8] Scorsese makes use of this sound stereotype to establish instantly the setting of his film – a realistic, yet symbolic urban environment. The siren also conveys violence, anguish and restlessness. The existence of an urban world off-screen is further corroborated by the tune that ends the scene. This tune functions as a score outside the story space; it has no obvious connection with the visuals, does not seem to be heard by the protagonist, and may therefore simply pass for non-diegetic music (*musique de fosse*).[9] However, it is source music coming up from the streets through the open window (*musique d'écran*).[10] Rock music played by loud radios and jukeboxes outside was indeed characteristic of hot summers in Little Italy as experienced by Martin Scorsese in the 60s. In a matter of seconds, Scorsese has thus turned a conventional urban setting into something which, although shot in California, is undeniably New York.

Charlie lies down on his back again. The movement is broken up into four shots, from medium shot to close-up; the tune starts on the third shot. The editing creates a visual echo to the music and the fragmentation of movement, whose effect is close to overlapping editing,[11] expands time. The unexpected combination of fast music with what feels like slowed-down motion draws our attention to a very subjective urban environment which is both stylized and ritualized. This will be the setting of *Mean Streets*.[12] With the exception of some commissioned scores like those for *Taxi Driver* or *After Hours*, the air of Scorsese's New York is saturated with rock and roll and Italian operas; these tunes help to endow his city with a nostalgic aura.

From nostalgia to idealization there is but one short step quickly taken by Woody Allen in *Manhattan*, *Radio Days* or *Alice*. His city usually comes alive to the sound of classical music or the rhythms of jazz. Woody Allen's two favorite types of music are combined in the prologue of *Manhattan* in George Gershwin's 'Rhapsody in Blue'.

The visuals are a simple, often seemingly random catalogue of black-and-white footage of the city taken by the second unit crew. No sophisticated editing, just a series of quick static shots culminating in one long take juxtaposed in a basic documentary-like fashion. And yet this sequence is undoubtedly one of the most beautiful declarations of love ever made to the city as a woman. The soundtrack – Gershwin's music combined with Ike's voice off and with the exclusion of any realistic city noise – exists outside the time and space suggested by the images. It is the indispensable ingredient that makes the alchemy work by providing a third dimension to a somewhat trivial urban canvas. With a few exceptions, the commentary is, overall, non-synchronous; more often than not, the scene addresses our sense of hearing so that the succession of everyday urban scenes that flood the screen is perceived by us in a blur. It is before the voice starts and after it stops that we can really see the city with its skyline and its festive night life. The success of the scene rests on a subtle yet simple interplay between sight and sound. It perfectly illustrates Robert Bresson's ideas: 'Image and sound must not support each other, but must work each in turn through a sort of relay. ... If the ear is entirely won, give nothing to the eye. One cannot be at the same time all eye and all ear.'[13] This scene also conveys one of the main characteristics of Woody Allen's style – the foundations of his screen city are words. In these two examples we see how sound is used not to reproduce but to actually originate urban space.

Chapter Three. '[They] adored New York City' and yet the two images of the city emerging from their films did not quite superimpose. I wish to focus on three privileged locations and city limits – rooftops, bridges, and the New York skyline.

The Roofs of New York
Both film-makers use rooftops in the same way. They are perfect places for organized or spontaneous parties, part and parcel of a Mary Poppins universe – a serenade for *Zelig* (1983), New Year's Eve in *Radio Days* or the wedding of Jake La Motta's brother in *Raging Bull*. In the latter scene, the rare few moments of happiness captured by a clumsy amateur cameraman belong to the home movie within the film. The score from Mascagni's *Cavalleria Rusticana* obliterates real time; it endows the faded images with a sentimental and nostalgic beauty belonging to a lost age of innocence.

Rooftops are also for Allen and Scorsese playground substitutes for young – or less young – boys who perform pranks and challenge the city at their feet like the brats in *Radio Days* or Johnny Boy in *Mean Streets* shooting out the lights of the Empire State Building.

Finally, rooftops are urban equivalents to hills; they are places for trysts and romances in *Who's That Knocking at My Door?*, and from *Annie Hall* down to *Husbands and Wives* and *Bullets over Broadway (1994)*. Woody Allen's New York evokes the city portrayed by the American Impressionists and the Ashcan School, in particular Robert Henri and John Sloan. In the rooftop scene in *Annie Hall* the protagonists and nature are harmoniously integrated within the urban environment. The two parts of the shot framing the scene remind us of Childe Hassam's engraving 'New York' (1931*),* in which a couple have tea on a flowered roof. Peter Conrad writes: 'The impressionist city is a picnic site. ... [It] renders sex pastoral.'[14] Woody Allen uses rooftops as privileged settings for urban pastorals. In *Alice*, where one shot reveals the protagonist eating a sandwich as she is walking around with her lover on a terrace overlooking Times Square, Woody Allen's homage to the Hollywood tradition becomes playfully irreverent.

There are three flashbacks on the roofs of Little Italy in *Who's That Knocking at My Door?* In the first one, a homage to *On the Waterfront* (1954), the rooftop remains a popular place for lovers. And yet the couple are jammed between chimneys; the handheld camera, the seemingly random editing and jarring horns contribute to a restless pace and a fragmentation of space. Outdoor location shooting does not prevent us from feeling trapped in the claustrophic microcosm of the asthmatic director. Besides, Scorsese's characters only seem at ease in the street, at sidewalk level, and when on a roof they will look down. Scorsese's New York calls to mind the low city of Edward Hopper. The camera – either close to the ground or in a high-angle shot position – as well as the narrow framing erases skyscrapers. With a few exceptions (one or two shots in *Who's That Knocking at My Door?*, *Mean Streets* and *Taxi Driver*) they are virtually absent and invisible.

Bridges and the El
Whereas rooftops provide the two cinemas with simple meeting places in the John Sloan tradition – the wedding scene from *Raging Bull* could belong to a film like *Zelig* – the use

Home movie – rooftop wedding party (*Raging Bull*)

Drinks on the terrace (*Annie Hall*)

Jammed between chimneys (*Who's That Knocking at My Door?*)

Dancing under the El (*New York, New York*)

Shoot-out under bridge (*GoodFellas*)

Hired assassin, Queensboro Bridge (*Crimes and Misdemeanors*)

of bridges, elevated highways and the El on the other hand brings out their differences. Overall, Scorsese makes little use of bridges and the El. They appear in *Mean Streets*, *New York, New York*, and *GoodFellas*. A beautiful seventy-two-second long sequence-shot in *New York, New York* shows Jimmy on the platform of the El. After celebrating V-Day, he finds himself alone; he has not managed to seduce Francine. He is watching from above a couple dressed in white – he in sailor's clothes – dancing together in the night, oblivious to the world outside. The passing train is suggested by moving shadows and clinking sounds. The scene shot in the Fox studios reproduces a station of the Third Avenue El, the only one still in use in Manhattan in 1945. We know how life under the El has always rhymed with hell on as well as off screen. From *The Crowd* (1928) to *Gloria* (1980), including *The Public Enemy* (1933), *The Wrong Man* (1957) and *The French Connection* (1971),[15] it has been synonymous with poverty and violence. Here the set is used in an original way. It both materializes the protagonist's solitude and functions as a place of poetry and magic in Scorsese's nostalgic homage to the 1940s musicals, and *On the Town*[16] in particular. What is remarkable is the combination of the dream world called forth by the visuals with the documentary quality arising from the soundtrack composed of train noises and devoid of any conventional score.

In *GoodFellas* life revolves around the shade of the 31st Avenue El in Brooklyn which fosters the outbursts of violence of the Italian community – the poor postman is beaten up, an ambulance picks up the man shot down in front of the pizzeria. All happens in accordance with the tradition of the gangster movie or the film noir. And yet Scorsese knows how to renew the tradition. Three shots: a long shot of a pink Cadillac under a bridge; innocent creatures playing under the threatening mass, a motif familiar to the Hollywood spectator;[17] a point-of-view shot which is a perfect example of audiovisual counterpoint. To the lively tune of Eric Clapton's 'Layla', a majestic tracking shot forward materializing the boy's voyeuristic stare unveils the blood-spattered faces of Mr and Mrs Roastbeef, gunned down in their car. Thanks to an original use of sound, Scorsese has achieved what Arthur Penn or Sam Peckinpah started in *Bonnie and Clyde* (1967) and *The Wild Bunch* (1969) through the use of slow-motion – he has distanced and stylized violence while at the same time somehow indulging in it. Is Scorsese here vindicating violence? In any event, the result is a powerful and disturbing shot, a shot simultaneously attractive and repulsive.

Just like Scorsese, Woody Allen appropriates the negative connotation of bridges shot from underneath. In *Crimes and Misdemeanors*, a single shot without narrative is enough for us to identify without the shadow of a doubt the stranger under the bridge as the hired assassin.[18] Yet, contrary to Scorsese, Allen uses bridges as landmarks. We recognize the Queensboro Bridge with Queens in the background. Unlike Scorsese, for whom New York is often an anonymous city in the tradition of the film noir – especially in *GoodFellas* – Woody Allen loves to explore the more or less well known sites of his city, just like the architect in *Hannah and Her Sisters*.[19] The major bridges of New York appear in his work. He uses them in two different ways, often simultaneously. First as dramatic props shown in low-angle shots or taking up the upper half of the screen, and thus dwarfing the lovers who meet there. Therefore the happiness of the couple at the foot of the Queensboro Bridge in *Manhattan* and in front of the Brooklyn Bridge in *Annie Hall* is not meant to last. The scene in *Annie Hall* relies on an iconography and a symbolism that was already well established in the 1920s – the bridge, the kiss, the foghorn. It follows in the wake of Mamoulian's magnificent *Applause* (1929).[20] Secondly and foremostly, to film the shapes of bridges in long and extreme long shots, in extended tracking shots, is a way for Woody Allen to celebrate and pay homage to his city: he thus offers to our appreciation the Verrazano-Narrows Bridge in *Annie Hall*, the Tappan Zee Bridge in *Manhattan*, the George Washington Bridge in *Broadway Danny Rose* and *Manhattan Murder Mystery*.

All these urban limits act as pretexts to display and enhance the city's shapely contours and her figure. This anthropomorphic temptation comes as no surprise, since cities have long been linked and likened to women; we recall Fitzgerald, Thomas Wolfe or Ezra Pound's New York,[21] Murnau's *Sunrise* (1927) or Italo Calvino's *Invisible Cities*. Woody Allen's films, and *Manhattan* in particular, are the descendants of the 'city symphonies';[22] they are hymns to New York, odes to the city in the tradition of Walt Whitman's *Mannahatta*, revisited in 1921 by Paul Strand and Charles Sheeler in their film *Manhatta*.

Fleeting moment of happiness, Brooklyn Bridge (*Annie Hall*)

The Manhattan Skyline
Another city limit is the all too celebrated Manhattan skyline. If Woody Allen sometimes indulges in its faded beauty, he nevertheless succeeds in giving this visual cliché a personal touch. He uses black and white in *Manhattan* or a fantastical and humorous coloring in *Alice* and in *Oedipus Wrecks*; in the latter work the dream of the city as a woman has gone sour and the urban landscape has turned into a 'castrating sionist'.[23]

The Manhattan skyline does not appear in Scorsese's work except once, in *Taxi Driver*, when Travis buys the material that will allow him to clean up the city. There is nothing touristy about the south Manhattan skyline seen from a Brooklyn Heights hotel. Framed behind the windows, the whole town is within gunshot; the venal city has become Travis's target in very much the same way as the prostitutes and actresses framed by Mark's killing movie camera in Michael Powell's *Peeping Tom* (1960). Martin Scorsese's New York is characterized by an absence of limits. It is sprawling, shapeless, often abstract so that the places linked by car become interchangeable; it comes to look like what, to Woody Allen, is the city of all evils – Los Angeles. Scorsese's New York is defined by an absence of establishing shots and extreme long shots of the city.[24] It is a 'meso-landscape' (a human-scale landscape) and a 'micro-landscape'[25] which exists first of all in the film-maker's cinematographic memory of New York.

Jewish mother, Manhattan skyline (*Oedipus Wrecks*)

Two Visions of the City
Woody Allen and Martin Scorsese belong to an American tradition of painters, writers, photographers and film-makers obsessed with the interpretation of New York. Woody Allen's New York is a one-of-a-kind, unique place. It is a town on a human scale where people walk and talk to each other. It is a magic melting-pot in which life mixes with the supernatural and comes to imitate art, as brilliantly exemplified in the homage to *The Lady from Shanghai* (1948) in *Manhattan Murder Mystery*. Scorsese's New York is an asphalt jungle, a labyrinth which symbolizes all cities. As suggested in the credit sequence of *Raging Bull*, it is both a cage and a window, a semi-abstract Francis Bacon-like construction. In *Life Lessons*, the plight of the Scorsese protagonist is perfectly evinced,

The city as target (*Taxi Driver*)

Homage to Hayworth and Welles, *The Lady from Shanghai* (*Manhattan Murder Mystery*)

New York – cage and window (*Raging Bull*)

A canvas-made-into-a-city (*Life Lessons*)

metaphorically, by the frenzied confrontation between the painter and his canvas-made-into-a-city.[26] And now, why not let Martin Scorsese – or is it Woody Allen? – have the last say: 'I lived in Rome for a while, and London, and Paris. But for me, the center of the world is here. New York. There is no other place.'[27]

Acknowledgements

Special thanks for invaluable audiovisual and printed documents: Ian Christie, BFI; Elisabeth Leedham-Green, Darwin College, Cambridge; Patrick Pleven, New York Mayor's Office of Film, Theatre and Broadcasting; Charles Silver, MoMA Film Study Center.

Notes

1. Serge Daney, 'Ville-Ciné et Télé-Banlieue', *Cités-Cinés* (La Villette: Éditions Ramsay et la Grande Halle, 1987), pp. 121-7.
2. Opening words of *Mean Streets*.
3. Martin Scorsese comments on the laser video of *Raging Bull*: 'Those fire escapes are in Hell's Kitchen somewhere, 44th Street and 8th Avenue or whatever.'
4. Herman Melville, *Moby Dick* (Harmondsworth: Penguin, 1977), p. 150.
5. This could be contrasted also with shots of the drunken and reeling Charlie who has no hold whatsoever over the room whirling around him (*Mean Streets*).
6. Peter Greenaway, 'Rien que le lieu, de préférence le lieu architectural', *Positif*, June 1994, p. 43.
7. Cf the opening shot of *Batman* which gives the gist of Gotham City – it is a drawing of skyscrapers accompanied by a cacophony of honking horns.
8. Michel Chion, *La Toile trouée* (Paris: Éditions de l'Étoile, Cahiers du cinéma, 1988), pp. 42.
9. Terminology coined by Michel Chion, *L'Audio-vision* (Paris: Nathan, 1990), p.71.
10. Ibid.
11. As practised by Soviet film-makers in the 1920s for example.
12. Slow motion and expresssionistic colors are recurrent stylistic motifs; bar meetings and fights are shown as rituals.
13. Robert Bresson, 'Notes on Sound', in Elisabeth Weis and John Belton (eds.), *Film Sound, Theory and Practice* (New York: Columbia University Press, 1985), p. 149.
14. Peter Conrad, *The Art of the City* (New York: Oxford University Press, 1984), pp. 87-92.
15. *The Crowd*, King Vidor, 1928; *The Public Enemy*, Howard Hawks, 1933; *The Wrong Man*, Alfred Hitchcock, 1957; *The French Connection*, William Friedkin, 1971; *Gloria*, John Cassavetes, 1980.
16. Both the Gene Kelly and Stanley Donen movie (1949) and the hit Broadway musical of 1945.

17. In *The French Connection*, for instance, we find a similar scene culminating in death beginning in the same way with a boy riding his tricycle under the El.

18. Ridley Scott uses the same symbolism in *Black Rain* (1989): at the beginning Michael Douglas is shown in his apartment *overlooking* the Queensboro Bridge; he is the hero who is going to win.

19. In making us share his love for a very idiosyncratic Rome, Nani Moretti on his vespa pays a magnificent homage to the American master.

20. In *Applause* the couple are filmed *on* the Brooklyn Bridge. The future is theirs.

21. 'A maid with no breasts', *New York*, 1912.

22. The original 1920s 'city symphonies' such as *Rien que les heures* (Alberto Cavalcanti, 1926); *Berlin, Symphony of a Great City* (Walter Ruttmann, 1927); *The Man with the Movie Camera* (Dziga Vertov, 1929); or later works like *New York, New York* (Francis Thompson, 1957).

23. This is how Ike describes his mother in *Manhattan*.

24. His Manhattan and Little Italy are light years away from the touristy settings established by helicopter tracking shots over the island and its bridges as, for instance, in Luc Besson's *Léon*.

25. According to the terminology 'méso-paysage' and 'micro-paysage' used by Jacques Mauduy and Gérard Henriet, *Géographies du Western* (Paris: Nathan, 1989), pp. 112-13.

26. Scorsese used Chuck Connelly's New York-inspired imaginary landscapes.

27. Martin Scorsese, 'Tapping the Intensity of the City', *The New York Times Magazine*, 9 November 1986.

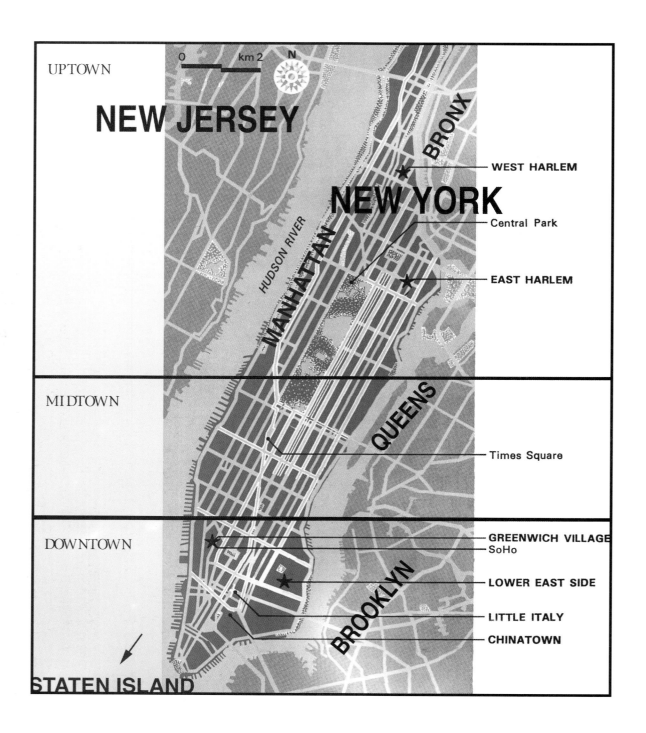

UPTOWN

NEW JERSEY

BRONX

NEW YORK

WEST HARLEM

Central Park

EAST HARLEM

HUDSON RIVER

MANHATTAN

MIDTOWN

QUEENS

Times Square

DOWNTOWN

GREENWICH VILLAGE
SoHo

BROOKLYN

LOWER EAST SIDE

LITTLE ITALY

CHINATOWN

STATEN ISLAND

PLACES AND NEIGHBORHOODS OF NEW YORK

	Who's That Knocking at My Door?	Mean Streets	Italianamerican	Taxi Driver	New York, New York	Raging Bull	The King of Comedy	After Hours	Life Lessons	GoodFellas	The Age of Innocence	Take the Money and Run	Bananas	Annie Hall	Interiors	Manhattan	Stardust Memories	Zelig	Broadway Danny Rose	Hannah and her Sisters	Radio Days	Another Woman	Oedipus Wrecks	Crimes and Misdemeanors	Alice	Husbands and Wives	Manhattan Murder Mystery	Bullets over Broadway	Mighty Aphrodite
UPTOWN	▲			△		■	◪	●		○	◪			■	□	■	■			■	■	●	■	■	■	■	■	■	■
CENTRAL PARK														□		■				■		■	□	■				□	□
MIDTOWN			■	△	◪	■	◪	○		■	◪		■		□	■	□	□	■	■	■		■	■	■	■	■	■	■
TIMES SQUARE · BROADWAY · 42nd STREET	□			■	▲		■							□	■	□				□						■			
LITTLE ITALY	■	◪	■																										
GREENWICH VILLAGE	□	◪		■				○		◪			■		■	□	□	□	□	●		□		■	■	■		■	■
SOHO								◪	◪	○						■			■			■			■	■	■		■
LOWER EAST SIDE · TRIBECA · LOWER MANHATTAN	□	◪						□	●	○		□		□		□						□				□	■	□	■
CHINATOWN																				□									
HARLEM				▲																									
BROOKLYN		△		□	▲			◪		●			□		□			○		■									●
THE BRONX					◪									□						○					□				
QUEENS										◪																			
STATEN ISLAND	□									○																			

| **MARTIN SCORSESE** | | **WOODY ALLEN** |

Legend

- ■ ▲ ● several sequences
- □ △ ○ ◪ 1 shot to 1 sequence
- ■ □ setting of fiction = place of shooting
- ▲ △ setting of fiction (≠ place of shooting [sets, other neighborhood or town])
- ● ○ place of shooting (≠ setting of fiction)
- ◪ ◪ ◪ composite space
  (a) (b) (a) mostly shot on location
  (b) mostly studio or one place standing for another
- ▢ blurred area

FILMOGRAPHY

MARTIN SCORSESE

1969	**WHO'S THAT KNOCKING AT MY DOOR?**
1972	Boxcar Bertha
1973	**MEAN STREETS**
1974	Alice Doesn't Live Here Anymore **ITALIANAMERICAN**
1976	**TAXI DRIVER**
1977	**NEW YORK, NEW YORK**
1978	The Last Waltz American Boy: A Profile of Steven Prince
1980	**RAGING BULL**
1983	**THE KING OF COMEDY**
1985	**AFTER HOURS**
1986	The Color of Money
1988	The Last Temptation of Christ
1989	**LIFE LESSONS in NEW YORK STORIES**
1990	**GOODFELLAS**
1991	Cape Fear
1993	**THE AGE OF INNOCENCE**
1995	Casino

11 NEW YORK FILMS out of
19 feature films

WOODY ALLEN

1969	*Take the Money and Run*
1971	*Bananas*
1972	Everything You Always Wanted to Know about Sex...
1973	Sleeper
1975	Love and Death
1977	**ANNIE HALL**
1978	*Interiors*
1979	**MANHATTAN**
1980	*Stardust Memories*
1982	A Midsummer Night Sex Comedy
1983	ZELIG **BROADWAY DANNY ROSE**
1985	The Purple Rose of Cairo
1986	**HANNAH AND HER SISTERS**
1987	**RADIO DAYS** September
1988	ANOTHER WOMAN
1989	**OEDIPUS WRECKS in NEW YORK STORIES CRIMES AND MISDEMEANORS**
1990	**ALICE**
1991	Shadows and Fog
1992	**HUSBANDS AND WIVES**
1993	**MANHATTAN MURDER MYSTERY**
1994	**BULLETS OVER BROADWAY**
1995	MIGHTY APHRODITE

11 NEW YORK FILMS +7 FILMS USING
NEW YORK AS A BACKDROP or *including
one or a few New York sequences* out of 25 feature films

Insiders and Outsiders

Latent Urban Thinking in Movies of Modern Rome

David Bass

'United Kingdom' sugar cubes

The seven hills of Rome (from Fazio degli Uberti, *Dittamondo*, 1447)

A special edition of sugar-cubes (illustrated alongside), entitled 'United Kingdom', highlights the difficulties and limitations of representing a complex entity in single images. Iconic buildings (Tower Bridge, Big Ben and telephone box), typical transport (double-decker bus and London taxi), characteristic clothing (bearskin, brolly and bowler hat); and national pastimes (polo and 'teatime') assemble like objects in a lost property office trying to describe their absent owner. Movies, too, attempt to build up a latent whole through the accumulation of fragments, but fragments which unfold in sequences over time, participating in narrative and other discourses.

A movie has neither presumptions nor obligations to encyclopedic completeness, and so its choice of fragments and their mode of assembly is relatively unfettered. What is selected for inclusion is often less revealing than what is excluded – lost, as it were, in the interstices between chosen fragments. Rome's enormous social and material complexity and its paradoxical relationship to time (its 'eternal' epithet attests to its ability to change) make the number of possible 'takes' on the city limitless.

Representations of Rome in other media also exercise the same rights of selection and assembly as film. A fifteenth-century drawing and a twentieth-century souvenir ashtray both extract fragments from the city (its seven hills in the case of the drawing, St Peter's and the Colosseum in that of the ashtray), obliterate the rest, and congeal them together to make a hybrid object that 'represents' the city.

The fragments from which such synthetic cities can be collaged may be merely characteristic of their source city or, like the Colosseum, unique and iconic. They may be arranged – like tourist souvenirs – without regard to the city's topography, or may follow it closely, like a jubilee year map from 1575 (The seven churches of Rome). Although it chooses not to show much of the city's contents, the map depicts the River Tiber, the Aurelian walls and (at massively magnified scale) Rome's seven pilgrimage churches and the lines of pilgrims traipsing between them, all in their proper relative positions. The map implicitly contains a 'narrative': the ritualised path of the pilgrims' visit. Other representations may warp the city's topography in deference to their overriding narrative or idea. Some replay its topography in miniature, like the Villa d'Este's Rometta fountain, whose representations of the Tiber and Rome's significant buildings are placed roughly according to the city's plan. Rometta acknowledges its own artificiality, being placed in the gardens for comparison with a view of the real city in the distance. Other representations such as the panorama and cinema work towards a more immersive and delusive simulation of the city.

Cinema's gearing towards the representation of action over time means that it can speak of the relationship between a city's life and its physical constitution in a way unavailable to earlier forms of representational media. Such a relationship lies at the core of this essay, which will largely ignore the conventional categories used in criticism of Italian films, in order to uncover six different latent spatial takes on the city of Rome. Of these six categories of urban thinking, the first is the almost exclusive preserve of the 'outsider' to Rome.

The Outsider's View: Taming the City

'This film was photographed and recorded in its entirety in Rome, Italy' – statement in title sequence of *Roman Holiday* (1952)

Outsiders' films of Rome violently warp the city's topography and present stereotypes of its culture and physical constitution. Such films are intimately tied to the phenomenon of tourism: filming on location is a form of visit, the plot concerns the exploits of outsiders visiting the city, and viewing represents a form of 'armchair tourism'.[1]

Anonymous, without obligations, and away from habitual activities, the tourist requires cultural and spatial orientation, or lapses into inappropriate behaviour. Though guidebooks existed for touristic predecessors in the pilgrimage and Grand Tour cults, Rome's first wave of modern mass 'tourists' in the 1944 Allied liberation of the city used masterpieces of cultural compression such as *Rome – 3000 years in 15 minutes*, and *Soldier's Guide to Rome* for this purpose.

20 Million Miles to Earth (1957), directed by the USA-based Nathan Juran, features perhaps one of the most unruly and unprepared of 'tourists': a monster from Venus. Tied up in Rome's zoo, it misses its native diet of sulphur and breaks free, pursuing an elephant out of the entrance gates. The creatures' haphazard route is typical of 'outsider' movies. First, they run past the neighbouring Villa Borghese, which lies beyond the Aurelian walls. Then, at the Porta Ardeatina five miles away around the city wall, terrified Romans are seen fleeing the city towards the sea, only for their illogical 'escape' to be barred by the appearance of the battling creatures. With the tourist's nose for the *centro storico*, monster and elephant then head into the city centre, setting geography and population in turmoil. At this point, the movements of crowds, creatures and the US army in hot pursuit become as hard to predict as they are to follow. Their routes jump-cut around the city, taking in all the major sights, in a visually glorious but topographically nonsensical sequence.[2] Although the Venusian has neither guidebook nor map, the director of this baffling chase clearly does.[3]

Most 'outsider' movies contain similarly out-of-sequence litanies of landmarks, usually encompassed within title sequences, chases or rides. Such films-within-the-film unwittingly emphasise the slippage between action and setting characteristic of this type of film: the film deals with the story, while the film-within-the-film states the location.

This type of movie is known in Italian as *film cartolina*: a moving postcard collection. Postcards or snapshots provide a validation – similar to *Roman Holiday*'s opening caption

'Roma' souvenir ashtray

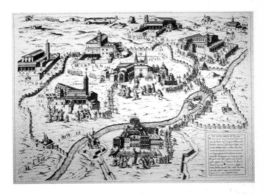

The seven churches of Rome (Antonio Lafréry, 1575)

Villa d'Este: Rometta Fountain (engraving by Venturini, 1685)

85

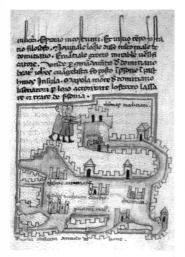

Topography warped by an overriding idea: Rome in the form of a lion (C13th)

Incident on the Campidoglio Hill (*20 Million Miles to Earth*)

Diagonal view of the Trevi Fountain (*Roman Holiday*)

(above) – that one was really 'there'. They provide surrogate memories of city fragments, and also fragmentary foreknowledge of the city. In a vicious circle of confirmation, collecting and possessing such prepackaged 'memories' can become the purpose of a typical holiday.[4] Like objects out of context or like pieces in a museum, postcards or film fragments may be arranged and ordered according to a number of overviews, the primary of which is an aestheticising gaze.

While sharing its subject-matter with the postcard and its predecessor, the engraved *veduta*, cinema has created new conventions for representing its chosen objects. It replaces the standard static view of the Trevi Fountain (viewed diagonally from Santi Vincenzo ed Anastasio) with a shot that emerges into the piazza from the narrow Via Lavatore to its side, so recreating the breathtaking effect of stumbling into this theatrical set-piece from the surrounding warren of alleys. The movie camera typically scans the Colosseum in sweeping, rotating movements that echo its form. The grandiose, unearthly Vittorio Emanuele monument is shown axially, often appearing through a dilating iris, thus echoing its overambitious and overbearing reworking of its context. Like the postcard, the *film cartolina* shows the tourist what to see, but adds the obligation of the 'right' way to experience Rome's landmarks.

Through montage, film can imply spatial adjacency between its moving-postcard monuments, and thus obliterate intervening tracts of real urban context as effectively as in any souvenir ashtray. In a scene from *Three Coins in the Fountain* (1955), one of a group of American women touring Rome asks, 'What's that?', as their car leaves the Piazza del Quirinale frame-left. The answer, 'That's the Fountain of Trevi', comes in the next shot, as the car enters frame-right to emerge from the Via Lavatore into the splendid sight. This smooth edit belies the fact that 300 yards of city separating these two places have been obliterated. Unwittingly an epicentre for jump-cutting, the Trevi Fountain finds itself in *Roman Holiday* implicitly placed next to the Via Condotti 600 yards away. Such 'postcard' movies warp and fold the city, ignoring and destroying swathes of urban context, to create a film-city of 'attractions' selected from the real city's obliging scenic reserve. The city of attractions is a lazy tourist's dream: a collection of desirable wonders, visitable without hot slogs through potentially boring, dangerous, 'non-places' in between.

As well as denying Rome's topography, the *film cartolina* alters its historical and cultural contexts. The same car ride in *Three Coins* ends up at a grand building which basks in sunshine, its terracotta-coloured walls contrasting with lush greenery and the blue sky. The next shot – a glass door with a sign reading 'United States Distribution Agency' – effectively hides the building's real identity (part of Enrico Del Debbio and Luigi Moretti's Foro Mussolini built to honour Hitler's visit to Rome, it contained Mussolini's private gymnasium and pool) and substitutes a domesticated reading.

The *film cartolina* tames the city by manipulating its scale as well as by massaging its contents. While, typically, panoramic establishing shots state Rome to be a grand but distant object, the protagonists experience the city as relatively small. The film-city's collectable sights neighbour each other, and frequent chance meetings and other narrative conveniences reduce the city's potential vastness. Each of the cinematically joined-up sights in this distilled 'city', on the other hand, is made to appear larger than life: shot frontally and full-frame (to eliminate its context), looking up (to simulate its effect on the overawed pedestrian), and with a lingering gaze (after all, such monuments are the reason the producers paid out to come to Rome).[5] Such films' manipulations of scale simultaneously enhance the city's ability to overwhelm, while reducing the threat of its size. In its transformation of intimidation into reassurance, the *film cartolina* parallels the early Grand Tourists' management of the sublime through 'Lorraine glasses', which made tolerable the sight of mountains, glaciers, seascapes and other monstrously vast and impure sights.

The *film cartolina* enframes, targets, shoots and captures its desired images, in a predatory strategy akin to that of the postcard or snapshot.[6] Following the Romantic literary convention of (male) protagonists who metonymically identify a city with one of its (female) inhabitants and must then possess her to come to terms with the city, the protagonist in Marcel l'Herbier's *Feu Mathias Pascal* (1925) seeks a similar double victory. Having repeatedly chanced across a woman on his jump-cut wandering around Rome, he 'spies' her again in the Foro Romano from the Lungotevere Marzio. This desiring gaze penetrates a mile of intervening city fabric. The *film cartolina* conquers not only people and monuments, but the whole city – remaking it, destroying the parts folded away in the interstices of its montage, and suppressing fragments or aspects that do not conform to its overview.

This cinematic mentality is paralleled by the city planning of regimes exercising extreme political or military power . In Paris, Baron Haussmann cut long straight streets through urban fabric to connect together the new empire's key monuments. Reducing in this way the medieval city's seemingly unknowable and amorphous character, he structured the experience of the new Paris as a succession of perspectively enforced vistas, each terminated by a political set-piece. His massive campaign of clearing and cleaning up also had militaristic motives, enabling troop movement and the suppression of subversion. In Rome, Mussolini hacked away with similar military and propagandistic intent, enabling favoured monuments or symbolic connections to be spelt out clearly, written through the everyday urban fabric. Pope Alexander VII's regime made urban surgery possible on a similar scale. He had '*tutta Roma di legno*' – a wooden model of Rome – in his bedroom, which he remodelled and played with like a train set. His notes to himself about the changes he wanted to see in the city make megalomaniac reading, It comes as no surprise that he proposed to move the fountain which would later be remodelled as today's Trevi to a new site in Piazza Colonna[7] – a feat later to be performed so often and casually on this hapless monument by cinematic jump-cutting.

Perhaps the tourists' most unproductive response to their holiday destination is to pay it no attention or to be bored by it. In *National Lampoon's European Vacation* (1985), visiting American children resent their parents' injunctions to trawl round a check-list of Rome's sights. Bruce Lee's *The Way of the Dragon* (1973) is probably the most extreme example of blasé cine-tourism. Though set in Rome, the film is almost totally oblivious to its setting. Otherwise centred on a Chinese restaurant, this kung fu *tour de force* features a journey through the city made when the visiting Lee is collected from the airport. As the monuments flash past in customarily disordered sequence, his hostess describes the difficulties a gang of extortionists make for her business. It could have been set in any other city, so complete is the slippage between soundtrack and visuals.[8]

'What's that?' (*Three Coins in the Fountain*)

'That's the Fountain of Trevi' (*Three Coins in the Fountain*)

Dialogue (*The Way of the Dragon*): Miss Chen: '...So I wrote to my uncle in Hong Kong. I thought he would send me a lawyer but now ... ' Bruce Lee: 'Hey, hey. I've told you I'm here to get you out of this mess. Miss Chen, don't worry. Just leave it to me. I'll get them.'

Bicycle Thieves

Bicycle Thieves

Bicycle Thieves

The tourist movie treats the city as a museum and reconfigures its decontextualised contents at will. A similar practise can occur in the design of real cities. Seeing inspiration in other cities, the architect-tourist proposes fragments of them – souvenirs of their visit – to be built in his/her native city. Such is the (purely aesthetic) basic of much post-modern 'that's nice, I'll have one of those' design. This kind of visual borrowing is at least partially blind to the real conditions of life in the 'donor' city. By restating conditions in the context of Rome, and not seeing it as a treasure-house of aesthetic delights available for plunder, the 'insider's view' seeks to redress such an imbalance.

The Insider's View: Urban Context
'Before choosing this particular child (Enzo Staiola), De Sica did not ask him to perform, just to walk. He wanted to play off the striding gait of the man against the short, trotting steps of the child ... It would not be an exaggeration to say that *Ladri di biciclette* is the story of a walk through Rome by a father and his son' (André Bazin).[9]

The outsider's view of the city can be characterised as a random itinerary of attractions, framed within the context of a visit. In 'urban context' movies, the insider sees the city as a strict itinerary of repulsions. If the *film cartolina* remakes the city in the service of the film, folding it to maximise the intake of touristic sights, then insiders' films of resistant urban context are made in the service of the existing city, their actions guided and squeezed by its intransigent topography and the character of its areas.

Traditionally symbolic of defence and unassailability, rusticated walls provide the unaccommodating background to an old man's wanderings with his dog around Rome's dusty streets in Vittorio De Sica's *Umberto D* (1952). The eponymous hero is nowhere at home – conditions are intolerable in his rented room, but poor-houses and soup kitchens are inimical to his need to maintain *figura* (the appearance of dignity) – and so he wanders the streets, finding precious little consolation.[10] Rome's glorious monuments are irrelevant to him, their visual order and grandeur contrasting cruelly with the old man's disintegrating life, and acting instead to heighten his discomfiture. Umberto D's greatest moments of embarrassment take place in the only two monumental spaces featured in the film. Designed as a grand welcoming space for foreign visitors, the Piazza del Popolo witnesses his pathetic attempt to raise some money by selling his watch. In front of the Pantheon, the viewer sees Umberto D trying for the first time to beg, and rhymes his cupped hand with the building's dome, which inverts and mocks the gesture on a monumental scale. This struggling citizen's world is the underside of a city which bends over backwards to put on a splendid show for its visitors.

Mobility allows a degree of freedom to those for whom the city would be an intractable and restrictive environment, enabling them to 'edit' it and offering opportunities to find more amenable places. A bicycle allows Ricci, the protagonist of *Bicycle Thieves* (1948), to advance himself socially by taking up a job in the city centre putting up posters advertising foreign films. His hopes are dashed when the bicycle is stolen on his first day at work. The film documents Ricci's subsequent grim search through Rome's flea markets and other unglamorous places for his vehicle of freedom. The director employs a number of parallels: between the search for a bicycle and the protagonist's struggle for freedom and identity – man and bike both being hopelessly lost, even torn to pieces by the intervention of external forces of injustice (poignantly, the bicycle frame is by Fides, or 'faith'); between structures which reinforce anonymity and uniformity – the blocks in Valmelaina where the Riccis live resemble the racks where pawned linen is stored and the pigeon-holes where crime reports are filed for police (in)action; and between predicaments and settings: Ricci questions an old man who he suspects to know the thief's identity on the Ponte Palatino, with the piazza of the *Bocca della Verità* (a kind of ancient Roman lie-detector) in the background, and finds himself in dark places – the tunnel under the Quirinale and under the Ponte duca d'Aosta – in moments of despair. Beyond developing such parallels and finding symbolic dimensions for existing places in the city, De Sica's main innovation is in how precisely he maps the father and son's quest through Rome. Their wanderings follow the city's topography accurately, reflect Italian ways of life, and adhere to the specific character of the various Roman districts and their inhabitants. *Umberto D*'s and *Bicycle Thieves*' engagement with a real, inhabited city of quotidian – if bleak – dramas is a reaffirmation of Roman Rome, in the face of the outsider's view of a city of past splendours.[11]

Poveri, ma belli

The Insider's View: Neighbourhood

'The fifties represent the worst period in the history of the Italian cinema – with the exception of fascism. It was a period of so-called pink neo-realism, of … *Poveri, ma belli*, of flat composite films put together for a quick profit. The Italian cinema was pervaded by mystifying optimism, escapism and happy misery' (Sandro Zambetti).[12]

'I portray things as they are. In my opinion, it is important not only to tell the truth, but also to show it as profoundly as possible.' (Dino Risi, director of *Poveri, ma belli*).[13]

The poor protagonists' struggles in 'urban context' movies are enacted in questing *vagabondaggi* – or wanderings – through the city. In such movies, the spaces of the city form a matrix in which urgent political messages are worked out in the context of everyday life. The characters in 'neighbourhood' movies are also poor, but are basically contented and so they rarely stray from home. Lacking political ambitions, the neighbourhood movie is frequently dismissed as trivial and dubbed '*pink* neo-realist' or 'Italian comedy'. Spatially, however, their observation is acute, revealing how Roman neighbourhoods are constituted, and how subtle but unspectacular relationships between private, semi-public and public spaces work as contexts for everyday life. Like many disdained types of film, the neighbourhood movie demands, on closer inspection, to be taken seriously.[14]

Dino Risi's *Poveri, ma belli* (1957) begins with the camera prowling around two neighbouring families' flats and their associated semi-public spaces and thresholds: the stairs and landings where casual meetings and avoidances take place, and the courtyard, overlooked by a balcony divided by railings into private areas for caged birds and drying clothes. Across these railings, the two 'poor but handsome' young men arrange to go out, then meet on the landing, and race down two flights of stairs (actually the same single flight repeated – families of such modest means would not live on the *piano nobile*). So far, a simple, densely inhabited repertoire of spaces. The next shot comes as a jolt: Piazza Navona, a grand space important to tourist and *film cartolina* itineraries. A moment later, the young men tumble out into the piazza (we see the building's front door, guarded by mothers, later on in the film) to start a day of half-hearted work, bantering with friends playing football in the piazza, and flirting with the new girl in the tailor's shop.

Poveri, ma belli

Poveri, ma belli

Nose-diving on the City (Tullio Crali, 1939)

L'oro di Roma

L'oro di Roma

Despite its great interest to the outsiders, the protagonists never comment on the piazza. It is simply their stamping ground.[15] The easy and unquestioning way they inhabit their spectacular location – characteristic of Rome, where houses cling to ruins, and 'significant' buildings are transformed and occupied unselfconsciously – enables the film to reclaim Piazza Navona's original meanings. The piazza is on the site of Domitian's stadium and follows its shape in plan, and even use as ancient supports for access stairs and superstructure as party walls (such as the one against which the young men's stair is built) between newer properties. Like its presiding church, S. Agnese in Agone, the piazza's name derives (via '*n'agona*' and '*campus agonis*') from the *agon* – or contests of various forms – which took place in the stadium. But instead of the sea battle re-enactments or athletic games it used to host, the piazza in *Poveri, ma belli* now houses contests of 'last one out's a cissy', football and love, demonstrating a cultural continuity more profound than that of mere physical configuration.

The easy but subtle choreography of private, semi-public and public realms parallels the intricate intertwining of lives within the neighbourhood and between the two families. After various unsatisfactory arrangements, including a difficult love triangle involving the tailor's girl (and considering the contemporary social necessity – affecting also the expectations of the film's primarily local intended audience – to displace the two men's implicit desire for each other), the film's implied ending in which the men start dating each other's sister seems inevitable.

Poveri, ma belli presents a cosily isolated view of its protagonists' neighbourhood as a microcosmic world blithely ignorant of external influences. Other 'neighbourhood' films acknowledge external cultural contexts and attempt to situate their particular district within them. *Un americano a Roma* plays on the contemporary Italian jealousy of America, while *Una giornata particolare* (an 'urban-block' movie equal to Alfred Hitchcock's *Rear Window* of 1954), situates life in Mario De Renzi's enormous Via XXI Aprile apartment complex in the historic context of Hitler's visit to Rome.

Two strategies have been adopted to situate the neighbourhood spatially within the larger context of the city: juxtaposing the district against more globalising views; and investigating the district's boundary. The title sequence of *Mignon è partita* features a pan across a map of Rome to find the district in which the protagonists' apartment block is housed. In 1955, *Racconti romani* started a spate of helicopter rides which invited the (primarily local) spectator to identify and situate his/her own neighbourhood within a Rome seen from above. Possibly inspired by Futurist *aeropittura*, or the related use of aerial reconnaissance in warfare, helicopters offered a new form of city spectatorship, which reached its apogee in Cesare Zavattini's 1963 project *I misteri di Roma*. This project for a *film inchiesta* (investigation) of a day in the life of Rome required an 'invasion force' of directors and 'a helicopter [which] will let us see how *our* city looks from above [at all times of day and night]'.[16] For Zavattini, the aerial view is for revelatory self-examination, not lazy tourism.

In *L'oro di Roma* (1961), Lizzani situates the Jewish ghetto in the city by examining its boundary conditions. Two telephone calls enframe the film. The first, shot through a window which reflects a panorama of wealthy Roman suburbs, shows a young Jewish woman, who plans to convert to Christianity, marry a gentile and leave the ghetto. Her state of suspension – about to leave the neighbourhood, its religion and society – is reinforced by the ambiguity of the superimposed image.[17] In the film, the ghetto's traditional boundary is blankly stated in maps over which the Nazis discuss the area's sequestration, and more subtly in the creation of a religious/moral topography across it. The lovers part by the Teatro Marcello at the edge of the ghetto. The fiancé always leaves from such partings back into the gentile city, going up the hill from the Teatro Marcello in the direction of the Campidoglio, where the Nazis have their headquarters. At the centre of the ghetto (in the twentieth century, at least) is the new synagogue, where the community gathers, and where *L'oro di Roma* starts. In the last telephone call, the woman says goodbye to her fiancé from the telephone box she normally uses by the Teatro Marcello. Despite having just been baptised into the church, she has decided to rejoin her people and be rounded up with them into vans by the Nazis. In this shot, the synagogue is framed in the window behind her, implicitly tying her back socially and spatially to the neighbourhood and resolving both the film and her inner predicament.

Accattone

The Insider's View: Periphery

'Via Fanfulla da Lodi, in the middle of Pigneto, with low shacks, peeling walls, there was a granular magnitude in its extreme meanness; a poor, humble, unknown alley, lost under the sun in a Rome that wasn't Rome' (Pier Paolo Pasolini).[18]

From the early settlement of *Roma Quadrata* on the Palatine, through successively expanding city walls and ring roads, Rome has been a bounded city. Areas beyond its boundaries can be considered 'out of bounds' – an exterior 'not-Rome'. Following the 'neighbourhood' movies' concern with local boundaries, a number of films characterised by a heavier tone and slower pace than their largely comic forebears examined the edge of the city itself. These films' intense gaze[19] is, however, more than an attempt to find the Rome which is not there. It tries to discover and scrutinise what *is* in the periphery.

The official 1962 *piano regolatore* also recognised the fact of the periphery, but sought to regulate its recent uncontrolled growth. The 'periphery' movie, however, seeks to uncover the poetry of the outskirts. It portrays its protagonists (who – as beggars, thieves, homosexuals and prostitutes – some may consider socially as well as geographically marginal) as allegorical or even mythical figures. Although its buildings are desperately expedient and its planning chaotic, the periphery's environment is shown – like its inhabitants – to be freighted with symbolism.[20] Unlike Ricci in *Bicycle Thieves*, the periphery movies' protagonists do not want to come into the centre to work and become respectable. If they do enter the city, they demonstrate their addiction to liminality by jumping off bridges into the Tiber, selling themselves or thieving.

Mamma Roma

Usually interpreted as the neglected underside of the nation's economic miracle, the ragged urban periphery of Pasolini's *Accattone* (1961) can be seen equally, in its raw vigour and authenticity, as the real emergent new Italy. Rome itself must have started this way. The heroic squalor of the present echoes the mythic origins of a heroic past.

Though often discussed as a single topic, Pasolini's movies present diverse perspectives on the periphery. The radical abjection of *Accattone*'s shanties, or *borgate*, is worlds away from the humane and careful design of the Tuscolano district INA-Casa developments featured in *Mamma Roma* (1962). The eponymous heroine frequently walks along the

Mamma Roma

Le tentazioni del Dottor Antonio

Dear Diary

La dolce vita

district's main street, between the entry canopy of Adalberto Libera's Tuscolano III at one end, to the cranked portal of Mario De Renzi and Saverio Muratori's apartments at the other. This opening, whose expressive concrete members negotiate a corner and continue the street through the apartment block, is an intense feature in an otherwise sober building. But Mamma Roma is always drawn to this fracture in the building, whose distraught gesticulation echoes her own state. She will never be accepted, or accept herself, in this place. Even though the view from her window, at which she despairingly throws herself as the film ends, seems Rome-like enough – the modern church of S. Giovanni Bosco's cupola appearing like a displaced St. Peter's on the horizon – it will never be the 'Rome' after which she is named. Tuscolano is not Rome, and Mamma Roma's work as a prostitute sits uneasily in its small-town 'not-Rome' cohesiveness. Pasolini is also uneasy in this kind of suburb: it lacks the rough and rancid reality of the true periphery.

If the Tuscolano quarter, with its displaced and disconcerting landmarks, can be seen as a ghostly 'not-Rome', the situation of Mussolini's third Rome, EUR, is even more complex. Also on the periphery – and therefore not Rome – EUR tries explicitly to be Rome, and isn't. Grandiosely conceived for an international fair, EUR's planning, monuments and orientation derive from a Fascist interpretation of what made Rome great, a reading in which the city is seen entirely as a configurational issue, and in which all but the rhetorically heroic aspects of its content are ignored.[21] Originally an instrument of a totalitarian state, Mussolini's new non-city has subsequently proven notoriously resistant to inhabitation. It attracts visitors, who take a perverse pleasure from being intimidated by its martial regularity, enforced perspectives, disconcerting scale and lack of patina, and derive a consolatory relief from knowing that this 'not-Rome' is not Rome.

Fellini plays on EUR's banal and terrifying unreality in *Le tentazioni del Dottor Antonio* (1962), making it the setting for other forms of escape from reality, such as dreams, cinema and advertising. The film centres on a prototypical form of cinema: a billboard of CinemaScope proportions featuring a giant Anita Ekberg advertising milk. Its crude speakers incessantly blare out the soundtrack – an insanely cheerful advertising jingle ('*Bevete più latte …*'). Enraged by the crowds drawn to this spectacle and by Ekberg's provocative pose, Doctor Antonio (one of EUR's dull, repressed inhabitants) becomes obsessed and, hallucinating, sees her descend from the billboard to tower over EUR's streets and taunt him. Away from the complex community and chaotic order of Rome's centre, in the peripheral region of obsessive regimentation and banal representation (first Fascist, then capitalist), monsters grow.

In a meditation on centre and periphery, Rome and EUR, old and new, Antonioni portrays EUR's double absence in the last sequence of *L'eclisse* (1962). Having arranged to meet at their usual place – a strangely nondescript crossroads in EUR – the protagonists Alain Delon and Monica Vitti fail to turn up. The camera does, though, witnessing their absence and observing – for seven increasingly anxious minutes as darkness falls – the comings and goings of this (non-)place. In the characters' absence, the crossroads – and, by extension, EUR – is forced, unprepared and unsuited, into the role of protagonist: a lonely and uneasy protagonist with nothing to say for itself.[22]

Recent films show how the periphery is becoming normalised, its bleakness, banality and despair decreasing as time brings inhabitation and erodes its veneer of newness. Nanni Moretti's *Dear Diary* (1993) features the director marking Rome's boundaries, visiting the commonly disdained garden suburbs and modern megastructures that encircle the city. As he wanders around on his vespa, a *motoflâneur* of the suburbs, his curiosity and enthusiasm for the ordinary uncover things to stimulate the imagination in the outskirts. Underneath Moretti's whimsical enthusings, there is still a darker side to the periphery. At the end of his *vagabondaggi*, Moretti makes a pilgrimage to the seaside location where Pasolini was murdered by the kind of boys from the *borgate* about whom he made his first films.

Fellini Roma

The Insider's View: The Metaphoric City

'I can be a good reporter only if I invent things' (Federico Fellini).[23]

In Roy Rowland's *Seven Hills of Rome* (1957), a sightseeing trip by helicopter ends with a cry of 'Look: Bernini's masterpiece', as it touches down in front of St Peter's and deposits its passengers in the piazza to count the columns in its colonnades. Fellini's *La dolce vita* (1960) also begins with the arrival of a helicopter at St. Peter's. Suspending a giant statue of Christ on a cable, it flies along the line of the ancient S. Felice aqueduct. Following in another helicopter, a journalist and a photographer try unsuccessfully to exchange words with women sunbathing on roofs beneath them. Before we have a chance to land and count the columns, the scene cuts abruptly to an Oriental dancer in a Via Veneto nightclub.

La dolce vita

In contrast to the neat scenario of Rowland's *film cartolina*, Fellini presents a complex and compromised vision, collaging ancient and modern, sacred and profane, public communication and private incomprehension. Eclipsing the news event that inspired it, Fellini's scene has become a new symbol of Rome. If the aqueduct no longer brings water to the city, and acts instead as a conduit for images, one could say that Fellini's city is made from images, which he brings to the screen in a theatrically heightened form.

Though tourist views, urban contexts, neighbourhoods and the periphery all occur in Fellini's films, his relation to individual locations in Rome is loose. He neither navigates nor jump-cuts knowingly around the city, but presents single scenes in succession which each investigate particular aspects of Rome and its life. Fellini collides his scenes together, like the succession of acts in a circus or variety theatre (both themes dear to the director). Rome is, for Fellini, a repository of 'acts', from which – like his satiric forebears Pasquino, Belli and Trilussa, or photographic anthologisers such as Bavagnoli – he selects one by one. In terms of a latent urban model, Fellini's Rome is akin to Rem Koolhaas's 'culture of congestion': a block structure of differences, placed opportunistically side by side.[24]

But his city is more than a haphazard collection of sideshow acts. Its various aspects, illustrated brilliantly in Fellini's vignettes, are drawn from a greater whole: a mythic/geographic entity called 'Rome'. So richly are the city's facets interrelated that each vignette has the power to recall this larger entity. Each of his scenes – whether an ecclesiastical fashion show in the Palazzo Spada, or dining in a piazza criss-crossed by tram-lines – serves as a metaphor of the city itself.

His frequent depictions of entries into the city also affirm Rome's status as a distinct place with which one has to come to terms.[25] *La dolce vita* starts with the helicopters' entry, but features a longer processional entry sequence of a more purely secular type – that of a celebrated American starlet (played by the Swedish actress Anita Ekberg). Ekberg's entry could be understood as an inverted version of that undertaken in 1655 by

La dolce vita

Mussolini inaugurates Cinecittà, 1937

Bellissima

Intervista

her compatriot, Queen Christina of Sweden. Instead of the foreigner's customary ceremonial entry route from the north down the Via Flaminia, Ekberg arrives in a more modern manner, from Ciampino Airport in the south and then up the Appian Way. After a series of adventures, she becomes part of the city by baptism' in the Trevi Fountain's waters, framed by the triumphal arch[26] embedded in the Palazzo Poli's façade which forms its backdrop. Many 'acts' in *Fellini Roma* work with the city/woman metaphor, not least the 'triumphal entry' of the camera crew, led by a phallic crane, into the city.[27]

From *La dolce vita* onwards, Fellini constructed his urban set-pieces in the studios of Cinecittà, isolated from potential contamination by the real city. The lack of surrounding city context in the studios emphasises the separateness of his individual city- 'acts', while enabling him to realise his visions in all their specificity. Occasionally he reveals these heightened representations' artificiality, and revels in demonstrating how the spectacle has been set up.[28]

The Insider's View: The City of Films
'De Sica, Visconti, Rossellini, Antonioni, whom all the world by now knows, almost as if they were the Colosseum or Piazza Venezia' (Cesare Zavattini).[29]

Designed like a modernist army camp and constructed with comparable haste, Cinecittà was inaugurated in April 1937. Over large white letters reading – instead of 'HOLLYWOOD' – 'CINEMA IS THE STRONGEST WEAPON', a 35-foot-high cut-out of Mussolini operating a movie camera 'directed' the ceremony, like a crazed but inanimate Dziga Vertov.[30]

But Cinecittà was more than simply a replacement for the CINES studios destroyed by fire shortly before, and more than autarchic Italy's place of resistance against foreign films. It was – as its name implies – a city in itself. Containing everything needed for making films, from studios and workshops to processing laboratories, Cinecittà's city-like diversity of activities was squeezed into a plan strikingly similar to Mussolini's new towns in the Pontine marshes and in newly colonised Ethiopia.[31]

As well as being a place where movies are made, Cinecittà has been employed as a location in films concerned with movie making and spectatorship, both as a fragment of Rome and as a city in its own right.[32] In *Bellissima* (1951), its studios are besieged by proud mothers entering their daughters in a contest to find the prettiest young girl in Rome. The film's central character, played by Anna Magnani, longingly watches pioneers' wagons in a Western screened in the courtyard of her apartment complex, fuelling hopes for her pilgrimage with her daughter to Cinecittà, the place where new frontiers open up, lives transform into film, reality is transcended and fortune beckons.
In *Intervista* (1987), Fellini shows a similar pilgrimage. A young reporter (a semi-autobiographical figure) visits the studios for the first time. His tram journey starts with a touristic sequence of landmarks which is replaced – as he comes closer to Cinecittà's field of transformational influence – by fantastic events: red indians, waterfalls, elephants … On arrival at Cinecittà, the camera lingers over its sole postcard-worthy view: the entry portal.

Fellini uses Cinecittà as more than a site of fantasy, a sight of Rome, or even a city: it is another 'Rome'. The reporter shares his surname (Rubini) with both Marcello, the hero of *La dolce vita*, and with Moraldo, that of Fellini's screenplay *Moraldo in città*, who arrives in Rome with similar hopes of finding fame and fortune. Fellini also begins *Intervista* with a misty aerial view of a model of Cinecittà, recalling the view of Rome through clouds with which he wanted *Fellini Roma* to begin.

Extending his fascination with revealing the construction of spectacle, Fellini's movies became increasingly concerned with film-making and taking film-making apart.[33] *Intervista* involves a number of films simultaneously: Fellini's half-hearted attempt to film Kafka's *Amerika*; a Japanese television documentary about Fellini; fragments of a fantasy-documentary about Fellini's youth; numerous films and commercials being shot in Cinecittà, in which Fellini occasionally intervenes to direct their 'directors'; a fragment from *La dolce vita*; and *Intervista* itself, the container into which these 'films' have been (albeit rebelliously) corralled. Cinecittà is employed at a number of levels in the film: as a model sitting in a room in the 'real' Cinecittà; as a site in Rome; as a place containing scenery and equipment for some of the movies enmeshed in the overall film and as a location in its own right for others; as a setting for the everyday life of actors and crew; and – unseen and unbeknown by the viewer – as the enclosure where places other than Cinecittà are reconstructed and shot.

Fellini allows Cinecittà to be present, transformed and represented at different levels, mediating and blurring levels of fantasy, dream, representation and reality and of memory, reconstruction and present actuality. These varying usages of Cinecittà parallel the ways in which film-making activities and sub-films are embedded within *Intervista* itself. Starting with his studio reconstruction of the Via Veneto for *La dolce vita*, Fellini used Cinecittà as the place in which he built his fragments of the city. Cinecittà is for him Rome-like in its transformational qualities, and a meta-Rome in its capacity (shared with this fifteenth-century Roman portal emblazoned with the city's seven hills) to contain representations of itself.

Italian movies have become increasingly media-aware and self-reflexive, starting with spoofs such as Sergio Corbucci's *Totò, Peppino e ... la dolce vita*, (1961) – a comic 'take' on Fellini's film – to such recent intertextual *tours de force* as *Intervista* and Maurizio Nichetti's *The Icicle Thief* (1989), which features frantic attempts to locate film within a mediated domain increasingly pervaded by television and advertising.

Similarly, it becomes difficult to locate a base-city on which media representations are founded. Representations alter reality: *La dolce vita* changed perceptions of the Via Veneto, and its real life and fabric altered accordingly. Relationships between Roman representations and reality are in such a playful state of slippage that Rome has become no longer a destination in itself for some tourists.[34] The aim of the *Roman Holiday* holiday, newly devised for the Japanese market, is to participate in a simulation of the eponymous film's 'visit' to a Rome that never was on a holiday that never was.

The weight of representations of Rome – which we have discussed in the form of different categories of film-city – is such that Rome is becoming a city of films and their directors, as Zavattini predicted, become the city's new monuments.

Intervista

Roma civitas septicollis, (C15th)

News item concerning the *Roman Holiday* holiday

Acknowledgements

I would like to thank the British School at Rome for granting me two periods as Scholar in Architecture from 1993 to 1995, which enabled me to work on this theme in Rome. I would also like to thank James Kabu for his constant support.

Notes

1. For instance: *Feu Mathias Pascal* (Marcel L'Herbier, 1925), *L'Age d'or* (Luis Buñuel, 1930), *Roman Holiday* (William Wyler, 1952), *Three Coins in the Fountain* (Jean Negulesco, 1955), *20 Million Miles to Earth* (Nathan Juran, 1957), *Seven Hills of Rome* (Roy Rowland, 1957), *For the First Time* (Rudolph Maté, 1959), *The Roman Spring of Mrs Stone* (José Quintero, 1961), *Rome Adventure* (Delmer Daves, 1962), *The Way of the Dragon* (Bruce Lee, 1973), *National Lampoon's European Vacation* (Amy Heckerling, 1985), *Little White Lies* (Anson Williams, 1989) and *Hudson Hawk* (Bruce Willis, 1991). *The Belly of an Architect* (Peter Greenaway, 1987) is a more complex and self-conscious variant. *Two Weeks in Another Town* (Vincente Minnelli, 1962) deals not only with the commonplaces of the 'tourist movie', but also explicitly with shooting on location in Rome and Cinecitta (see subheading: The City of Films). *Night on Earth* (Jim Jarmusch, 1991) and *My Own Private Idaho* (Gus van Sant, 1991) are exceptional in this regard and untypical as 'outsider movies'.
2. By some law of averages, a few moments of strange appropriateness occur, such as the elephantine iconography of Armando Brasini's zoo gates, and the elephant's death beside Marcello Piacentini's Casa Madre dei Mutilati (the headquarters of the association of the war-wounded). Probably more knowing is the choice of the Colosseum as the place where the monster is finally slain.
3. *Un marziano a Roma*, by Ennio Flaiano, was not published until 1960.
4. John Urry, *The Tourist Gaze* (London: Sage, 1990), pp. 139–40: ' … much tourism becomes in effect a search for the photogenic; travel is a strategy for the accumulation of photographs. This seems particularly to appeal to those cultures with a very strong work ethic. Japanese, Americans and Germans all seem to 'have' to take photographs – it is a kind of leisure equivalent of the distorting obligations of a strong workplace culture.'
5. These techniques extend Piranesi's practice in his etchings of the *Vedute di Roma*, in which, to reinforce the 'magnificence' of Rome's monuments, bystanders are depicted at half size in relation to their settings, casual irregularities are made orthogonal, and perspectives are exaggerated.
6. Susan Sontag links photography and the *flâneur*. Photography 'first comes into its own as an extension of the eye of the middle-class *flâneur* … The photographer is an armed version of the solitary walker reconnoitring, stalking, cruising the urban inferno, the voyeuristic stroller who discovers the city as a landscape of voluptuous extremes.' Susan Sontag, *On Photography* (Harmondsworth: Penguin, 1979), p. 55.

7. Richard Krautheimer, *The Rome of Alexander VII, 1655–1667* (Princeton, NJ: Princeton University Press, 1985), p. 79: 'Shift the fountain of Piazza Colonna to Piazza S. Marco, the one here on Monte Cavallo to Piazza SS. Apostoli; move the obelisk from Campo Marzo up here to Monte Cavallo; bring the horses [possibly the Quirinale Dioscuri] to flank the watergate planned by cutting the corner of that wall [possibly the entrance to the Quirinale gardens at the end of the proposed Via del Babuino extension] … finish Porta Pia and place opposite it that watergate; bring the show façade, the mostra, of the Trevi Fountain to Piazza Colonna; finish work on Piazza S. Pietro … ' Square brackets contain author's explanatory notes.

8. Although – as in *20 Million Miles* – the law of averages supplies a moment of appropriateness: the final showdown again takes place in the Colosseum.

9. André Bazin, *What is Cinema?* (Berkeley and Los Angeles, Calif.: University of California Press, 1972), Vol. 2 pp. 54–5.

10. For intelligent discussion of a number of films in relation to Italy's post-Second World War economic and political climate, see P. Adams Sitney, *Vital Crises in Italian Cinema: Iconography, Stylistics, Politics* (Austin, Texas: University of Texas Press, 1995).

11. Within the context of neo-realism, such films as *Bicycle Thieves* (Vittorio De Sica, 1948), *Roma ore undici* (Giuseppe De Santis, 1951), *Sciuscià* (Vittorio De Sica, 1946) and *Umberto D* (Vittorio De Sica, 1952) show an (unconscious?) parallel between the protagonist's struggles and those of the under-resourced director trying to get his film made. Other films, such as *Roma città aperta* (Roberto Rossellini, 1945) and *Paisà* (Roberto Rossellini, 1946) parallel the struggle of the city itself in the face of foreign invaders with that of the beleaguered Italian film industry in the face of almost crippling foreign competition.

12. Sandro Zambetti, in Adelio Ferrero (ed.), *Storia di cinema* (Venice: Marsilio, 1978), Vol. 3 p. 58.

13. Dino Risi, quoted in Aldo Vigano, *Dino Risi* (Milan: Moizzi, 1977), p. 11.

14. For instance: *Sotto il sole di Roma* (Renato Castellani, 1948), *Guardie e ladri* (Mario Monicelli and Steno [Stefano Vanzina], 1951), *Un americano a Roma* (Steno [Stefano Vanzina], 1954), *Racconti romani* (Gianni Franciolini, 1955), *Poveri, ma belli* (Dino Risi, 1957), its sequel *Belle, ma povere* (Dino Risi, 1957) and *I soliti ignoti* (Mario Monicelli, 1959). Certain films made after the 1950s also explore neighbourhoods, but are less susceptible to such categorisation or to accusations of triviality: *L'oro di Roma* (Carlo Lizzani, 1961), *Una giornata particolare* (Ettore Scola, 1977), *I ragazzi di Via Panisperna* (Gianni Amelio, 1989) and *Mignon è partita* (Francesca Archibugi, 1989).

15. As are, occasionally, the bathing establishments under the Ponte S. Angelo nearby. Trips further afield are few, and provoke crises such as a feeble threat by one of the men, when spurned by the girl from the tailor's shop, to throw himself off Mussolini's Ponte Flaminio.

16. Francesco Bolzoni, *I misteri di Roma di Cesare Zavattini* (Rome: Cappelli, 1963), pp. 13–32 (author's italics and bracketed paraphrasing).

17. This shot – and a number of others in the film – shows a strong alignment with some of Antonioni's cinematic techniques. For a discussion of Antonioni's use of glass, see David Bass, 'Window/Glass: Reflections on Antonioni', *Scroope* 7, 1995–6.
18. Quoted in Sitney, *Vital Crises*, p. 180.
19. For instance: *Accattone* (Pier Paolo Pasolini, 1959), *La commare secca* (Bernardo Bertolucci, 1962), *L'eclisse* (Michelangelo Antonioni, 1962) and *Mamma Roma* (Pier Paolo Pasolini, 1962).
20. In *Accattone*, for instance, a pan down a blank wall finds a man at its base, who asks: 'Isn't there a saint who protects the hungry? If you're there, help out.' His question is (not) answered by a pan back up the unspeaking wall.
21. It is interesting to observe how the vision of ancient Rome put forward in Carmine Gallone's contemporary *Scipione l'Africano* (1937) corresponds to that of EUR, but with the buildings sporting a more explicitly ancient Roman fancy dress. The portrayal/remaking of ancient Rome in movies is, however, beyond the scope of this essay.
22. For mysterious reasons, people even now tend to behave uneasily at this point where Viale della Tecnica and Via del Ciclismo cross: they halt, cross and recross inexplicably.
23. Giovanni Grazzini (ed.), *Federico Fellini – Comments on Film* (Fresno, Calif: The Press at California State University, Fresno, 1988), p. 119.
24. See Rem Koolhaas, *Delirious New York: a Retroactive Manifesto for Manhattan* (Rotterdam: 010 Publishers, 1994), especially pp. 123–25, 152–58.
25. This theme occurs in Federico Fellini: *Lo sceicco bianco* (1952), *Le notti di Cabiria* (1957), *La dolce vita* (1960), *Otto e mezzo* (1963), *Toby Dammit* (1968), *Fellini Roma* (1972) and *Intervista* (1987), as well as in screenplays such as *Moraldo in Città* (1954).
26. An architectural motif originating in, and subsequently associated with, victorious entrances into the city.
27. For a more detailed exposition of this theme, see Peter Bondanella, *The Cinema of Federico Fellini* (Princeton, NJ: Princeton University Press, 1992), p. 197.
28. Fellini's passion for ad hoc transformations of reality into moments of spectacle has its origins in the travelling show featured in *La strada* (1954), and can be seen in virtually all of his films, most notably in *La dolce vita*'s 'field of miracles' sequence, and in the billboard construction in *Le tentazioni del dottor Antonio*. This interest later focuses on the construction of cinema itself, seen most explicitly in *Otto e mezzo* (1963) and *Intervista* (1987), which is discussed later.
29. Francesco Bolzoni, *I misteri di Roma di Cesare Zavattini* (Rome: Cappelli, 1963), p. 21.
30. The political role and militaristic overtones of the film studios and of Mussolini's cinematic ambitions are clear, but more subtle and complex in practice than they may superficially appear. See James Hay, *Popular film culture in Fascist Italy* (Bloomington: Indiana University Press, 1987).
31. The spatial regime of theatrically enforced representations to be found in Mussolini's new towns relates more to cinematic conventions than to the connection with de Chirico that is usually inferred. Paul Virilio's statement in *The Lost Dimension* (New

York: Semiotext(e), 1991), p. 26, is provocative: ' ... More than Venturi's Las Vegas, it is Hollywood that merits urbanist scholarship, for, after the theater-cities of Antiquity and of the Italian Renaissance, it was Hollywood that was the first Cinecittà, the city of living cinema where stage-sets and reality, tax-plans and scripts, the living and the living dead, mix and merge deliriously.'

32. For instance: *Bellissima* (Luchino Visconti, 1951), *Two Weeks in Another Town* (Vincente Minnelli, 1962), *Le Mépris* (Jean-Luc Godard, 1963), – set in a 'Cinecittà', but not filmed in the real one; *Intervista* (Federico Fellini, 1987); and *Nestore l'ultima corsa* (Alberto Sordi, 1993).

33. For a more detailed exposition of this theme, see Bondanella, *The Cinema of Federico Fellini*, pp. 150–226.

34. Carla Pilolli, 'Vacanze romane con replicante', *Il Messaggero*, 8 February 1995.

PART THREE

The Modern City II

People In Space

Introduction

Maureen Thomas

Marcel L'Herbier's 1924 film *L'Inhumaine* shows how the screen can be conceived of as a space to be filled with movement, where human figures interact with architectural elements in such a way as to provide both a visually splendid aesthetic experience and an emotionally engaging drama. The music of Cine Chimera led by Richard McLaughlin completed the wonder and delight of the show.

Non-dialogue film with live music calls on us to enjoy cinematic pleasure not by contemplating an imitation of life, but by moving beyond our humdrum daily experience to enter a world intensified, where we hear and see and feel with extra clarity. We are invited to release ourselves, as ancient Greek plays and Wagner's music theatre also urge us to do, into a mode of heightened awareness where we fully participate emotionally as well as intellectually in the drama.

In his paper, Ian Wiblin shows how this special combination of thought and feeling is not only the end result of the photographer's art but also an integral part of its inspiration. Through his own response to cities unpeopled – the very absence of human presence which implies the story behind places designed by human beings to be inhabited – he examines the way great film-makers, particularly Antonioni, construct scenes of poignant emotion. Just as in the great non-dialogue movies, he sees the relationship in the films he analyses between the people and the architectural spaces they occupy – or have just occupied – as a crucial factor in evoking an emotional reaction in the audience or viewer.

Tim Benton looks at a similar issue from the opposite point of view. He shows how different techniques of documentary meet the challenge of creating for the audience watching a screen a real perception of how an architect develops a vision and makes it into a three-dimensional reality. He demonstrates various approaches which allow the film-maker to include in the audience's experience a sense of the architect's feeling for space, people and ideology, as well as a knowledge of the historical place, function and significance of a particular architectural achievement. Le Corbusier is his subject, but the question he tackles is how architecture can be successfully documented through moving images.

In looking closely at the achievements of the architects Jean Nouvel and Christian de Portzamparc, both extremely conscious of the impact of film imagery to the extent of using it in their own work, the architectural journalist and film/video-maker Odile Fillion demonstrates that in representing architecture on the screen and using the language of moving images to convey the intentions, inspirations, moods and originality of a specific architect, a whole series of visual metaphors and perspectives open up which have only just begun to be explored. Not only is the medium a very particular version, in this case, of the message, but the emotionally charged spatial world of the film set and heightened location mediated by designer and cinematographer (as discussed by Diana Charnley and Christopher Hobbs) can itself inform the spaces an architect creates to provide the setting for real life.

Le Corbusier's film *Le Poème électronique* (1958), Thompson's *New York, New York* (1957) and Brakhage's *The Wonder Ring* (1955) all reinforce the perception of Wiblin, Benton and Fillion that architecture and film have more in common that simply the cross-translation of two-dimensional and three-dimensional space: they also share the desire to give living, feeling human beings their proper place in a constructed world.

The Space Between

Photography, Architecture and the Presence of Absence

Ian Wiblin

I would like to start by describing a short, simple scene from Michaelangelo Antonioni which comes near the beginning of *L'eclisse* (1962). The effect of this sequence of images is strangely powerful, despite their minimal content.

Vittoria (Monica Vitti) – a thin young woman with shoulder-length blonde hair, wearing a simple black dress, a small handbag and an article of clothing (perhaps a shawl) dangling from one arm – says goodbye to her now ex-lover outside her apartment. They stand facing each other framed by the concrete pillars of the building. Seen from behind, Vittoria leans back against one of these pillars. The man, Riccardo, eventually seems resigned to the termination of the relationship. He exits with a swift swing and resounding clang of a metal gate. Vittoria now stands in front of the clear glass doors of the apartment block – which we are seeing for the first time – and watches Riccardo walk away. After a short pause, she turns and enters through the glass doors. Cut to a tracking shot which begins to the side of the glass doors. In this shot, the action is seen from outside, through large plate glass windows. The camera follows Vittoria as she walks quickly across the open space of the lobby. Her clipped footsteps are heard, muffled by the glass barrier between her and the camera. The interior wall opposite is seen to be of bare brick and the floor to be laid with very large dark tiles. The generous white grid between these tiles is very evident, as is the mortar of the brickwork. The building has a precise, modern, though slightly austere, character. The short track halts as Vittoria mounts a concrete staircase that is now seen at the far left of the frame. The sound of her scuffed steps disappears. In the next shot, now from inside, the camera fleetingly strays across the width of a concrete pillar at the top of the stairs. For a brief moment, Vittoria seems hemmed in by brickwork. She moves quickly through the space and unlocks her door. In a wide shot, from outside once more, Vittoria is now seen entering the space of her apartment. An unremarkable domestic clutter is revealed. A lamp, a dark half-sphere on a long thin stem, is the most striking object. Vittoria lets her bag, along with the unspecified piece of clothing, drop down on to a chair. She then continues across the room. The camera, in a track that follows Vittoria's movement, shifts from its view through the window and travels briefly across the exterior brickwork – the shot describes the interior space, from outside. Momentarily, Vittoria is lost from view. The camera comes to rest framing Vittoria in an ambiguous space. A column of brickwork dominates the centre of the image, visually

Ian Wiblin, *Inside*, 1995

confining Vittoria to the far right of frame. The interior space above her head is masked by the horizontal struts of a shutter pulled partly down over a window – the window through which the camera is now looking. This serves to further crop the visual space around Vittoria and emphasises her low position in frame. She is not seen full-figure but is cut off at mid-thigh by the bottom of the frame. With a sort of sighing gesture, she leans into the space that is hidden by the brickwork at the far left of the room. Her position suggests that she is now looking out of a window. A strip of curtain and part of a framed picture are visible behind her. Outside the space, to the left of the central column of bricks, is a dark mass of dense foliage that shifts around in an otherwise unperceived breeze. A small area of open sky completes this vertical third of the frame.

L'éclisse

It is the enclosing feel of this final composition, in which Vittoria seemingly pushes towards the eerily moving dark mass of tree, that gives it a particular 'edge'. The swirling of the foliage seems strangely poignant, contrasted as it is with the brutal geometric order of the architecture. The quality of sound – just a faint isolated rustle is heard – is, of course, crucial to the feeling or emotion that this shot transmits. The meticulous portrayal of Vittoria's brief ascent to her apartment has reached its logical conclusion. Halted by the far wall of her room, she has nowhere else to go. The shot eventually cuts abruptly to a noisy city street, a car rushing towards the camera. The scene has lasted little more than a minute.

There are many significant shots in Antonioni's films that feature balconies and windows – single characters looking up at, or down from, apartments, and the like. In views from windows, main characters are often seen as small, isolated, and vulnerable figures on the streets below. I again think of Monica Vitti, this time as Claudia, in *L'avventura* (1959). Jeanne Moreau, as Lidia, in *La notte* (1960), is similarly framed. The opening scene of *L'eclisse* develops as a confrontation between two characters within the interior space of a modern apartment; At a certain point, curtains are opened revealing the distance and strangeness of the world outside. What the curtains have been drawn back on is a landscape dominated by a bizarre water tower. In a scene in *L'avventura*, shutters are abruptly closed to blot out the architecture of the town. This action takes place immediately after the character Sandro, who is a former – or perhaps failed – architect, has deliberately knocked a pot of ink across a student's carefully observed drawing of an impressive church tower.

Often, in the films of Antonioni, ideas that are bound up with the narrative are conveyed directly and purely through images – without any definite or obvious anchoring to a story, though the ultimate strength of the images relies, in part, on the legacy of the narrative that has already been played out. The final minutes of *L'eclisse* work in this way. The film's main character exits six minutes before the end – although, of course, we do not know this for sure and perhaps expect her to reappear. As she leaves, a street corner then becomes the star of the film. Vittoria's final gaze leads into a montage of images depicting the various arrangements of objects at this location and describes the activities taking place there. It is a location that has been important earlier in the film, as a rendezvous point for Vittoria and her would-be lover. During this final sequence familiar objects are seen again – an object that floats in a drum of water was dropped there by Vittoria in an earlier scene but this time the people are absent. So the sequence still serves

L'éclisse

Ian Wiblin, *Wroclaw*, Poland 1989

Ian Wiblin, *Jerusalem*, 1994

to describe the relationship that has been at the core of the film, and its aftermath. Now the world goes on without either of the protagonists as night falls and people go anonymously about their business.

Despite the fact that many of the shots do contain movement, because of their generally unconventional cinematic form and the absence of an obvious continuation of the narrative, Antonioni's collection of images has the feel of still photography. His montage of images projects an urban environment that is incomplete and unresolved. The unfinished and perhaps abandoned state of the buildings mirrors the state of the human relationship, as it has been described in *L'eclisse*. These images – the building materials arranged and framed so they mirror a skyscraper skyline; the scaffolding poles sticking out of the building covered with matting turning it in to an abstract sculpture; the dark 'presence' of the round-topped trees; the strange beauty of a random arrangement of objects, a water tank and planks, and so on – have an overall lighter touch than any one-to-one symbolism might achieve. They provide a succession of visual ideas pertinent to the fate of the film's characters, and provide further, more abstract, reflection on the human condition. The presence of a 'story' is maintained in tiny non-character-centred narratives – the object floating in the water tank, water leaking from the tank, making a path toward the gutter and finally flowing down a drain. As the sequence progresses, people pass by, some of whom were seen earlier, some of whom resemble the film's main characters. Finally, a bus comes and goes, its braking interrupting the quiet of the scene, adding an almost violent edge that jars with the emptiness, the lack of activity. The urban space has eventually won out over the characters and the narrative thread has finally been dissolved.

I am a photographer. Or rather, I am an artist who uses photography. I make this distinction because I feel it is relevant to my 'sensibility' – a vague something inside that motivates my particular response to the environment around me and forms the way I 'look'. It determines the sort of places, spaces and objects that will move me enough to want to photograph them and explains why I am moved by a particular sort of cinema.

Architecture seems as integral to the films I watch as it does to the photographs I look at or take myself. In all the films that have made a strong impression on me, buildings feature prominently and seem as indispensable as the characters. Cinematic imagery leaves such a strong impression that surely our way of looking at the city space around us is influenced by certain films and film-makers. I am not an architectural photographer, but my subject is usually 'the city'; the buildings rather than the people. Although at first glance my work might appear to fit into a documentary genre, I consider that it is essentially subjective and personal. The images represent no more than my direct experiences of particular spaces and places at the very moment I photographed them. What I hope to convey is an emotional response to what I see. As I have already suggested, what I respond to initially are buildings. Indirectly, what motivates this response is the discernible 'presence' of the anonymous and transient inhabitants. The final photographs depict spaces where the people are both imaginary and absent. The images, in common with much still photography depicting empty buildings and streets, have the potential to be read as scene-of-crime photographs or location stills for films. Something has happened – or is about to happen. It is just such narrative potential that is somehow stored in seemingly empty architectural space that provides a link between photography and cinema, particularly in the work of Antonioni, the master of suggesting presence on the screen by its absence.

My photographic 'investigations' are usually within streets and buildings that are unfamiliar – where I am conscious of being an outsider or even an intruder. In these locations I can feel threatened as much by the mass of a wall or the void of a courtyard as by any more tangible or direct human presence. From this viewpoint – of someone who does not belong – I react to the space that I find myself in. I evaluate it in an emotional way. It is this response that the resulting photographs are intended to document rather than the streets and buildings themselves. In these (mostly) unpeopled images I hope a human presence still persists, perhaps emanating from the façades of buildings or from objects left behind in the street. The use of architecture in cinema can operate in a similar way, evoking emotion in the audience which the director can connect with characters or ideas.

Paul Strand, *Wall Street*, New York 1915

There has usually been a specific historical or archaeological concern that has motivated my own photography. My first serious use of a camera was in the Polish city of Wroclaw. Added to my initial direct experience of this city was the knowledge that it had had a previous identity. Before 1945 it had been the German city of Breslau. This fact provided me with my starting point. The photographs I took represented my attempts to reveal the layers of recent history. As I naively explored the city it was inevitably difficult to avoid a German past that projected from its buildings and streets. The inhabitants of Wroclaw, almost necessarily, became a more distant element in the work. The ultimate absence of people from the images also echoed the sense I had of a city strangely underpopulated.

It is this sort of 'edge' that architecture can transmit that interests me – the sense which buildings project of being witnesses of events and history, their resilient presence as symbols of a humanity evolving, decaying or unresolved. Such an edge must be inherent to buildings deliberately constructed as objects of oppression and intimidation. It can also be felt in more mundane architecture. It is potentially there wherever concrete forms a barrier between people. Architectural space provides a potent backdrop for countless photographers and film-makers as they explore and dissect human life. In Paul Strand's photograph 'Wall Street' (1915), it is clearly the physical presence of the building that impresses. Its huge, sharp-edged form and dark, shadow-cloaked recesses dominate and threaten the ant-like figures that hurry beneath it. In 1921 Strand made a film, together with Charles Sheeler, which includes a similar shot as a moving image. This film, *Manhatta* (1921), is a seven-minute portrait of lower Manhattan. Strand has described it as an attempt to do with natural objects what in *The Cabinet of Doctor Caligari* (1919) – Robert Wiene's classic of early German cinema – was done with painted sets.

There is of course a dynamic emphasis, suggestive of cinema, visible in the images of many still photographers. The work of André Kertész and László Moholy-Nagy springs immediately to mind. Although working independently and with different influences, both produced images primarily concerned with the idea of the modern city and used architectural form in equally surprising ways. Utilising extreme views from, as well as of, buildings, their images imbued the mundane and the everyday with startling abstract qualities. In them, the human figure is often enveloped in the patterns of architecture.

André Kertész, *Place Saint Sulpice*, 1934

Eugène Atget,
*Corsets,
boulevard de
Strasbourg*, 1912

Karl Blossfeldt,
Papaver Orientale
(c. 1900)

August Sander,
Coalman, Berlin
1929

Such images are strongly suggestive of sequences in the films of Antonioni – the end of *L'eclisse* in particular. Architecture is, of course, a vital component of his cinematic language. His use of architecture could be described as expressionistic, though he clearly demonstrates that buildings need not have blatantly expressionistic characteristics to express emotion on screen successfully.

Antonioni's films are undoubtedly specifically cinematic. Their form is completely about cinema. Despite this, or perhaps because of this, many images and sequences of images, within Antonioni's films, do have a strong affinity with still photography. Of course, film-makers do look at photographs and use them. A famous photograph appears in Ingmar Bergman's *Persona* (1966). It is of a small boy in the Warsaw ghetto, his hands raised above his head, a soldier to the side of him with a gun and a grin. Many images and sequences in *Persona* seem indirectly to be about the process and ultimate disquieting power of the photographic image. The layered imagery exploits specific technical characteristics of photography – such as depth of field and shifting focus – to create the veiling layers of identity.

Antonioni's *Blow-Up* (1966) is overtly bound up with still photography through its photographer protagonist. Many film-makers undoubtedly take photographs obsessively themselves. Notably Alain Resnais did while researching for many of his films, some of which were never finally realised in cinematic form. What remained of them were the collections of images – of streets, anonymous corners and abandoned objects from various cities around the world. In the introduction to a book of these photographs, *Repérages* (1974), the images were described as 'studies of an imaginary cinematic city'.

Much photography that is less directly connected to the cinema can seem equally cinematic. This is true even of extreme and consistently rigorous documentary photography. For example, the work of Eugène Atget, August Sander, Karl Blossfeldt, Bernd and Hilla Becher and Thomas Struth. At first glance this may seem an odd selection of photographers. After all, to varying degrees all of them have adopted an objective, almost scientific, approach to their work that seems to have little or nothing to do with constructing narrative. But there is something about their 'collections' of objects – whether buildings, industrial features, people or even plants – that transcends the individual image's status as merely being a document of a particular object.

This, at least in part, has to do with a simplicity and pureness of approach. These images all seem to be about the 'presence' of architectural structures. I would say this even of Blossfeldt's plants. To an extent I would even say this of Sander's people. Of course I initially focus on his specimens of German society. I study what they wear, the way they hold themselves, their expressions, the way they look back at me. I am wrapped up in their particular histories. Eventually, though, I find myself drawn to the fragments of kerbs, doorways, walls and windows visible behind the people. These insignificant and obscured details seem to emphasise the extreme poignancy of Sander's work. His portraits, like the Bechers' endless water-towers, gas-tanks and blast-furnaces, like Struth's empty streets, like Atget's buildings, possess a quiet emotional force.

As well as occupying the depicted present, these photographers' subjects, whether made of flesh, stone or steel, seem also to unwittingly project a past and a future. Filmed architectural space too has this capability. It is most strongly realised in the works of Antonioni, Godard, Fassbinder, Bresson, Ozu and Tarkovsky, for example.

I have already mentioned Antonioni. *Il grido* (1957), *L'avventura*, *La notte*, *L'eclisse*, *Il deserto rosso* (1964), and *The Passenger* (1975) – we recall them instantly and vividly, because of the strong and particular use of architecture employed in each film. Architectural form often dominates the frame and ultimately the film. It controls the emotional force of the narrative. The buildings seem to simultaneously project a sense of the characters' histories and to be knowing of their fate.

Jean-Luc Godard makes very specific and original use of architecture. He succeeds in creating a spontaneity that seems to spark around and within a framework which is crucially provided by architectural space. This is repeatedly evident in many of his earlier films: the hotel rooms of *A Bout de souffle* (1959), the CinemaScope modern apartment of *Le Mépris* (1963), the 'futuristic' labyrinthine corridors of *Alphaville* (1965), the ramshackle interiors of *Pierrot le fou* (1965), the anonymous rooms of *Vivre sa vie* (1962).

Le Mépris

Rainer Werner Fassbinder's use of architecture is more directly oppressive and enclosing. Endless stifling interiors imbue much of his work with an intense sense of confinement. A bleak tenement-block hopelessness pervades such films as *Why Does Herr R. Run Amok?* (1969), *Katzelmacher* (1971), *The Merchant of Four Seasons* (1972), *Fear Eats the Soul* (1974) and *Berlin Alexanderplatz* (1979). The implied confinement reinforces the inevitability of the characters' circumstances. It confirms the actions of Herr R. and explains the fear that must eat the soul.

In the films of Robert Bresson, which are equally uncompromising in their style, there is a sense of architecture evident simply in their pared-down construction. This finds echoes in the quiet significance of such literal built spaces as the prison cells in *A Man Escaped* (1956) and *L'Argent* (1983).

Yasujiro Ozu made simple, carefully observed and brilliantly effective use of domestic interiors in his films. These predominant house-based sequences are broken with shots of trains, factory chimneys and other images of the modern industrial city. His use of architecture, as ever-present and understated as that of Bresson, is consistent throughout his films. *The Record of a Tenement Gentleman* (1947) and *Tokyo Story* (1953) – his best known film – are obvious examples of Ozu's presentation of cultural and emotional detail through clear architectural relationships and contrasts.

Katzelmacher

Conscientiously objective documentary photographers – such as the Bechers and Struth – necessarily employ a standardisation of visual approach. The working methods of some film-makers, perhaps Bresson and Ozu most notably, can be equally self-restricting. The consistency of height and angle of view of the camera is as apparent in Ozu's filmed interiors as it is in Struth's cityscapes, as is the use of specific fixed-focal-length lenses. The restrained, deceptively expressionless acting in the films of Bresson also mirrors the coolness of approach evident in 'objective' photography.

In the films of both Bresson and Ozu, architectural space frames narratives that are built with precision and purpose. In Bresson's *L'Argent* this sense of construction is evident in every movement and gesture. One, brief, simple scene describes the journey of an envelope as it is passed round a table. Its unhesitating circular passage echoes the enclosing confinement and inevitability of prison life. The significance of the envelope's contents and the inhumanity of the censoring process are conveyed in a deliberate, totally unsentimental and matter-of-fact way. This minimal treatment, stripped of any overstatement, has a cohesion and structural emphasis that could be described as

Tokyo Story

Thomas Struth, *Shinju-ku, Tokyo 1986*

architectural. This quote from his short book *Notes on Cinematography* (1975) underlines Bresson's approach: 'Not beautiful photography, not beautiful images, but necessary images and photography.' These words perhaps represent the cinematic equivalent of the architectural maxim, 'Form follows Function'.

Even though modern functional buildings predominate in the films of Antonioni, his use of such architecture is, at times, undeniably expressionistic – even when it is not precisely visible. Antonioni's book, *That Bowling Alley on the Tiber* (1986), is a collection of thirty-three story-sketches or ideas. One of these 'narrative nuclei' is entitled: 'Where There Aren't Any Houses': 'A flat expanse of land on the Po delta. A village of low, coloured houses. The sidewalk continues beyond the end of the street. No more houses flanking it, only the sidewalk proceeding all by itself toward the embankment. At night there's always a small empty truck, as though its owner lived there, where there aren't any houses'.

Antonioni's alternative titles for this book were 'A Pack of Lies' and 'Nothing But Lies'. His reasoning was that as long as the films were not realised, such 'narrative nuclei' only represented partial truths and therefore, not the whole truth – a form of lie. The house theme of Antonioni's conveyed partial truth is echoed in *The Anarchy of the Imagination* (1984), a collection of interviews, essays and notes by Fassbinder: 'I would like to build a house with my films. Some are the cellar, others the walls, still others the windows. But I hope in the end it will be a house.' Although perhaps I am interpreting his implied sense of construction a bit literally, Fassbinder's statement suggests something that is coming together, being resolved, making sense. Houses as depicted in the films of Antonioni by no means project such a sense of harmony. A modern house, perhaps derivative of Frank Lloyd Wright, built beneath huge boulders in the desert, appears at the end of *Zabriskie Point* (1969). In a series of static, repetitive shots, but from several viewpoints, the house explodes. The individual particles of the shattered house and its contents can be studied in great detail as they twist gracefully through the air in slow motion.

The house, as an image, also appears memorably in the films of Andrei Tarkovsky. In *Ivan's Childhood* (1962) there are the ruins of a house blown up in war. In *Solaris* (1972) there is a house, seen from space, isolated on an impossibly tiny island. In *Mirror* (1974) there is a wooden house – or maybe it is a barn – on fire. In *Stalker* (1979) there is the house of the guide to the mysterious and expansive 'Zone'. In *Nostalgia* (1983) there is a house that is a family's prison and there is a Russian house that stands inside the ruins of an Italian cathedral. In *The Sacrifice* (1986) there is a model of a house. The real house burns to the ground at the end. This grand finale at the end of *The Sacrifice* develops slowly, in a very long single shot. Remaining at a distance, the camera is a quiet witness, as the house burns in 'real time'. The characters are seen as no more than tiny figures, isolated in a flat landscape, immediately surrounding the blaze. Their bizarre interaction, as the fire takes hold and the house begins to decompose, is recorded dispassionately. The camera, even from the edge of the action, seems to methodically plot and emphasise the space around or between the characters. It charts mental as well as physical geography and the buildings themselves seem to stand as symbols of community which may or may not survive.

I should like to end as I began with an extreme and uncompromising cinematic sequence from a film by Antonioni – the conclusion of *The Passenger*. The camera, in a long and meticulously choreographed single movement, impassively describes the space that the central character's world has been reduced to. In a room of a small hotel, we see Locke (Jack Nicholson) resting, stretched out on a bed. The camera then inches almost imperceptibly out of the window and veers off around the building. Various, apparently innocuous, activities are partially glimpsed on the periphery of frame, the faintly audible accompanying sounds apparently merely illustrative: a car arrives ... people get out of it ... the car drives away again ... . The camera completes its calm, surveying circuit, eventually entering again through the same window. We discover, perhaps inevitably, that Locke has been murdered. This almost scientific dissection of space and plotting of activity has created an invisible metaphysical architecture. The camera has, through its unhurried, assured and fluid movement, demonstrated a freedom that is way out of reach of the film's protagonist. In so doing, it has confirmed the totality of his incarceration and the irrevocability of his fate.

L'avventura

Antonioni's use of architecture is neither so neutral nor so pure. In his films, the use of architectural space – the projected physical mass and presence of buildings, the framing of figures – is crucial. Even so, I can still see, or perhaps I should say feel, a connection between the imagery of Antonioni's cinema and the rigidly 'objective' photographs of Eugene Atget and more recently of the Bechers and Struth. What links their images, despite the apparent differences in motivation and approach, is the 'presence' of the buildings depicted, whether in the single frame of the photograph or in the twenty-four frames a second of the film, often implying the absent character or story. They share a clarity of vision that enables the mundane to articulate simultaneously the aspirations and limitations of humanity.

L'avventura

Much of Antonioni's cinema does rely heavily, and at times very directly, on architecture as a key visual element. Architects and engineers also appear as lead characters. There are building-sites in *L'avventura*, *La notte* and *L'eclisse*. In *Il grido* and *Il deserto rosso* there are factories and industry. Antonioni, of course, makes use of grand classical architecture; a striking image from *L'eclisse* is provided by the interior of the Rome stock exchange, the vast width of a pillar forming an immense barrier between the film's two main characters before the start of their emotional entanglement. Antonioni's use of modern architecture, even buildings under construction, is perhaps even more notable, as in *L'eclisse*, where the final six minutes describe the layout of, and general activity around, a street corner on an unfinished suburban housing project.

Jean-Luc Godard, in answer to the question 'Do you feel that all your films, irrespective of the way they are handled, are about the spirit of adventure?', put to him during an interview about *Pierrot le fou*, replies: 'Certainly. The important thing is to be aware one exists. For three-quarters of the time during the day one forgets this truth, which surges up again as you look at houses or a red light, and you have the sensation of existing in that moment.' This statement seems to be as suggestive of the films of Antonioni – the final frames of *L'eclisse* are filled with the exploding glare of a street light – as of those of Godard himself.

Bernd and Hilla Becher, *Gas Tank, Bonn, D 1992*

L'éclisse

Godard's words would equally encapsulate the motivation and mental working process of many still photographers – the street images of the American photographer Lee Freidlander come particularly to mind. Though they fit awkwardly with much of the documentary photography I have alluded to, in some respects the end result is the same, despite the sometimes extreme differences apparent in the approaches of many of the image-makers I have been concerned with. It is ultimately the architecture itself that has the stored potential to express human experience and emotion. In images of built space – whether still or moving – it is the discernible presence of humanity implied by the direct absence of people that is so moving.

Representing Le Corbusier

Film, Exhibition, Multimedia

Tim Benton

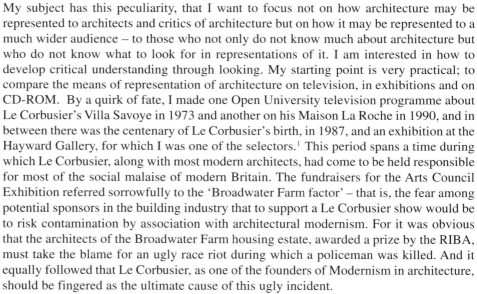

My subject has this peculiarity, that I want to focus not on how architecture may be represented to architects and critics of architecture but on how it may be represented to a much wider audience – to those who not only do not know much about architecture but who do not know what to look for in representations of it. I am interested in how to develop critical understanding through looking. My starting point is very practical; to compare the means of representation of architecture on television, in exhibitions and on CD-ROM. By a quirk of fate, I made one Open University television programme about Le Corbusier's Villa Savoye in 1973 and another on his Maison La Roche in 1990, and in between there was the centenary of Le Corbusier's birth, in 1987, and an exhibition at the Hayward Gallery, for which I was one of the selectors.[1] This period spans a time during which Le Corbusier, along with most modern architects, had come to be held responsible for most of the social malaise of modern Britain. The fundraisers for the Arts Council Exhibition referred sorrowfully to the 'Broadwater Farm factor' – that is, the fear among potential sponsors in the building industry that to support a Le Corbusier show would be to risk contamination by association with architectural modernism. For it was obvious that the architects of the Broadwater Farm housing estate, awarded a prize by the RIBA, must take the blame for an ugly race riot during which a policeman was killed. And it equally followed that Le Corbusier, as one of the founders of Modernism in architecture, should be fingered as the ultimate cause of this ugly incident.

We have created a culture in Britain in which, compared with France or Italy, architectural values are far from political or popular ones. Inconceivable here is the image that I saw on French television of two French Presidents and the widow of a third jostling for the microphone to claim that they had achieved more for the arts. Inconceivable the prospect of Margaret Thatcher or John Major, or indeed any durable politician on the British scene with the possible exception of Michael Heseltine, being caught in the open expressing a view about architecture or staking their careers on architectural as opposed to capital investment projects. When the history of the current heir to the throne is written, his not entirely ignorant interventions in the field of architecture will probably be seen as a sign of political naivety, an indicator of instability, possibly madness, rather than one of praiseworthy cultural sophistication. And this is not only because architecture, as well as planning and public welfare, loses votes but because of a deep-rooted ignorance of

Maison La Roche, exterior, 1923–5

architecture which runs through public life. And this contrasts with the level of knowledge and understanding of literature, music, politics, the sciences and technology. And of course, the National Curriculum has done nothing to introduce a proper understanding of architecture into our schools.

I write, therefore, from the perspective of a teacher committed to increasing understanding of architecture, its purposes and meanings and the intentions of architects. We have shown, at the Open University, that the history of art and architecture can attract as much attention and interest as 'school subjects' such as literature or history. We have been able to do this, not only by using TV and video, but also by integrating the study of the arts into interdisciplinary courses and making them comprehensible at an introductory level. The realisation that buildings supply evidence of historical and cultural change and that judgements of architectural quality can be informed by understanding causal conditions in society provides the stimulus to learn more. Of course, most people who visit National Trust properties or parish churches, or who take an interest in their built environment are well aware of these things without the instruction of television.

Villa Savoye, hallway, 1929-30

In the context, then, of increasing understanding of architectural issues, television programmes, exhibitions and multimedia offer tantalisingly different but overlapping elements of communication and representation. Both television programmes and exhibitions are public events, just as architecture is necessarily public. In the case of television, there is an inbuilt emphasis towards popularisation, simplification and vividness of exposition, at the expense of depth and complexity. Exhibitions, on the other hand, rely on a kind of magical illusion, in which special objects are placed before an audience as if self-evidently important, and the public is left to make what it can of them. The discussions which inform the choice and exclusion of objects are largely occluded from the visitor, who will have to buy a catalogue to uncover a context and narrative informing the selection. TV is essentially *ersatz*, exhibitions obsessed with the authentic. TV saturates images with attached meanings (voice-overs, narratives, juxtapositions) while exhibition curators turn pale at any texts above fifty words. Television is governed ruthlessly by a single narrative while exhibitions allow some latitude for individual choices in circulation and intensity of observation. In our culture, most exhibitions seem to turn into 'Art' shows (assessed by aesthetic criteria) while TV programmes about the arts always seem to turn into historical explanation or contextualisation.

In exhibitions, the buildings themselves, of course, are necessarily absent, represented by drawings, models, sometimes installations. But architectural drawings are often difficult to read, unimpressive from a distance (at the scale of gallery design and hang) and require an understanding not only of process but of architectural intentionality. An architect can 'see' a building or fragment of building which will result from a drawing, and can imagine moving through it. Non-specialist members of the public cannot. Models are too easy to read as volume and too difficult to interpret as architecture. Reconstructions of rooms are expensive and difficult to get right.

In 'Le Corbusier Architect of the Century', the main elements of exhibition were drawings, some original photographs, some few modern photographs, some models (both original and purpose-made), some reconstructions of parts of buildings and an exhibition design which reinforced a Corbusian aesthetic. The exhibition carried some information

Le Corbusier Architect of the Century, Hayward Gallery, 1987

Detail of concrete mouldings of terrace,
·Villa Savoye, 1929–30

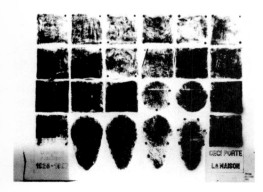

Detail, Collage of sections of pilotis supporting the
Villa Stein-de Monzie, 1926–8

about the architect's life and work and, with the addition of paintings, sculptures, furniture and applied arts, was able to present enough startling contrasts to raise questions for the most inattentive observer. I believe that the exhibition did quite a good job of putting Le Corbusier's work into its context. I am aware, however, that most of the objects which were of most absorbing interest to the specialists were least likely to register with the public. There was a wonderful sheet of details, at a scale of 1:1, of the concrete profiles of the Villa Savoye. Drawn in green chalk on elephant-sized tracing paper, this represents Le Corbusier providing the modern equivalent of Vignola's or Serlio's orders, standing to these as a Picasso stands to a Raphael. Another drawing which could have given pleasure to very few non-architects was a quite extraordinary sheet of card, onto which Le Corbusier had fixed pieces of tracing paper representing the cross-section of every concrete piloti in the Villa Stein-de Monzie. Here was *firmitas* separated from *venustas* and *utilitas*, an ironic and surreal joke about functionalism. Nobody laughed. And yet finding work like this is what makes an exhibition interesting for the participants.

And then of course there are the original photographs, which in many cases the architects themselves control. Many of the photographs of Le Corbusier's buildings are 'signed' with his motor car, his spectacles or some purist object, authenticating his presence and his direction of the photograph. So we know the angle, we know the values of light and shade that he wanted us to see. Furthermore, we have the abstract from his lecture in Argentina in which he takes us on a 'promenade' around the Villa Savoye, and in it we have the very simple statement:

Arab architecture teaches us a valuable lesson. It's best appreciated on foot. Walking, you have to walk through a building with a changing viewpoint, to see the articulation of the building deployed. It's the opposite principle to that of Baroque architecture, which is conceived on paper around a fixed theoretical axis. I prefer the teaching of Arab architecture.[2]

And this, in the end, is the basic argument for film as opposed to photography or drawing as a medium of representation for architecture. A building, as a series of volumes and spaces, textures and effects, wide and close views, needs to be performed, like a score. To walk through a building, or to film it, is to produce a particular reading which instantly throws away more than it selects. But without this performance the building remains removed from the senses, unrealised, dead. But if an architecture exhibition is like exhibiting the score rather than hearing the music, filming a building enshrines a particular view and a selective narrative in a medium which discourages critical attention. At least, in an exhibition, a selection can be supported and contextualised by catalogue essays. A challenge exists to find a means of combining the vividness and visual depth of film with possibilities for discursive, exploratory and layered exposition.

Multimedia might appear to offer useful possibilities. Virtual-reality technologies are complex and currently expensive. In a multimedia group at the Open University, we have been exploring low-cost possibilities for developing means of presenting architectural spaces in an accessible and interactive mode. Using sequences of still photographs, some of them organised in panoramas, the user can be allowed to move through a building, zooming, panning and tilting as required. Sequences of timed holds, zooms and 'movements' can be linked together into voice-over clips which, while lacking true movement, provide an effective spatial exploration with decent sharpness and no more distortion than compressed video. These sequences can be used wherever introductions and teaching loops demand a fixed commentary. The major use of the CD-ROM, however, would be in interactive mode, in which the user would explore the spaces and interrogate the fabric of the building. A toolbox would allow the user to pick different tools for interrogating the environment: a data icon (for investigating historical information), an iconographic icon (for calling up comparable images from a database), a structure and materials icon for a glossary of materials and teaching loops on structural properties of different architectural forms. A fundamental principle is that the user should be placed in control of the virtual space represented in the CD-ROM. Thus, hot spots should be placeable anywhere and documented by the user. The user should be able to get at the database of images and the database of indexed text segments. An editing facility should allow the user to make her own animation sequences and record commentary over them. The student of the future should be able to make her own exhibitions, multimedia essays and illustrated talks as part of a fair exchange with the teacher. Whether these are communicated across the Internet, recorded on appropriate media or communicated through some shorthand reference system as a supplementary to a written essay remains to be seen.

There will always be a place for exhibitions of original drawings, models and photographs and for beautifully crafted films which interpret buildings in visual terms. Artificially constructed wireframe or rendered architectural environments clearly have a place in architectural research but are too expensive in labour and processing power to be readily communicated to students. More significantly, it is important to teach students skills of investigation and probing which correspond as closely as possible to the experience of walking around a building, guide book in hand.

Notes

1. A305 (History of Architecture and Design,1890–1939), Open University, 1975: *TV 13 Le Corbusier's Villa Savoye*; A316 (Modern Art Practices and Debates), Open University, 1985: *TV 14 Le Corbusier: Maison La Roche*, Le Corbusier Architect of the Century, Arts Council of Great Britain, 1987
2. Le Corbusier, *Précisions sur l'état present d'architecture* (Paris, 1929).

Life Into Art, Art Into Life

Fusions in Film, Video and Architecture

Odile Fillion

For the last twenty years, I have been working in France as a journalist, mostly specialising in architecture. Through my work I have come to know a large number of architects and, over a considerable period, grown familiar with the world of architecture. Gradually, I have come to the conclusion that most of our well-known architects are fascinated by cinema and by film-makers.

Jean Nouvel

This fascination was lasting in the case of Jean Nouvel, who used, as a boy, to slip out of the house at night, clad in his pyjamas, to sneak to the local cinema. It may even have been responsible for some of the remarkable physical features he later developed. If I tell you that, at an early age, Jean Nouvel once chanced to meet Orson Welles at the Paris restaurant La Closerie des Lilas, you may then be struck by a curious resemblance between these two monumental figures, both of whom habitually appeared wearing black hats and smoking cigars.

In fact, in his notes and publications, Jean Nouvel quite early on starts to remark upon the similarities between the way a film-maker manages a team of specialists, from lighting designers through cinematographers, sound designers and technicians to designers and performers, and the way an architect works with a team of specialists, in lighting, acoustics, colour and engineering.

Progressively, Jean Nouvel started to claim the right to 'steal' images for his architecture from a range of sources, finding inspiration in such fields as car technology or aeroplane and train design, as well as the work of various artists – painters or sculptors, for instance, such as Joseph Beuys or Yves Klein, and film-makers. The German director Wim Wenders was probably one of the most decisive influences in Nouvel's work.

The first direct reference to cinema in Nouvel's architecture was in a bar for the Theatre at Belfort, completed in 1983. Nouvel said he conceived it as a copy of a scene by Wenders, with wet asphalt, red neon light, a stainless-steel counter and Coca-Cola crates – he even suggested that walking into the bar should give the same sort of feeling as walking onto a film set. This direct reference to Wenders recurs in a proposal for a nightclub at Nogent sur Marne in 1987, whose lines were stolen straight out of *Der Stand der Dinger/The*

Jean Nouvel inside the Palais des Congrès, Tours

State of Things (1982), Wenders's film about the difficult making of his *Hammett* (1983), and included asphalt, great bright lights, wrecked cars, industrial surroundings, highways, flashing lights and big screens.

Jean Nouvel constantly claimed both that images of this kind were a source of enrichment in the work he created, and that the technologies themselves behind the images inspired him – it was, for instance, from video technique that he borrowed his concept of materiality, or rather non-materiality. His dream is to include big screens as real components in architecture, a dream he might have realised, had his design for the Grand Stade competition (1995) won.

In 1989, Jean Nouvel finally met Wenders in person, and was totally enchanted by the film-maker. The two became friends, and Nouvel conceived the idea of asking Wenders to make a film on the construction of *La Tour sans Fin*, the 'infinite tower', the famous 400-metre high cigarette tower which was to have been built at *La Défense* in Paris. In fact, as can be seen in *Until the End of the World* (1991), Wenders included the *Tour sans Fin* in his vision of Paris in the year 2000. But, as the construction of *La Tour sans Fin* itself was broken off, the idea of making a film about it never reached fruition.

Alongside this inspiration from the work of Wenders, Jean Nouvel continued to borrow from different films, such as *2001: A Space Odyssey* (1968), *Alien* (1979), *Blade Runner* (1982), and *Brazil* (1985), the gleams of whose strange worlds clearly appear in buildings like the Opéra at Lyon, or the Palais des Congrès at Tours.

The influence of film, however, also affected Nouvel's work at the level of the architectural/spatial concept. He started to contemplate the notion of movement in architecture. He no longer regarded architectural space as simple volume, or combinations of sets of images, but rather as a series of sequences. 'Cinema', he says, 'has taught us to see images in relation to time. A town is now read through motion, travel. Today, architectural composition refers to sequences. Most contemporary architects take into consideration the journey of the human being through space. The notion of the journey is a new way of composing architecture.'

Last year, for an exhibition at the Kunstverein in Hamburg, I made a video which tried partly to explain this idea of movement and the complexity of the references in the work of Jean Nouvel. As exhibition material, it was conceived as a collage of images which were simultaneously projected onto three big screens, alongside an interview with Jean Nouvel.

We had virtually no budget, and ten days to complete the entire shoot, which had to be more or less spontaneous – we had no real opportunity to do proper reconnaissance before we went out with the camera. I had to select the images as I came across them, trying at the same time to think how we would compose the three simultaneous sequences for the three screens.

In fact, in order to set up the final sequences, I had what we had shot printed so that I could view it and construct the tapes for each screen, almost like putting together a collage for a book. It was a weird process – I had to bear in mind all the time that there was no way the people looking at the screens, turning from one to another, would necessarily make the connection between one shot or building and another. It was a representation of

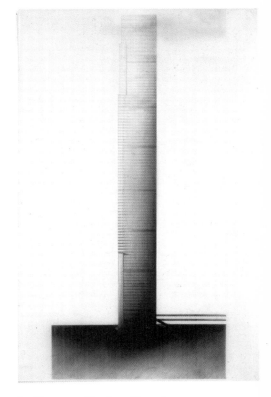

La Tour sans Fin, Jean Nouvel

Opéra de Lyon, Jean Nouvel

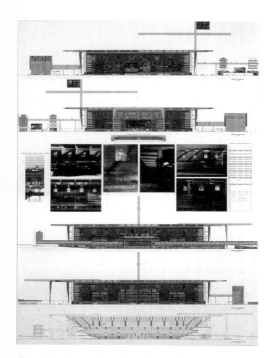

Grand Stade, project, Jean Nouvel

Médiathèque d'Orléans Pierre du Besset et Dominique Lyon

Nouvel's overall concept of movement, the striking characteristics of his personal signature, that I tried to achieve. So we produced a portrait of the architect through his architecture.

Christian de Portzamparc

To make a video portrait of Christian de Portzamparc, who won the Pritzer Prize in 1994, I used a very different style, because he has a very different approach – his work represents a more realistic and autonomous architectural claim. For him, cinema was a revelation, when, in the 1970s, he discovered Jean-Luc Godard and Michelangelo Antonioni. He had turned against the academic modern architecture of the time; it was, he says:

> … the cinema which freed me from the obsession of harmony. Films by Godard and Antonioni were showing a "modernity", in new situations, in cities where past and present coexisted. The richness of urban phenomena appeared there in a new way, beyond modern formalism and its pretensions of putting the world in order. I could no longer believe in a city model founded on harmony and copying.[1]

From this revelation, Christian de Portzamparc set out to work on an urban model based on the idea of a multipolar universe, with telescoping buildings. That was the concept behind the Cité de la Musique, on the edge of the Parc de la Villette in Paris, which was built like a little town, with different buildings, colours and shapes. In the Cité de la Musique, he explains, 'there is great diversity of places, of contrasts, it's an exploration of the city, of the way I experience the city today. I think it is crucial to invent a contemporary poetics of contrasts, a poetics for this diversity of location.'

I have made two pieces on Christian de Portzamparc, his work and his approach. One is on the National School of Music, made for a programme about communication and architecture in 1991, produced by Richard Ugolini. The other was done at Christmas 1994, for French Television (FR2), and for that I worked with a steadicam operator.

The Cité de la Musique includes a concert hall with several different buildings – housing, offices and a museum – around it. The plan of the building spirals like a snailshell – in fact Christian de Portzamparc gives a shell-name to the public space, which he calls '*la conque*'. I tried to express this architectural composition in the video itself.

Video and CD-ROM

In 1994, a young partnership of French architects, Pierre du Besset and Dominique Lyon, were holding an exhibition at the French Institute of Architecture. They asked me to make a video for it. Although they cited no films, they made constant references to video games. For young people, this culture is a natural extension of, perhaps a substitute for, the cinema culture of earlier times.

I, personally, am very interested in the possibilities of new imaging techniques, and fascinated by the method of exploring space most often used in video and now CD-ROM games. Professionals call it 'tunnels' – you have the feeling you are travelling endlessly through a dreamscape, a world with no boundaries. The architecture of Dominique Lyon and Pierre du Besset includes cartoon and graphic novel references, and they use bold, bright colours. We used 'tunnel' motion to speed through the environment they create, giving the impression in our piece of the video-games world which feeds their imagination.

Conclusion

I began by showing how, in the 1980s, Jean Nouvel incorporated direct inspiration from the figures and environments of the cinema into his architecture, fusing the world of moving images and the film set with design in the real world. When I created a portrait of his work and his ideas, I used his own technique in reverse, evoking his buildings through moving images and their relationship to space and time. The challenge of making really interesting and appropriate moving image representations of architectural spaces and concepts, at the same time as portraits of the human architects themselves, has come to fascinate me. It is a creative genre which has, unfortunately, been very little explored, probably because most producers have not yet realised the potential and enthusiasm which new appreciations of screen worlds and environments are generating. It is still difficult to get funding for work in this new region of documentary. But the borderlands between the domain of the film director using traditional tools and the realm of the architect using video or synthetic imaging to reveal real or fantastic spaces are beginning to offer, as Jean Nouvel saw, a fruitful two-way interaction. It has drawn me into experimenting with trying to find inventive and appropriate visual languages to convey the excitement of what is happening.

Acknowledgement

Most of the productions mentioned here were realised with the support of major institutions such as the Centre Georges Pompidou, the Institut Français d'Architecture and the Caisse des Dépots, who have been most generous in their support of my work.

Note

1. Private communication.

PART FOUR

The Virtual City I

Architecture In Movement

Introduction

François Penz

In the following papers on the Virtual City the worlds of architecture and film-making find themselves confronted with the use of new digital tools which will affect our vision and our practices. In Part Four we deal with architects both in education and in practice moving from the world of education towards multimedia and the virtual representation of the city.

The Case for Architecture
Film-makers often go to great lengths to construct elaborate sets to achieve their vision, for example the reconstructed modern city in Jacques Tati's *Playtime* (1967). By contrast architects and students of architecture have already got a number of elements which are what I would call 'ready-made sets' or 'natural film sets', such as drawings, physical models and often nowadays computer models of spaces; but they may not necessarily realise their potential. If we want to carry on the analogy with film, I would then suggest that for architects the narrative structure is the design philosophy, and the intentions and motives the storyboard. For architects to express themselves through moving images requires, in fact, little effort because so much visual material is already at hand although not captured on camera.

Films and videos about architecture have been shown for some time now, usually in the form of documentaries. The image in movement has been used for presentation purposes and for the communication of ideas in a 'post-production' phase; but it has only become very recently possible and feasible to use moving images in a more upstream way as part of the architectural process through the use of digital tools; I am not here referring only to computer-animated spaces but to the general ease of working with animated images from all sorts of sources (video, film, stills, computer animations, and so on) and combining them and editing them with relative ease thanks to increasingly user-friendly and reasonably priced software running on equally user-friendly and reasonably priced personal computers, in a way which was unthinkable even five years ago.

Of course film purists may balk at the quality of the images, but for a quick and evocative *mise en scène* of architectural spaces – equivalent of rough hand-sketching – the technique has enormous virtues and will in the future almost certainly affect the way architects work, even in practices. The creative use of the *caméra-stylo* (as coined by the *nouvelle vague* directors) is already having an impact on architectural education, for example in my own Cambridge department, where 'video-computer-animation' projects can be an integral part of the curriculum, or through the work of Annie Forgia's and Earl Mark's students. But to date perhaps some of the most interesting examples of the creative use of digital tools come from the world of museums, as well as in the entertainment and music industry, as illustrated in the papers by Michael Eleftheriades and Joachim Sauter, below.

Finally, I want to make it clear that the point here is not to turn architecture students or architects into film-makers (or vice versa), but to give designers an opportunity to explore new design tools to evaluate and explore spaces, and that, given recent advances in digital technology, experimentation has become easier and easier.

Architects have a lot to learn from films and the collaboration with film-makers and the interdisciplinary nature of the work can only bring to both professions a new impetus in their creative drive.

Using Digital Techniques and Videos in Architectual Education

Annie Forgia

Introduction

The work we are developing now in the Laboratory of Representation of the School of Architecture of Paris-Conflans has been formulated and defined gradually through the progressive teaching of the use of computers in architectural design for the students of the school. The introduction of the teaching of digital images has set new problems in the organisation of studies and therefore of the CAD (computer-aided design) Laboratory. I first studied Arts and Architecture, and was later admitted to the French Institute of Advanced Cinematographic Studies (IDHEC), which at the time was one of the few such centres in the world. I then started to work as a designer for films and then for TV.

After about ten years, I began to think that my experience could be used to design architecture. I subsequently obtained a research contract on 'The Use of Pictures in Simulating Architectural Space'. At the time digital images had not yet arrived. I was convinced from the beginning that the appearance of digital images was going to develop the use of video in new ways.

To teach how to work with digital images means studying at the same time how to make a video, and the problem of mixing digital images with analog images.

In 1981, for the first Festival of Architectural Film in Bordeaux, I was invited to organise an exhibition for the 'Plan Construction'. The Plan Construction is an interministerial organisation for the development of construction, which supports many programmes of research, especially in the field of digital techniques applied to architectural design. The great difficulty in organising such an exhibition was to find a logical thread to link together the different research results I had to show. At the time I was studying the different approaches of representation, and a consideration of the process of architectural design as a system seemed to offer a possible script for the exhibition.

From this point of view, it was like a puzzle, each piece falling into place. Since then, my research work on representation using new technology in the process of architectural design, as well as my architectural teaching using new systems of representation have been based on a systemic approach. Techniques are changing and evolving very quickly. We cannot teach softwares and video and photography without a purpose and a link between them, which is why we have organised our laboratory and teaching to take into account of all these elements.

Organisation of studies

In the fourth year of study there is a one-term certificate of 150 hours, during which graphic software (Arc+, very much used by French architects), digital images by way of a 3D Studio and Photoshop, video and photography are all studied. Lectures are also given about the methodology of representation. The purpose of this certificate is to train the students in the different techniques so that they are able to follow the seminar of the fifth year named 'Prospective of Architectural Design'. These two certificates are specific to our School of Architecture.

The seminar is organised within the framework of a case study, generally an urban case. This study involves lectures on the theory of the process of architectural design applied to the case, and on the methodology of representation and communication.

This seminar is divided into three stages:

1. How to analyse the site, the potentialities of the site, and how to take the necessary data, using photography, video and computer graphics.

2. How to design using hypotheses and not an architectural 'parti' (concept). This method permits a dialectical process between the evaluation by simulation of the different hypotheses and the analysis of the data. At this stage we use computer graphics, digital images and other devices which allow us to simulate the hypothesis.

3. How to communicate the hypothesis chosen as a definite concept?

A communication goal needs to be clearly defined by each student, who has to communicate their ideas using digital images, photography and video.

To achieve the organisation of such a teaching programme, we have succeeded in having in the same building a computer laboratory for computer-aided design and for digital images; a video laboratory with devices for both traditional and computerised montage; a photographic laboratory; and a workshop for traditional models. As a result of this the students can work, moving freely from one place to another according to the needs of their project.

The teaching team consists of four tenured staff responsible for the whole teaching concept, plus specialists for photography, video and Photoshop. There are also six visiting teachers who are practising architects and also specialists in different softwares. Our four tenured staff and three reseach workers have created a research group working in the field of digital images in architectural design. The general title of this research is 'Virtual Space of Conception'. The laboratory plays a major part in teaching computer-aided architectural design in the School of Architecture.

Moreover, the laboratory now accepts postgraduates studying for a doctorate in the problems and methodology of representation in architectural design and town planning. This organisation of the laboratory allows us to train graduate architects to produce digital images. This one-year training is developed in co-operation with the French National Audiovisual Institute (INA).

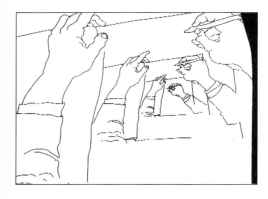

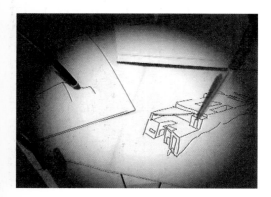

Fragiles esquisses

The candidates are chosen by interview, and we admit about ten each year. During training they have to produce a short video of a few minutes in which both analog images and digital images are mixed. The aim is not to turn architects into producers, but to impart new capabilities in the field of representation and communication. The training covers two main directions: the teaching of the production of digital images, and the production of videos.

In addition, there is a course on the methodological implications of using digital images and video in the process of architectural design, and a course on communication: for example, semiological analysis of the image, sociological approach of communication, how to compose a scenario (structure, narration, dramaturgy, and so on). This training has existed since 1987, and is financed by the Direction de l'Architecture in the Ministère de l'Équipement.

This organisation has formulated a general policy of development of teaching computer graphics and digital images in the Schools of Architecture. While not every School follows this policy, it is now increasingly popular. Other former students are in research laboratories. There are at present six research laboratories in different schools of architecture, which work on digital images in the field of architecture. Others work in companies which specialise in the production of digital images or have started their own companies.

In France many companies specialising in the production of digital images are managed by architects or are working with architects. For example, Renault's laboratory which produces images to simulate virtual cars, or to make communication products for the company, is managed by a young architect, Bruno Simon.

Comments

First of all I think it is preferable for our purpose to teach with 'light systems' such as PCs, and software such as 3D Studio and Photoshop, rather than with more complicated systems. What is essential is to get a good mastery of methodology. If the students know what the problems are regarding light, colours, textures and so on, and how to solve them, then they will know which are the right questions when they meet other systems, or more complicated systems. I also think that, with digital images, animated images will in the future, play a great part in the process of architectural design and town planning. They will greatly help the architects in communicating with clients.

Space cannot be described only by means of geometry. For example, people generally remember the Place de la Bastille in Paris as a circular space, when the geometrical reality is that it is more or less a square.

The use of digital images will compel architects to define not only the building geometry, but also the colours, the lights (their origins, directions and intensity), the material texture, and so on, in a new way. The multiplicity of views allows architects to explore a future reality. Thus, it is now possible, in a way, not only for the architect to communicate this future reality, but also for the client to take possession of it, and to verify the proposed hypothesis of an anticipated reality.

Even if the digital images are constructed according to the laws of perspective, the possible multiplicity of views will change for ever the use and the the concept of perspectival space in architecture. The following quote from Jean Mitry illustrates the point:

> The characteristic of film images is to be animated … It is the motion itself which shows the object as we see it and produces not its image but an average image without even photographic reality … This thing, seen on the screen, does not exist objectively on any image of the film … In the change the thing disappears behind the motion which is presented to our eyes; it leaves only an 'idea' of itself which is as an 'average' of the successive perceptions that we have of it while it moves.

The use of montage allows one to present the general features of an architectural or urban space and at the same time some significant details which could qualify the whole. The possibility of connecting the images with each other and the fact that the connections give sense or a new sense to the images related by the montage is one of the major aspects of the use of animated images in the field of architectural representation. The size of video screen and of the digital images are standardized.

These images have a frame and ought to be composed according to that frame. This presents a new subject in the teaching of digital images and their use: the introduction to a culture of images through the history of painting and the history of cinema. It is important not to leave the students under the influence of an aesthetic developed only in the field of publicity and spectacular films.

The Videos

The videos described here are the works of graduate architects produced during their training in the laboratory. They were left free to choose the subject of their work. The last session was generally oriented towards painting and painters, even if these subjects were correlated with architecture and the representation of space. It is generally very difficult to ensure that these videos mix digital with analog images. Each architect produced an incredible number of digital images (3,000 to 4,000), and very often had difficulties in following the initial storyboard and realising the montage in the way initially chosen.

The illustrations show images from three of these videos which, with their qualities and faults, seemed representative of the kind of works that our students produce. The first video, *Fragiles esquisses*, is inspired by the work of the Portuguese architect Alvaro Siza. The first part of this video presents Alvaro Siza and his taste for sketching to prepare his designs. This part is illustrated by an animation in 2D and 3D, which is pleasant and even skilful. The last part shows a building designed by Alvaro Siza, in 3D digital images, as if it was a classical architectural model, filmed in analog images. This is interesting because it shows one of the difficulties for architects, whose culture is founded on a tradition of drawings and models – using digital images in an original way. The second video, whose title is *2 mille 36 Joiseaux*, is related to paintings by different painters and to Le Corbusier's conception of space. It has in fact a relatively complex storyboard, and the result shows in a particularly interesting way how a very tight montage allows the author to use in the same short video both fixed images and animated images. The interest of the spectator is sustained by a strict choice of paintings used to construct the scenario.

2 mille 36 Joiseaux

Fotoplastikon

The *Fotoplastikon* is a thoughtful decomposition of the optical box of Hoogstratten. Beside the obvious virtuosity of this piece, the three-dimensional anamorphosis of the images of the panels of the box, the references to the colours and the light of the Dutch painting of the seventeenth century show the possibilities of software like 3D Studio, and the value of such tools in the teaching of digital images.

Acknowledgments

I wish to acknowledge the French National Audiovisual Institute (INA) and particularly J. Martiné for the collaboration without which these videos could not have been produced. I also wish to acknowledge my colleagues at the Computer Laboratory of the School of Architecture of Paris-Conflans, who did not stint of the time they gave to the students. I also wish to acknowledge the financial support of the Direction de l'Architecture which was so necessary in organising this teaching for graduate architects. Finally, thanks (on behalf of my colleagues and myself) to the architects who agreed to undertake such a lot of work: B. Silva Pinto for *Fragiles esquisses*, A. Nagy for *2 mille 36 Joiseaux*, and M. Kozucki for *Fotoplastikon*.

References

Einsenstein, S. M., *The Film Sense* translated and edited by J. Leyda, (London: Faber and Faber, 1968).

Francastel, P., *L'Image, la vision et l'imagination, de la peinture au cinéma* (Paris: Denoël Gonthier, 1983).

Mitry, J., *Esthétique et psychologie du cinéma* (Paris: Éditions Universitaires, 1963).

The Physical and Conceptual Assembly of Architectural Form

Earl Mark

La Belle et la bête

La Belle et la bête

A richly ornamented building may be simulated by the animation of just a few architectural details. The viewer is led to presume the existence of many more details than actually lie in place. Cocteau's cinematic treatment of architectural space in the movie *La Belle et la bête* (1946) provides some instructive examples. This is evident in the entrance hall of the Beast's *château*. Well-placed lighting transforms a relatively empty stage set with just a few architectural details into the illusion of a richly ornamented hallway.[1] The architectural qualities of the hall are suggested by the few details that we actually see. These architectural details appear to characterise those spaces that we cannot see because they lie hidden in shadow.

Similarly, when movie-making is used to explore architecture, a few well placed details can be used to describe the overall character of a building. For example, a few components of a block and bracket structure can be used to represent how the overall shape of a roof is determined in traditional Chinese architecture. The animation of a few details depicts more generally how the upward corbelling curve of the roof's outer edge is determined by the placement of the modular blocks and brackets. The blocks and brackets seem to account for both the roof's physical structure and its conceptual organisation.

Kits of Parts

The 'kit of parts' idea is rooted in traditional design methods based on wood and other physical modelling materials. For example, the kit used within an architectural design project might consist of some wooden models at a small scale, such as a model of a type of column, or a type of wall, or a type of window. A part such as a column may be physically duplicated and tested in different orderings. This technique is occasionally used within an introductory graduate design studio, where the kit is presented to students and they perform some variations on it.[2] In some cases, the students are expected to design the kit itself as well as the possible configurations of it.

In the film *La Belle et la bête,* Cocteau created a *château* from a kit of a very few parts consisting of candelabras, fireplace ornaments and other architectural details. His animated kit reinforces selective architectural and narrative aspects of the Beast's *château*. In an early film sequence, the arms holding the candelabras move and direct the Merchant to a dining table. In a later film sequence, the busts in relief within the fireplace (played by two actors) move their eyes back and forth and give emphasis to the repetitive pacing motion of Beauty waiting on the late arrival of the Beast to dinner. The animated architectural elements express common purpose in similar motion, a synchronisation of parts moving to the action of a character or to otherwise reinforce a part of the narrative.

The moving kit of parts can help to characterise a space-time continuum. For example, as the Merchant comes to a stop at the front door of the Beast's *château*, his shadow continues to move independently. The unusual treatment of light and shadow is carried along by a kit of candelabras in the scene that follows. It appears in this following scene that the Merchant moves through the entrance hall and candelabras mysteriously become lit so as to direct his way, but some trick photography may be at work.

This sequence of the Merchant moving past the entrance and through the front hall was apparently recorded in reverse motion. That is, the Merchant stepped backwards while the candelabras were in turn blown out. The film was then physically reversed in the final print. The film reversal creates the effect of a series of candelabras becoming lit in a specific direction that guides the Merchant towards the dining-room table. He pauses along the way to look round the room and discover yet more additional candelabras motioning him back to the table. With all the time that expires, we hardly take notice of the fact that the dining table is sitting unusually close to the entrance of the *château*. The camera's attention to the slow lighting of the candelabras may divert us from more directly assessing the short distance.

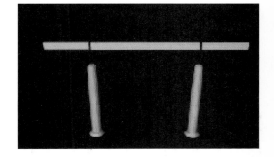

The candelabra sequence may work to extend the apparent passage of film space-time such that it seems that the Merchant walks farther to reach the dining table than actually is the case.[3] More generally, Cocteau's kit of real physical parts is suggestive of how a computer graphics kits of parts may also be animated to change the perception of space-time. The space-time usage by Cocteau in *La Belle et la bête* is similar to an animation 'walk-through' of a building. The walk-though of a building may not just be a straight run, but may include small vignettes of where a person is likely to dwell. We get a sense of the whole composition from the small vignettes. The overall space-time order may be suggested but not fully simulated.

Still, computer graphics kits are more physically flexible than real physical kits. Each individual part easily changes scale, colour, and orientation. As an architectural design tool, a computer graphics animation can be choreographed with purposeful object transformations, which put emphasis on key components of a design proposal, or which shows how they are conceptually ordered or physically assembled.

As suggested in the illustrations, the conceptual and physical assemblies of architectural form are created with a minimal set of parts. The sequences provide a selective reading of the architectural space. In some cases, the space-time experience is implied by selective shots rather than more exhaustively treated. The animation tells about what is important and how space is conceived, rather than presenting space in a neutral form.

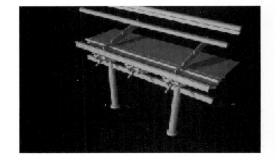

Instances and Animation
The physical description of each part within the computer graphics kit is represented by a so-called 'parent'. Clones of a particular parent are referred to as 'children' or 'instances'. The process of creating an instance is referred to as 'instantiation'. Each child can be

Animation of block and bracket system

133

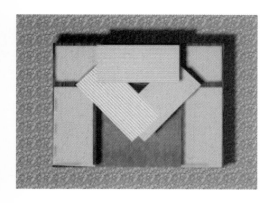

Animation of Tatami mats

instantiated in three-dimensional space through the specification of an x, y, and z Cartesian co-ordinate location (for example, the child of an object *column 1* placed at Cartesian co-ordinate location x = 4, y = 4, and z = 0). Within computer graphics animation, the form of each child is similar to that of its parent, but it can vary in scale. That is, the x-scale, y-scale and z-scale of the child can be determined independently of the parent's x-scale, y-scale and z-scale. The child instance can also be rotated differently from its parent, and assigned its own distinct material properties which result in its own individual texture, colour, light-reflection and light-absorption qualities.

The computer graphics animation can consist of sequences where the size, rotation, and location of many child objects are visually transformed. Such freedom in the physical parameters of objects gives a designer the means with which to alter the general appearance of a place more radically than is possible with a real physical kit consisting of wooden parts. For example, the walls within a kit can very easily change size, spatial orientation, colour, or texture. Particular properties of an object within a single part of the kit can be transformed gradually while other of its properties are held constant. The geometrical modifications of the original kit and of the spatial relationships between its parts may arouse very divergent conceptions of an architectural space.

Various Kinds of Kit Applications

A kit of objects that are relatively fixed in scale is animated in the construction of a traditional Japanese tea-house at Katsura. In the beginning of the sequence, a parent Tatami mat is instantiated into several child instances. The instances are then rotated into place so as to lay out the floor plan. The floor plan of the tea-house appears to emerge additively from the modular assembly of each mat. The animation of the mats provides a kind of visual logic to the ordering of proportions within the floor plan of the tea-house. The object of the computer animation is to have the viewer take notice of the relationship of the smaller mats to the whole composition. Similarly, as the Merchant enters the home of the Beast in Cocteau's film, he takes notice of a certain aspect of the entrance hallway as guided by the animation of architectural parts. That is, the Merchant is motioned along his way by a series of moving candelabra arms that point in the direction of a dining table. He takes in an aspect of the architectural space, but not necessarily the whole space.

Within another animation sequence of the Japanese tea-house, the layering of different structural elements and textures is the predominant sequence, where one structural system frames the next subsystem. For example, the columns are animated into position first. The columns then frame the screen walls, which are animated into position next. The screen walls then frame in turn the bamboo screen windows. In a similar sequence, wooden beams frame the roof substructure, which then frames a thatch covering, which in turn supports the roof cap. The visual effect of this animation is to characterise the wall system as the layering of these different components. This layering sequence depicts the association between closely interconnected parts, as compared to the animation of the Tatami mats, which consists of separate parts that are placed alongside one another.

Neither the layering of the wall system and its subsystems nor the side-by-side placement of the Tatami mats is necessarily more characteristic of the tea-house construction. For example, as you enter the fully constructed and textured tea-house in another animation, the textural variety of different wood, paper and bamboo materials juxtaposed may give way to yet another sense of how to read the architectural composition, one based on a balanced composition of materials rather than on the layering of structural systems or the side-by-side placement of similar units such as Tatami mats.

Through animation, an observer may view a building as the creation of different part-to-whole systems, none of which are strictly determinant. An animation can also represent an assembly sequence where the series of motion picture frames is timed so as to pause at important moments in the development of the composition. The kit of parts is in effect a proposition on how the overall architectural design is assembled. It presents a set of possible subdivisions for a design. The kit may consist of small independent forms that can be combined in one composition. It can consist of modular elements that are scaled at different sizes. For any particular element of the kit, or for a set of elements within the kit, the animation can depict variation in material properties. The material properties are controlled by coefficients for transparency, shininess, roughness, colour, orientation of grain, and so on. The animation of these properties within a kit provides different ways of altering and understanding a design and the materiality of its parts.

The animation of the Japanese tea-house is based on the assembly of and ordering of discrete building construction elements. Alternatively, the animation of Kahn's Salk Institute, is not based on such construction elements, but describes its translational and bilateral symmetries. Here the kit of parts begins with a single pavilion. At first a row of pavilions is created by animating the translational symmetry of one pavilion. Next, two opposite rows of pavilions are created by animating the bilateral symmetry of the single row. Light delineates other modulations with the Salk Institute where areas of shadow delineate modular components of the design. These shadows change with an animated simulation of sunlight moving throughout the course of a day.

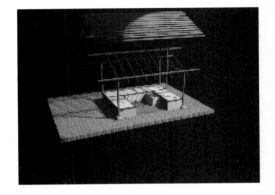

Another kit of parts is based on material continuities of a passageway under Jefferson's Rotunda at the University of Virginia. Here the kit is composed of carefully detailed windows and bricks. These establish rhythms that become apparent when observed by a camera in motion through the passageway. A strong simulated natural light creates shadows which modulate between the kit of windows, the walls, and the brick texture. The light delineates these distinct elements within a common space. The modulation of the series of Palladian windows is emphasised as the camera moves forwards and the edge of camera frame is bordered alternately by shadowed and non-shadowed parts of the walkway.

A kit of parts can be made up from the architectural grid elements of Le Corbusier's Carpenter Center at Harvard University. Rhythms are established by the changing sunlight pattern against the *brise soleil*. The changing position of the sunlight throughout the day is simulated in time-lapse intervals. The shadows within each cell of the grid deepen as the sun sets.

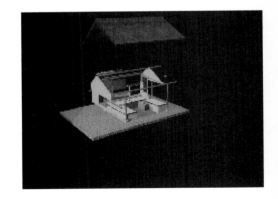

Animation of a traditional Chinese wooden column structure demonstrates both the high level of craft and the aesthetic refinements evident in its construction. These qualities are apparent from even an ordinary view of the completed work. However, we may not appreciate the entire structural system from its external appearance as well as when given a chance to see its assembly. For example, the animation of a column's construction reveals its hidden aesthetic elements.

Animation of tea house structural system

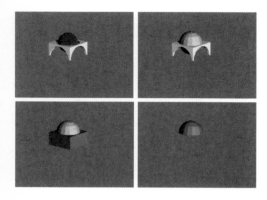

Animation of Pendentive

A conceptual assembly of a pendentive[4] is animated on the basis of solid modelling. Note that this sequence does not represent the physical construction of a pendentive. Rather, the solid modelling technique reveals its pure geometrical and formal organisation. The above examples illustrate the similarity in appearance of a computer-animated model to a real physical model. However, a computer model may be more easily constructed than one with real physical materials. In some architectural practices, therefore, a computer generated walk-though is a practical alternative to moving a video camera through a real physical model. The computer animation has the effect of taking a video camera, and passing it through a small wooden or chipboard model. Still, a computer animation can be more dynamically altered than a real physical model. Its dynamic capability can be used to visualise physical and conceptual assemblies which are difficult to show with real physical kits of parts.

The animation of physical assembly and conceptual assembly, however, does not have as its primary purpose the provision of a surrogate visual experience as might be recorded by a camera moving through a model of a building. Rather, within the projects cited above, animation is used to visualise the many relations that exist and which can be altered among the formal parts, material attributes and range of shapes that constitute a building or other design. The computer based 'kit of parts' requires the viewer to participate more actively in a form of model-making through animation, where the relationships between physical and conceptual components are explored.

Notes

1. Jean Cocteau, *Beauty and The Beast: Diary of A Film* (New York: Dover Publications, 1972) portrays the stage in photographs that indicate the spare use of architectural detail.
2. The introductory graduate design studios at the University of Virginia, Department of Architecture, include a design problem based on a real physical kit of parts.
3. Cocteau, *Beauty and the Beast*. See the photographs of the stage set.
4. Prof. William Mitchell used the example of the pendentive to introduce solid modelling to his students at the Harvard Graduate School of Design. This animation was recreated after his example. Solid modelling consists of performing unions, intersections and subtractions of solid-like objects.

Architecture or Cinema?

Digital 3D Design and the World of Multimedia

Michael Eleftheriades

Background

The story I am telling is of one person's experience of the evolution of computer- aided design and presentation in architecture over the last ten years. It illustrates the way the skills of an architect need to extend into the realm of moving images already occupied by screen directors if we are going to use the emerging technology to its fullest advantage. One of my abiding fascinations is motion. I'm absolutely gripped by the relationships between light and motion. My other passion is for the third dimension.

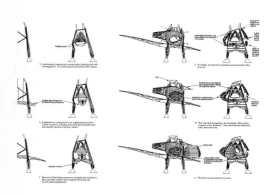

This is a project from my student days concerned with the South Bank of the Thames. I went and measured the site and created a 3D model using a computer. I could then go and look at every part in detail and from all angles. I proposed to build a sumo wrestling theatre next to County Hall, which would be the focus of the configuration. The building itself was developed both as a computer model and as a card model, because in 1987 computers were so difficult to use. Now, because it's a sumo wrestling theatre, it takes a lot of its cues from the sumo wrestler – it has a very low centre of gravity, and all the weight is taken up by the back legs.

The building was generated on the computer in all its details, a good use of computer graphics, because this is a component building: you can take it apart and put it back together again, and see how it all evolves.

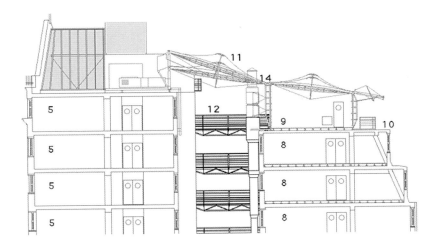

After a year with Michael Hopkins I joined Imagination, where there was a real interest in doing new things and developing new ways of imagining and working. I was familiar with Herron Associates when they started designing the Imagination building, and the point about scale Zbig Rybczynski makes in his paper (pp. 182–197) was pertinent – on the computer there's no perception of scale; it can work at 1:10,000 of an inch resolution while at the same time working to 1:1,000 or 1:200 or 1:10 or 1:1. Moreover, it doesn't need to create the consistencies our eyes are used to. Herron Associates were printing full-size versions of the building, so if you went into their office you could see a print-out of the whole of the gallery at 1: 1.

Defining relationships between objects and showing how moving parts work turned out to be another advantage of computer graphics software – I designed a robotic lamp with Ron Herron, who is very interested in the idea of 'walking cities'. In order to achieve what we wanted in design terms, we experimented with taking data from one piece of software and going into another, so our models were done in one package and then developed in another.

The Imagination building was complex, partly because of its geometry in the atrium, and here the use of the computer was invaluable and enabled us to design and to actually work out the trusses in the roof and the different angles.

Multimedia

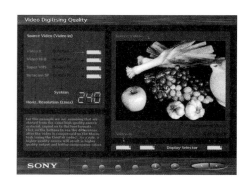

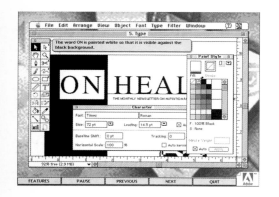

After working at Imagination for three years as an architect, I was offered a new position as a multimedia designer. Having always intended to make my mark in architecture, of course I hesitated – but finally decided to try the option, because I was convinced there was a lot of new potential in multimedia which needed exploring, and I realised my opportunities to explore them would be greater if I joined the multimedia world.

But what is 'multimedia'? So many different things. In some respects, I always was a multimedia designer in so far as anyone who mixes different media is. But what multimedia is really about, particularly on a personal computer, can be said to be three things: interactive input (you can make decisions about where you are and where you want to go); visual interface (relating to where you are or allowing you to interact with the computer); and control (which is probably what makes this medium unique). Multimedia work is particularly important because it can involve any and every other medium. That may sound like saying it's nothing because it's everything, but I think it is more positive than that – it has the potential to develop many different existing media conventions in new ways, something that really relates to the 20th century, only possible now because of modern computer technology.

Multimedia work has many facets – animation, video, product design, computer-based presentations and marketing, working with textures, working with three-dimensional spaces.

Here is some of our work illustrating the diversity of multimedia: a project for Adobe Systems Europe, a design for cars – interactive for Ford UK and a project for Sony.

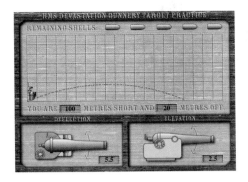

It's no accident that most of the really interesting developments in terms of computers and 3D are happening in games, because games are incredibly popular and 3D worlds are what people naturally relate to. It's what people want, what people are used to; it's what people know how to navigate. It's interesting to see how rapidly the graphics have already evolved and developed, from the early days to the present. In games, the computer can generate an environment with real people composited within it, a technique which would allow both designers and clients to immerse themselves in three-dimensional simulated worlds to experiment with ideas or to explore sites and buildings – or maybe even design structures organically by 'being' inside them. A game might take five man-years to produce, including a three-dimensional computer-generated world the player can navigate through, and even when the graphic style is more inventive than the usual 'clean' look we identify with computer graphics – having textures, very real-looking – a 'number one' game in terms of popularity, I'm sorry to say that the architecture can still be absolutely dreadful.

However, the fact that such games do become number-one sellers despite their shortcomings demonstrates forcibly that people like playing as well as working with well-designed three-dimensional spaces, even if they exist virtually. There is real excitement in the unique quality of the space, the light, the objects, the trees, their textures and character. Meanwhile, even the most impressive of games still lack good architects to take them seriously enough, or understand them well enough, to design imaginative environments.

Here are illustrated some of our games; one for the Maritime Museum and a three-dimensional virtual game designed to teach children safety in the home.

The Internet

On the Internet I have experimented, for example, with a drawing that was simultaneously drawn by myself in London with three other people, one based in Paris, one based in California, and one in Chicago. We called it the 'electronic mural', or the 'global interactive network'. We had a 'virtual' drawing which could be on any one of these sites, and people would link together electronically and work on it simultaneously. This is a very fascinating thing to do, because it completely changes your perception of the computer as a machine you work on by yourself. It becomes a doorway you can use to relate to others, pointing the way to the future.

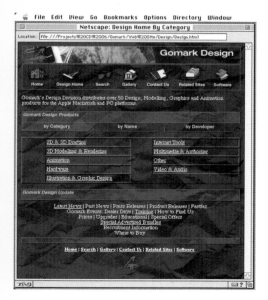

The computer is increasingly developing into a communications medium, a funnel through which data, information and video are all pouring in. The Internet already gives global access to things like a pictorial tour of the White House. It is really the global marketplace where artists and designers can show their work as illustrated here with the Gomark site.

The Future

   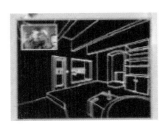

I have looked at the development of digital technology in its relationship to spatial representation and moving images over the last decade. But what about the future?

How might a designer-client relationship work with the aid of the Internet? Someone looking for an architect could make contact, show the designer her space, ask what the architect would propose, see it in virtual reality, and decide whether she thought the idea would suit her. The client and the architect could be anywhere on the globe. This is already practicable in the current state of technological development.

As a conclusion I would say that I think it will become standard as computers become pervasive consumer items in our culture, and the realm of architecture will merge imperceptibly with the world of cinema.

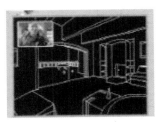

Experiencing Virtual Reality

Joachim Sauter

Introduction

Art+Com is a research and development centre for computer-aided design and communication. Its main purpose is to promote co-operation between the arts and the sciences. It was founded in 1988 as a non-profit organisation and has currently an average of twenty-five to thirty employees and voluntary workers, and is financed by research funds and grants.

This organisation was established with motives and ideas that remain valid today. To illustrate the point we will consider the case of a Renaissance painting.

The Renaissance was an epoch in which art and science converged. The artist became a scientist and the scientist an artist – or at least, as we would say today, they were working towards each other in an 'interdisciplinary' relationship. We at Art+Com follow the same principle. Here artists, designers, computer experts, scientists and engineers work together on projects which can no longer be clearly categorised into one of these disciplines. In other words, we are neither pursuing traditional scientific research nor studying art in the traditional context of studios, galleries and museums.

In Renaissance times the closeness of the sciences to the arts meant that science had a strong influence on the evolution of painting. This was manifested in the development of central perspective. For the first time the foreshortening of space was correctly portrayed from the central point of view of an imaginary individual standing in front of the picture.

The illustration shows one of the first examples of this development. Incidentally, it also shows the result of interdisciplinary co-operation between an engineer, who designed the architecture in the painting, and an artist friend who painted the figures.

A second important shift of paradigms in the representation of space and objects appears during the second half of the last century with the invention of photography and film. Here the picture is no longer based on a single viewpoint but on several different ones at once. Cubism, for example, reflected this in its use of filmic forms of representation, such as double exposures and time-lapse photography.

Today we can observe yet another shift of paradigms in spatial representation. The computer enables real-time representation of space independently of the observer's viewpoint. In other words, we no longer have a fixed viewpoint outside the representation; instead, the observer can interactively select any viewpoint within the spatial representation. This can be done by measuring the head position. Also, the user can communicate his or her desired viewpoint to the computer with a different input interface.

This paradigmatic shift in spatial representation is one of the focuses of Art+Com's work: to what extent can these spaces be used for the organisation and communication of information? To what extent can narration can take place in these spaces? Will this form of representation possibly give rise to a new idiom, a new media language, a new dramatic form?

The Iconoclast Project

Before we discuss further results of our work which address those questions, let us consider the Renaissance painting illustrated. The most interesting detail in this portrait is the flower, in the form of a pair of eyes, that the woman is holding in her hand. This external interface brings her into contact with the viewer of the painting; at the same time she is looking very intently at the flower itself. This look, as well as the development of new interfaces between representation and observer, is another focus of our work at Art+Com. By placing a computer behind the painting we were able to track down the observer's eye. In doing so the 'eye-tracker' modifies the painting in an interactive mode.

Our motivation for this project was the fact that, at the end of the 1980s, people were still looking at the computer primarily as a tool and not as a medium. The painter has exchanged his brush for the light pen, but he has used it to do almost exactly the same things that he once did on an analog basis. For us this was art with computers, not the beginning of computer art. We saw the same thing happen with the architects, who turned in their drawing boards for digitisers, or with film-makers who have replaced the camera with a mouse. With the installation 'Iconoclast' we have tried to propagate one of the most important qualities of the computer, namely interactivity, in a classical situation for the reception of art.

Along with interactivity, we see two other qualities that distinguish the computer as a medium rather than a tool. These are multimedia capability (the integration of various media) and interconnectivity (the linking of several computers to form a network). We have attempted to examine these properties in our projects – as in one of our first projects, 'New Media in Town Planning', in 1989.

To this end we designed a tele-interactive multimedia application which would provide spatial and historical information for town planners, architects, citizens' initiatives, and planning authorities. Ordinary PCs from their offices were connected via broad-band ISDN to a mainframe, laser disks, and later on to real-time computing hardware in an information centre. We enabled the user to navigate through a network of browsers in search of information clusters. One such cluster was Potsdamer Platz, located in the centre of Berlin in what was once the no-man's-land, the 'death strip,' between the eastern and western halves of the city. We can access film clips from the video disk along with textual information, hypertextual links, still pictures, maps, and so on. In this case we have tele-interactively called up a computer animation from the video disk which takes us down into the subway station at Potsdamer Platz, once a deserted 'ghost station' that was closed for thirty years. We reconstructed it in the computer and combined it with video material we shot shortly after the Wall came down.

The Iconoclast project

145

In a second project phase we offered the user out of the same application a tele-interactive access to a workstation and with it the possibility of moving interactively around the underground station using a mouse. The mouse position was sent via broadband ISDN to the workstation, and the image, generated in real time, came back over the same line. This real-time representation was made possible by a 'Radiosity Renderer' developed by our programmers, and which later gave us the chance for a joint project with Jeron Lanier and VPL, who were then the leading virtual reality developers. Using their interfaces and our spatial representation software we then developed a common virtual reality system.

Our interest at the time was to use the virtual space not only for simulations but also to examine its capability for communication. To what extent can it be used to organise information – information which can then be called up by users? It meant developing the preconditions for an interactive and multimedia system. One of our objectives was to enable the user by activating an object to reach another hyperlinked place of information as well, bringing multimedia events into the virtual space by activating these objects. Out of this work we published a number of video textures in virtual space.

Virtual Reality Modeller

The organisation of information in space is not new – the Greeks made an art out of it, and it is still known as 'mnemonics' today: the idea of using places and active vivid images for the dynamic, active storage of things and words.

All these experiments were useful for the simulation and organisation of information, but we quickly recognised that, in terms of investigating a virtual reality (VR) architecture, we had made one of most basic mistakes: all we were doing was producing copies of the real world or at least worlds which had the inherent potential to exist in the real world too.

This mistake was an obvious one. We were working with Euclidean modellers, and therefore our construction tools were based on geometry. Geometry, of course, means nothing other than measuring the world, the real one. We started to look for modellers and construction principles which were not based on Euclidean geometry. We started to work on the principle of planned coincidence – on stochastic modelling. One of our first ideas in this direction was to give objects time characteristics. We provided our objects with surfaces which randomly generated themselves in space and time.

Following the development of our virtual reality system in 1991, the Art+Com architects were invited to take part in the planning competition for the Potsdamer Platz area, and alongside their physical model proposals we developed a system for presenting the city centre and its urban history.

We are also trying to provide a historical simulation by giving the user the ability to morph three-dimensionally through the architectural history of the city. By choosing a point in the city, and by moving the data glove, you can roam backwards and forwards not only in space but also in time.

Another important element here is the integration of interactively accessible multimedia information. If the user, for example, moves to the square in front of the old Berlin Palace, he or she might find there an active link which plays a film shot here in 1990. In other

3D modelling of Berlin

words, the information is organised in time and space. We have also modelled the old Berlin Palace as it was in 1900. It is a model on a 1:1 scale made out of canvas to show the public how the reconstructed palace would look. We called this 'real virtuality'.

Let us now move from urban space to inner space, to the project 'Home of the Brains'. In this project the concept of the museum as a public place for discussion is transposed into the realm of the virtual. The visitor enters a space and finds himself in a linear dialogue conducted by four media philosophers and computer scientists: Minsky, Weizenbaum, Flusser, and Virillo. One corner of the space was fitted out with interactive objects for each thinker. The user can intervene in the discussion via these objects, thus defining his or her own position in respect to the space and the debate itself.

We have also continued working in the area of interfaces, attempting to develop adequate interfaces for specific projects. One example is to navigate in the 'virtual city'. The user can fly around a virtual Berlin simply by moving a 3D sensor over an aerial photograph of the city, and a monitor shows the rendered view from the sensor's position. This kind of interface was very successful because it is a very direct way to navigate through a city space. For example, at the first Radio and Television Trade Fair after the reunification in 1991, residents from both parts of the city explained their neighbourhoods using this system, forgetting very quickly the complex technology behind it.

Moving on to another project, we showed two years ago tele-interactively a model of Berlin in an exhibition in Tokyo. Japanese visitors to the virtual Berlin were navigating with a sensor over the aerial shot located in Tokyo. The data was sent via telephone to the computers at Art+Com in Berlin, which rendered the pictures in real time and sent them back via satellite to Tokyo. The system also allows you to penetrate and navigate into some buildings.

But we were still not fully happy with the interfaces and set ourselves the task of removing them altogether! We then developed in 1992 a system which, for the first time, allows movement through virtual space without a material connection between man and machine. For this purpose we used the 'eye-tracker' already mentioned and designed the so-called 'eye-fly'. The user can move through the virtual space by means of eye movements – he or she selects the place to which he or she would like to go by looking at it.

This experiment was important for us because we were able to eliminate completely the material connection between man and machine. We didn't develop this further, but in the near future we believe that many everyday interfaces will have no physical connection.

TerraVision Project

Today at Art+Com we are focusing on the development of special interfaces for special applications. One example is the TerraVision project. TerraVision is our most up-to-date application project. With this we are trying to make locally dependent data visually and interactively accessible from a virtual Earth generated from satellite photos and altitude data.

The so-called 'earth-tracker' interface was devised from an architecture project which was designed last year for the Ars Electronica Center in Linz. The project is a proposal for an interactive façade and our first VR project in the public space. It is called '*Netzhaut*', which is the German word for 'retina'. In literal translation it means 'network skin'.

'Home of the Brains' project

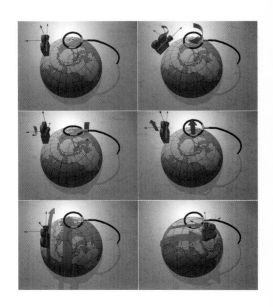

TerraVision project: earth-tracker interface

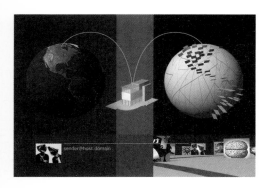

'Network skin' project

The Ars Electronica Center is a museum for new media in art and science, and we decided that the entire networked computer community should have a part in the design of this façade. Our plan is to invite them via different Internet channels – 3W, news, and e-mail – to send a virtual representation of themselves to the museum. These representations will then be placed on a virtual globe corresponding to their place of origin. This virtual globe, with hopefully thousands of contributions by network users, will then be projected on the outside of the building and can be moved by the visitors with an earth-tracker which is located in front of the building.

In conclusion, I think that VR research has solved two of the three big 'I's of virtuality. The first 'I' stands for immersion. Today there are already many affordable interfaces and computer platforms which are both more 'immersive' and less obtrusive and which allow the users to immerse the model completely in a virtual scenario.

The second big 'I' stands for interaction. There are already systems which allow users to interact and tele-interact with objects and even with virtual representations of real people.

The main challenge in the near future will be the exploration of the third big 'I': involvement. Here the task will be to involve the user in a virtual scenario by means of an idiom or media language which is specific to this new medium. At this moment we are not much further along in this respect than film in the era of the Lumière Brothers.

This condition is summed up in our first image, the Renaissance painting, which shows a boy who is holding the first child's drawing documented in the history of art, or the picture within the picture.

PART FIVE

The Virtual City II

The Marriage of Art and Science

Introduction

Henning Camre

'There is a perceived polarity (however artificial) between technology and the humanities, between science and art, between right brain and left. The burgeoning field of multimedia is likely to be one of those disciplines, like architecture, that bridges the gap', says Nicholas Negroponte.[1]

Personally, I welcome the close collaboration between the powers of art and science. Like Zbig Rybczynski, I am a cinematographer by training, and have always relied on my technical skills to support my creative energy in both fiction and documentary filming. Zbig's thoroughly practical and at the same time idealistic concept of a perfect technique to bring the visions of the mind's eye to the screen, unrestricted by the physical limitations of lens mediation and material architecture, is fascinating and inspiring. The haunting image in his *Orchestra* of the interlocked couple floating weightless around the heights of the cathedral roof symbolises fittingly the much-desired embrace of art and science.

In fact, all the papers in Part Five are about convergences of one kind or another. It has been particularly gratifying to see how Paul Richens has used his expertise in architecture and in the field of 3D computer software to bring together screen set design and simulated lighting for the camera in the context of moving images. The digital tool he is developing will significantly expand creative possibilities for students, and his work illuminates important issues for the future of computer-aided film-making. Diana Charnley's presentation of the issues of illusion and drama at the heart of the work of the screen designer, and Christopher Hobbs's revelations of how contemporary digital techniques continue the tradition of what he calls the art director's repertoire of 'lies', serve to demonstrate how, in fact, art and science in film-making have always yearned towards each other.

These four papers come under the heading 'The Virtual City'. In my view, they combine to show how the screen has always been a place where human aspirations, ideologies and perceptions are able to find a unique form of expression. The digital era and the emergence of multimedia are allowing us, as Joachim Sauter as well as Zbig Rybczynski demonstrates, to go on from working with computers as tools to engaging with them as a fruitful moving-image medium. Michael Eleftheriades shows how, for him, tool and medium have developed hand in hand. Like the move from silent to sound film, the step from lens-based screen art into the world of synthetic imaging is a great one, whose consequences we cannot judge immediately. I like to hope it is a step towards the kind of complete achievement dreamt of by the great classical artists, philosophers and scientists Zbig Rybczynski refers to. I believe it has always been the dream of all the great architects and film-makers who have laboured to make real and substantial their vision for others.

Note

1. Nicholas Negroponte, *Being Digital*, (London: Hodder and Stoughton, 1995), p. 81. Negroponte is Director of the Massachusetts Institute of Technology Media Lab.

Production Design As Process

Diana Charnley

The Cohen brothers' hyper-real *The Hudsucker Proxy* is the portrayal of an imaginary urban environment. Because it is created entirely by the determination of plastic space through the set design, much of the imagery is centred around the consciousness of space and its relationship to time, maximising the power of architectural spatial tools.

In the opening sequence, the camera drifts through a grand canyon of high-rises, finally coming to stop at the 45th floor of the Hudsucker Building. All the buildings in this sequence were constructed at 1:24 scale, while the window and ledge along which Tim Robbins crawls was a full-size set piece, and the clock that the camera pans off at the end of the shot a 1:6 scale model. These three elements were composited digitally to appear as one seamless whole.

The production designer recreated the illusion of a mythical 1950s Art Deco New York by combining sources of images from different scales, using models in vertical and horizontal compositions to facilitate camera movement. Such effects require a studio set-up with a motion control camera rig, set up in this case to move in parallel with the studio floor.

Education and training in screen design must now embrace not only traditional screen grammar and an understanding of the historical evolution and techniques of production design, but also the new possibilities for the visual imagination offered by innovations in the virtual and digital domains. The issue of computer-aided work for the screen is addressed in detail by Paul Richens and Zbig Rybczynski. My main task is to demonstrate the ways in which designers have traditionally worked to achieve the illusion of architectural space and reality on the screen, focusing on the issues where new approaches are beginning to absorb old concepts and reincarnate them through electronic tools.

The most elemental dichotomy of film aesthetics may already be said to exist in the difference between the work of the Lumière Brothers and Méliès, where the inception of production design as a process locates itself. Our modern concept of design is reflected in Méliès's exploration of the moving image primarily through artifice and illusion in the telling of stories, as opposed to the recording of events as they unfurl before the camera, unmediated by a designer's intervention.

Here I propose to offer three different case studies which illustrate the process of production design, demonstrating its ephemeral nature and artificial character, and thereby highlighting the artifice common to both physical sets and the possibilities offered by the virtual world. Production design in both education and practice needs to embrace the potential offered by the digital domain. In design education, two areas where the computer can be a very fruitful tool are emerging.

One is the investigation of design possibilities for student live-action drama productions at the planning stage, both in the 3D simulation of proposed physical spaces and in the pre-visualisation of camera positions prior to their realisation either on locations or in studios. The other is in theoretical sessions, where aspects of a script can be developed to their fullest visual potential unhindered by the limitations of resources, and narrative evolved through the simulation of form.

Production design for moving image art and entertainment, whether cinema or television, currently ranges from the artificial construction of a heightened and magnified form of realism to the dramatic evocation of spaces past, future or distinctively contemporary. An inherent irony of the production designer's vision and the art director's craft is its duality – sometimes it is clearly visible, claiming a distinct presence, and at other times utterly imperceptible, constituting the primary plastic form of the production.

That vision and craft are about giving the written word form, interpreting the script and narrative structure into a three-dimensional physical entity – for the time being anyway. Originating a concept and evolving a form, identifying a style which complements the psychological motivation of characters and their interactions as depicted in screen stories, are important aspects of design. This involves the creation of a world – entering into the mind of a character, making a physical space within which they can evolve organically and communicate psychology and emotion to the audience as effectively as possible. In other words, ideally the designer works from inside the script outwards, rather than imposing a form onto a neutral space.

Once into production, the designer's job is to link the disparate visual strands of the film-making process, linking scenes shot entirely on a sound stage to prepared and adapted existing locations – which might be 100 miles apart – so that they form a cohesive whole.

Mary Reilly, directed by Stephen Frears, and *Copy Cat*, directed by John Amiel, were both in post-production prior to intended release in 1995–96 when I prepared this paper. Both were made for mainstream cinema distribution, and can be used to illustrate and demonstrate production design as process.

The design of *Mary Reilly*, which evokes and recreates the Edinburgh of the 1880s, is almost entirely constructed on the sound stages at Pinewood, using craft techniques and construction methods which have evolved with film-making, and haven't really changed in their nature since the 1930s. Made by Warner Bros., *Copy Cat* is a suspense thriller, the story of an agoraphobic played by Sigourney Weaver, filmed in San Francisco in 1994. The production design and ensuing organisation of space create a three-dimensional metaphor where the mental conflicts of the central character's internal world are charted. It depicts a contemporary environment, meshing location spaces with those realised entirely on the sound stage.

Production Design for *Mary Reilly*

At an early stage in the design process, during pre-production, all the sets are delineated in block form. These are planned as one large composite, to include and combine the main exterior of Jekyll's house with its library and staircase interior, plus an exterior courtyard and lane. The whole thing was built on a sound stage measuring 100 x 41 metres, over a period of twelve weeks, by a crew of sixty, and remained in its finished form for about six weeks' filming.

The designer's sketches, drawn quickly to give the director an idea of the design intention and framing possibilities, with the elements of foreground, mid-space and background, are important for the rest of the design department – the construction manager, the set decorator, and art directors. For example, a sketch might represent a long shot of the completed lane, with bridge over.

The illusion of depth is here created through accelerated perspective – the steps themselves are three-dimensional, the end building a scenically painted cloth with a perspective cut out to the right.

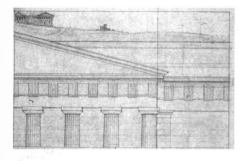

The illusion was created painstakingly, using measured drawings requiring a very precise degree of detail and calculation to plan the painted backing. These drawings are executed by a team of skilled draughts-people, working quickly, predominantly in graphite – rarely in ink! Too many script changes, usually.

Another combination of two- and three-dimensional elements creates the illusion of space – a crescent, in fact – by combining perspective painting with three-dimensional fluted columns.

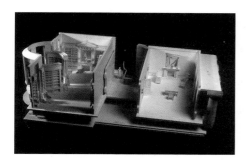 

With the inclusion of the human figure for scale, white card models are not only an important part of the design process, they are needed by the camera and lighting departments in the planning of shots.

From models through sketches to the final result – the constructed and dressed library – the three stages of the process happens very quickly once the key decisions have been made, usually within weeks rather than months.

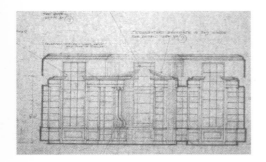

Another crucial aspect of design is the detail – the planning and positioning of objects within the space once the basic form has been made. In Jekyll's library objects were chosen to reflect the character of Jekyll, and suggest his social and economic background. They need to be placed in such a way that they work textually within the frame, articulating and punctuating the space with furniture, and also graphically in the creation of an illustrative, balanced composition. At the same time, they must accommodate the intricately choreographed movements of actors, the camera, and lighting equipment. The design constitutes all the surfaces of the composition to be lit, from the large spaces to objects.

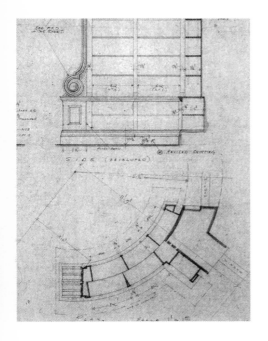

Working drawings showing necessary construction details, including an elevation of the library wall and details of the shelves. The construction process takes place from the drawings when they are finally completed – usually after a series of lengthy discussions between the designer and construction manager, in which a fine balance between time, resources and budget is agreed.

Once the set is built, the views the director needs – for example of the courtyard from the house – illustrate the importance of composition in the design, using mid-space and foreground elements to create depth and balance for the camera. Smoke is added to the space, diffusing light to create the required atmospheric effect.

Behind the scenes, however, there is nothing so substantial as Edinburgh stone. The back of the set reveals a basic construction of flattage – plywood on a simple timber frame supported by a scaffolding rig.

The courtyard itself, quite sculptural in the modulation of form, demonstrates the importance of building up layers for the camera, by articulating foreground with mid- and background-elements, alongside a range of sensitive textural finishes. Casts were taken from stone in Edinburgh, made in plaster in the studio, and finished by using a range of monochromatic washes.

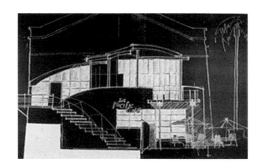

Copy Cat

A hundred years on – on the screen – *Copy Cat* shows the contemporary (1994) story of a female agoraphobic, a woman who suffers from the morbid fear of public places and open spaces. As the film progresses, the character's sanity re-emerges, and the production design reflects this change physically in the transformation of the designed space in which she resides. The designer literally builds a metaphor, which illustrates graphically a mental state. The protagonist is a criminal psychologist whose professional life has been concerned with the study of the serial killer and of death, and who has retreated entirely from the outside world into the inner sanctum/refuge of her physical house. The designer chooses, poignantly, a location which juxtaposes the vast panoramic expanse of the Golden Gate Bridge with her apartment.

This emotionally resonant juxtaposition is achieved by identifying a location which offers a suitable existing building with a flat gable end elevation, onto which a rendering of the exterior of the character's apartment can be grafted, required on location for a number of days' filming only. The interior of the apartment is built on the stage, separately.

Early sketch models exploring aspects of the proposed exterior apartment in relation to the mass of the existing building and bridge.

In thinking about the form of the trapped agoraphobic's apartment, the designer investigated fenestration as a boundary between the interior and exterior world. The search led to references that include Pierre Chareau's *Maison de verre*, in the division of horizontal and vertical spaces whose proportions suited the widescreen format of the film. Shot on the West Coast of America, Frank Israels and William Owen Moses' dramatic compositions of light, space and material also influenced the design.

The five-metre-high curtain wall constituting the front of the woman's home is dressed with aerofoil window shutters, which progressively allow more light into the apartment as her mental state improves. At the beginning of the film, the shutters are closed, creating a fortress-like space, closed off from the panoramic external world provided by the choice of location and the spatial relations it confers.

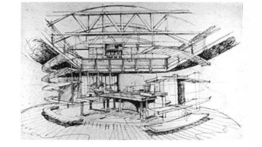

The agoraphobic's study was conceived as the hub of the set, an inner sanctum formed by a series of sliding mobile semicircular screens, used as storage units. This approach created a space which was flexible for the duration of filming, which worked dramatically by combining the dual functions of haven and secluded den-like environment, capable of sheltering the inhabitant, but capable, equally, of concealing an intruder.

The Crying Game

Another approach by the same designer, Jim Clay, is exemplified by the production design of Neil Jordan's *The Crying Game* (1992). The concept alludes to a form of realism. The glasshouse where the IRA keep their hostage prisoner was constructed three-dimensionally twice: once in the studio, for a number of weeks of filming scenes set in its interior, and then again on the back lot, on a site selected so the existing trees could be used as elements in a spectacular attack.

The stone wall around which the structure is built and the apparently ancient remnants of tangled climbers and rotting leaves are present by design, not default. The evocation of this place, its realisation by eradicating all signs of its manufacture, all evidence of its unreality, create on the screen the illusion of a form of realism. This is another facet of production design centred around a textural and painterly approach in the rendering of surfaces, colour palette and composition.

Conclusion

The conceptual work which has gone into evolving the concrete methods and techniques used by the designers whose films I have examined, to manipulate and shape architectural space in order to create a screen world of heightened emotion which is convincing and consistent, will always be the foundation for the new structures being made possible by digital domain technology. The paradox of Georges Méliès's realisation that space on the screen is not the same as space in the natural world, alongside the Lumière Brothers' conviction that actually to place the natural world on the screen is the highest aim of cinematographic science, lies behind all of it. Every designer in every era, with whatever tools are to hand, hopes to find the balance that best suits the production of the moment, combining art and science in a unique blend of the ephemeral and the lasting.

Notes

The Hudsucker Proxy is the work of production designer Dennis Gassner, whose credits include *Field of Dreams* (1989), *Millers Crossing* (1990) and *Barton Fink* (1991).

Mary Reilly was designed by Stuart Craig, whose work includes *The Elephant Man* (1980), *Memphis Belle* (1990), *The Secret Garden* (1993) and *The English Patient* (1996).

Copy Cat and *The Crying Game* are designed by Jim Clay, whose work includes *The Singing Detective* (1986), *Queen of Hearts* (1989) and *A Kiss Before Dying* (1991).

Film Architecture

The Imagination of Lies

Christopher Hobbs

Wizard of Oz

The Tower of Babel

Film architecture doesn't really exist – it's a lie. Welcome to the Land of Oz, where nothing is what it seems. The wonderful Emerald City, which everyone who has seen *The Wizard of Oz* (1939) remembers, glimpsed tantalisingly across a field of poppies, the symbol of the unattainable dream we still all hope will come true, is actually hardly more than a sort of Art Deco brooch painted on canvas.

Although the Emerald City seems real enough on the screen, in fact film architecture bears no load, has no foundations or loos; its staircases go nowhere and its corridors end in painted perspectives.

The lies began long ago. The Tower of Babel, the vertical city, an illusion created for the screen by Otto Hunte for Fritz Lang's *Metropolis* in 1926, is now being considered in reality for the first time in Japan.

The grand and gigantic have always appealed to film-makers – Manhattan is the inspiration for endless designs. On the screen, Babel meets Manhattan. At the bottom of the city are the simple structures of the workers, then the skyscrapers and traffic of New York, and finally the great tower, Babel itself. Amazing – when you realise that this is just a glorified doll's house, dressed with Dinky toys. It is our imagination, the film-makers' most valuable and cheapest resource, that creates the vast Metropolis of Fritz Lang's vision.

Another screen child of New York is to be found in Batman's Gotham City. The large figure at the end of the street is not some Cronenberg character – The Attack of the 100-Foot Propsman – but a set dresser spraying the streets with oil to simulate wet surfaces. None of the buildings along the street has a back or a roof. Lies, all lies.

On the screen, verisimilitude is unnecessary. In Fritz Lang's *Siegfried* (1924), the city appears as Symbolist vision. It is a sort of Teutonic Oz, quite as insubstantial as its later counterpart, and just as strong a manifestation of dream – in this case, of the romantic glories of the Germanic past as conceived by nineteenth-century revivalists.

Slags

The Last Laugh

Loser Takes All

I would say that there are two traditions of architecture in film: the monumental, and the florid. To begin with the florid: by now the image of a future Los Angeles seen in *Blade Runner* (1982) has become very familiar. The effect of thousands of tiny lights, convoluted buildings, finer and finer detail, is actually created by filming again and again onto the same strip of film – a sort of visual lasagne.

In real life, you could get the whole thing onto a couple of ping-pong tables. The great pyramids are tiny colour slides cut out and propped up, although there were also large models for close-ups. Incidentally, in the fly-past over the city, you may like to know that the triangular skyscraper is the Millennium Falcon from *Star Wars* (1977) redressed as architecture. Waste not, want not.

I rather cheekily add here my own version of the *Blade Runner* city, made for *Slags* (1983), with Dawn French and Jennifer Saunders. It was made almost entirely of car transmissions perched on beer barrels and cost about fifty quid – not bad, considering.

Star Wars

At the other end of the scale from the elaborate design choices of *The Wizard of Oz*, *Star Wars* and *Blade Runner*, is extreme simplicity. The worker's city from *Metropolis* is simple, functional and very effective. Curiously enough, in another film, *The Last Laugh* (1924), made just a few years earlier than *Metropolis*, we find almost identical architecture.

There is another sort of simplicity of course – that based on poverty. In *Loser Takes All* (1956) we could not afford Monte Carlo nor to recreate the Casino interior as it really is, so at Pinewood we draped a small stage with black velvet, put cheap red carpet on the floor, constructed huge truncated pillars on raised, wheeled plinths and built an arch gilded with the sort of foil found in chocolate wrappers. With tables, lights and aspidistras it was possible to create the illusion of a huge interior by moving the columns into different configurations. Bars, private rooms and corridors could all be created easily on the same patch of cheap carpet. The set bears, of course, almost no relationship to real architecture – except in the imaginations of the audience.

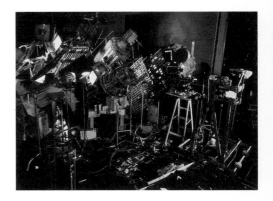

Star Wars

More trickery was used to construct the sinister industrial city of Blastburn, created for *The Wolves of Willoughby Chase* (1988). The first image of the city is actually made with the help of a water-filled tank. This was augmented by real locations – at a semi-derelict coal mine in Bohemia, called Godvalt III. As it turned out, rather embarrassingly, the mine was in fact a Soviet forced labour camp, a fact we only discovered on our last night of filming there – so our images, though put together as illusions, are a very close to an uncomfortable truth.

Blastburn was perhaps a romanticised view of the industrial city, but of course the great romantics have always been the Germans. Murnau's *Faust* (1926), like Lang's *Siegfried*, contains wonderful and sinister city images – like all romantic art, they represent a truth: but as architecture, they are nonetheless lies.

In *Siegfried*, we see a band of noble knights crossing a perilous gorge. In reality, they are only a bunch of thespians on nags, crossing a ditch. The gorge which creates the drama was a little model placed just in front of the camera. The film-maker's task is to understand what dramatic effect is wanted, and deploy the resources of screen illusion to achieve it. Building in miniature and combining the model with live action makes the impossible possible.

The Wolves of Willoughby Chase

Mighty Siegfried himself quests amongst the immemorial trees. He's just about to meet a huge dragon – actually full of people pulling levers. He is seen even more to advantage as he prepares to confront the monster, with the light streaming through the foliage far above. What has this to do with architecture? The trees were built of concrete, and had a tin roof on top. The sun's rays have been painted in by hand. The heightened effects necessary to give the scene its emotional charge have been achieved without risk to real forests from heavy equipment and with the ability to control the weather. Images like this, for all their trickery, often linger in our subconscious more than we realise. The illusory cities in some films look architectural without containing load-bearing walls; in others, a designer can employ real architectural strategies to create the illusion of unspoilt nature on the screen.

In that seminal screen city, *Metropolis*, the great forum of the elite is created, as the slightly wobbly line across the image reveals, from real action and a model matted together. The actual Foro Italia of Mussolini in Rome, built many years later, bears a striking resemblance to the Metropolis model. Is this coincidence, or was Mussolini perhaps paying a compliment to his German ally?

The game of screen architecture *sans frontières* can be played *ad infinitum.* In Fellini's wonderful *Casanova* (1976), for example, Italy pretends to be Germany. The theatre set is dazzlingly architectural in form if not in function, all light and patterns. The chandeliers are one of my favourite images in film, and have already been stolen several times by lesser designers. They do remind me of another architecture, however, largely created by Cedric Gibbons of MGM, for Busby Berkeley. Real cities and architectural detail can inspire remarkable flights of fancy on the screen.

Indeed, in the ordinary world as well as the screen world, the boundaries between reality and fiction can sometimes become blurred. The architect Lutyens created something very like a film set at Castle Drogo. He built a large gatehouse and flanking walls of canvas in order to persuade his client to further extravagance – a technique often attempted by film designers with their producers, alas too frequently with no more success than Lutyens achieved on that occasion.

The *sets* for *Thief of Baghdad* (1924) were immense, although largely topless. Douglas Fairbanks's magic carpet, incidentally, was a steel plate on wires suspended from the enormous crane. In *Things to Come* (1936), the whole upper part of the set was suspended, and a miniature hung near the camera, then lined up with a more modest full-scale set where the actors played, farther away.

I used the same trick in *Orlando* (1993), where old London Bridge is in fact a 25-foot-long miniature, lined up with real arches, only 12 feet high, behind the actors.

Things to Come

Les Enfants du paradis

Neon Bible

Edward II

Reality and dream become ultimately mixed at the original California Disneyland. The Sleeping Princess Castle is, we are reliably informed, the last resting place for Uncle Walt himself, who lies cryogenically preserved, a popsicle King Arthur in his concrete Camelot.

To descend from Camelot to the streets – to be precise, to the Boulevard du Crime from *Les Enfants du paradis* (1945). We can compare the elegant drawing of the set with the filmic reality. The beauty of the street is not so much its architecture, but its texture – the wonderful texture of the crowd.

Texture is vital to the screen designer. As in real architecture, it can be manipulated to catch the light or model form. In *The Long Day Closes* (1993), the street in Liverpool needed for the film had long since been demolished. I had to recreate it in such a way as to suggest childhood memory. Everything was artificial, from the bulging cobble to the birdshit, and everything is exaggerated – the road heaves and dips so that puddles will collect, the railings writhe, drainpipes are intentionally warped, rust is as thick as paint-clogged cornflakes. On film, which tends to flatten surface anyway, the effect is far less weird than one might expect – and I hope evokes the richness of memory. Behind the scenes, it can be seen that the whole street was built in the grounds of a derelict hospital near the Rotherhithe Tunnel in London's East End.

Even in extreme close-up, as in *Neon Bible* (1995), shot in Atlanta, Georgia, texture helps create atmosphere on the screen. In fact, in *Edward II* (1993), which I designed for Derek Jarman, there was little else. I built two huge walled spaces with rough plastered walls, and filled them with rough-cast towers on wheels, each 16ft high x 12ft x 12ft. That was the whole set.

In one scene, the Queen and Mortimer have a long dialogue and need uninterrupted walk. I parked the columns against the walls, and had all the space I needed, with plenty of interesting shapes for the cinematographer to light. If I wanted a room, or a corridor, or a cathedral, I only needed to move the columns together or apart, and add a desk for a

Edward II

library, a bed for a bedroom or a tomb for a cathedral. All you need is a couple of wedge-shaped ramps and light – and the audience does the rest.

For me, however, the ultimate design, incorporating form, texture, simplicity and complexity at their best, is John Bryan's work for David Lean's *Oliver Twist* (1948).

All the sets, interior and exterior, were specially built for the film – I can only assume that the spectacularly rotted beams, like the one framing the scene of the children and Fagin on the staircase, were salvaged from blitzed buildings – it would be hard to find them now! Again, actors are used as an integral part of the architectural form, a pavement far more exciting than my cobbled surfaces in *The Long Day Closes*.

On the screen, it takes only seconds to move through time, from the past to the future, and the designer is as much of a charlatan in carrying images from time to time as in juxtaposing them from place to place. Here, for example, are those concrete trees from Lang's 1926 *Siegfried*, perhaps, turning up in my own designs for Dennis Potter's (posthumous) *Cold Lazarus* (1996), which takes place two hundred years in the future from now. Paul Richens of the Martin Centre, Cambridge, as part of his research into synthetic images for set design for the National Film and Television School, worked up digital images as design aids from drawings I had made for the set. Of course, digital imagery is increasingly being used in film and television, and gives us wonderful new ways of deceiving our audience.

Finally, as a coda, I should like to mention Derek Jarman's spectacular designs for Ken Russell's *The Devils* (1970). If you wonder why Derek chose to cover his medieval town with white lavatory brick, the answer is that it was the cheapest surface he could find in the plaster shop. His work for Russell is film architecture as sculpture, and very beautiful, too. Destruction is a major motif in the film, and Ken Russell directed it with passionate focus. In fact, when the walls were to be pulled down, he was operating the camera himself, in order to avoid any mistakes. Someone behind him dropped a box, Ken turned, his arm raised in irritated response, and the crew took this to be the signal to destroy the walls. Unfortunately, the camera hadn't been turning and it took several days to rebuild the set before they could be destroyed again properly.

Cold Lazarus

To sum up, a great part of the power of the screen is its ability to transport the audience into a new universe, where it can experience delight and danger in an unexpected but convincing and above all emotionally resonant environment. Our task is to create those screen universes by whatever means we can, exploiting every trick of the illusionist's trade. You can't trust anything on a film set, least of all the architecture.

Filmography

Blade Runner, US 1982, d. Ridley Scott, des. Lawrence G. Paull

Casanova, Italy 1976, d. Federico Fellini, des. Danilo Donati, Federico Fellini

Cold Lazarus, GB 1995, d. Renny Rye, des. Christopher Hobbs

The Devils, GB 1970, d. Ken Russell, des. Robert Cartwright, Derek Jarman

Edward II, GB 1993, d. Derek Jarman, des. Christopher Hobbs

Les Enfants du paradis, France 1945, d. Marcel Carné, des. Alexandre Trauner, Léon Barsacq, Raymond Gabutti

Faust, Germany, 1926, d. F. W. Murnau, des. Robert Herlth, Walter Roehrig

The Last Laugh, Germany 1924, d. F. W. Murnau, des. Robert Herlth, Walter Roehrig

The Long Day Closes, GB 1993, d. Terence Davies, des. Christopher Hobbs

Loser Takes All, GB 1956, d. Ken Annakin, des. Christopher Hobbs

Metropolis, Germany 1926, d. Fritz Lang, des. Otto Hunte, Erich Ketelhut, Karl Vollbrecht

Neon Bible, US 1995, d. Terence Davies, des. Christopher Hobbs

Oliver Twist, GB 1948, d. David Lean, des. John Bryan

Orlando, GB 1993, w.d. Sally Potter, des. Christopher Hobbs, *et al.*

Siegfried, Germany 1924, d. Fritz Lang, des. Otto Hunte, Karl Vollbrecht

Slags, BBC TV 1983, French and Saunders, d. Sandy Johnson, des. Christopher Hobbs

Star Wars, US 1977, w.d. George Lucas, des. John Barry.

The Thief of Baghdad, US 1924, d. Raoul Walsh, des. William Cameron Menzies

Things to Come, GB 1936, d./des. William Cameron Menzies

The Wizard of Oz, US 1939, d. Victor Fleming, des. Cedric Gibbons, William A. Horning

The Wolves of Willoughby Chase, GB 1988, d. Stuart Orme, des. Christopher Hobbs

Computer-Aided Art Direction

Paul Richens

Introduction

Computer-aided design (CAD) for architects began to be possible about twenty-five years ago; in the last five it has become commonplace. In a few years time, it will be as ubiquitous as the word processor is today. But the construction industry as a whole is not a sophisticated user of information technology. The state of affairs in the film industry is quite different; computer graphics of the utmost sophistication play an increasingly important part in the production of film, but comparatively little in their design. Is it possible that an opportunity is being missed?

This paper is written from the standpoint of a designer of architectural CAD software, and seeks to explore the extent to which computer graphics techniques, which have proved useful in architecture, could be used in production design, and the simulation of cinematography. Several experiments, using commercial software of the sort that architects find useful, have led to the conclusion that much is possible, but that a full realisation of the benefits would require software specially adapted to the task. The bulk of this paper describes the nature of this adaptation; it is in the nature of a preliminary specification for software for computer-aided art direction. The initial investigation centred on the needs of film students; it has since broadened to look at the needs of established practitioners.

Objectives

The main use of CAD in architecture, though the least interesting, is for drafting the huge quantities of final drawings that tell the builder what to build. Film designers also produce large-format blueprints to describe sets to the construction crew. To an architect they are strange, not only for being invariably dimensioned in feet and inches, but because they show only the inner, visible surface of the set, and give almost no information about its construction or structural support. This, of course, reflects the way responsibilities are divided between the designer (how it looks) and the rigger (how it stands up), which is quite different from that found in architecture (at least in Britain, and at the present day). So the volume and complexity of construction drawings required in set design is less, and standard packages for drafting could be used without difficulty.

Much more interesting is the use of preliminary drawings, renderings and models in the process of arriving at a design. In architecture, extensive use is made of three-dimensional computer models and rendering systems for presentation to clients. Use of a computer for conceptual design is rather unusual; when it does happen the software employed is likely to be lightweight, easy to use and fast to respond – it is more likely to be running on a Macintosh than a high-end workstation. A number of engineering disciplines rely extensively on computers – such as structural design, artificial lighting, heating and air-conditioning.

In the screen world, we can expect geometric modelling to be helpful in set design, computer rendering to be useful for lighting design and cinematography, and animation for simulating camera movements and special effects. To the professional designer (who we can assume knows how to do the job without a computer), the most useful result will probably be the assistance that computer simulation gives in negotiating a design with the director and other members of the production team. Students will find a much wider range of benefits – the simulator will teach them about set design, lighting and photography, in much the same way that a well-made desktop publishing program teaches its users about page grids, fonts, point sizes and leading – all the esotericism of the sub-editor's craft. Indeed, the realisation that a software application could be constructed as a teaching machine – to teach both its own behaviour and some area of craft skill – is one of the profound insights that underlies the Apple Macintosh, and the modern Graphical User Interface.

The primary aids to negotiating a film design at present are drawings, scale models and story-boards. A computer simulation would act like a scale model, but with the added advantage of being able to simulate lighting and the camera's eye. Discussions can centre on the simulation, the model can be adapted as they proceed, storyboards or key scenes can be produced as a sequence of stills from the simulation. Indeed, a computer based storyboard could go further by mixing stills with animation clips, for example to show the effect of a moving camera. In education, it is likely that such an elaborated storyboard could be used to develop narrative skills.

Modelling

Very sophisticated geometrical modelling techniques are used for industrial design, and indeed in film animation. Architectural modellers tend to be simpler, and would be quite adequate for set design. Modellers such as ModelShop or UpFront, which are popular in architectural schools and tend to emphasise simplicity and speed over geometrical precision, show the way to go. The model is composed of 'primitive' shapes such as blocks, spheres and cylinders, combined with more elaborate extrusions and solids of revolution. An elementary spline-surface element is desirable for more organic shapes. These basic elements can be produced in any shape and size, and 'grouped' to make composite objects which can be repeated, scaled and oriented as needed.

Sets frequently include 'floaters' – pieces which can be removed temporarily to gain access for lights or camera. Obviously, the geometrical model should have similar flexibility. It may also enable checks to be made that such apertures are big enough, for example to allow a crane to operate.

Two things which occur frequently in film sets (but have hardly been seen in architecture since the ending of the baroque) need special treatment. Both are to do with representing objects in the distance. In an urban exterior, parts of the scene in the foreground (containing

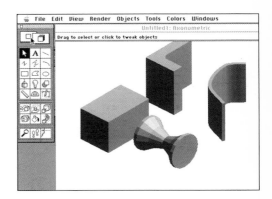

Primitive shapes in Modelshop.

Computer generated backcloth behind a computer generated set.

Bump mapping.

Texture mapping for a variety of materials.

the action) will be built full-size. Background buildings may be painted on a cloth. In between, the set may contain scale models of objects in the middle distance, or more elaborate perspective pieces built with some degree of foreshortening as well.

A modeller adapted for set design should be able to render a 3D model of the background onto a surface, and then use the image as a backcloth. It should also be able to calculate perspective pieces from the full-scale geometry and a given camera position. It will also be able to simulate the strange distortions that result if the camera moves from the centre of projection, or if an object or actor approaches too closely.

Texturing

When a set is built on a stage, the first task is to construct the bold forms; this corresponds to the geometrical modelling described above. The second is to apply surface texture, which may be done by applying vacuum-formed plastic sheet, by rendering with cement or plaster, or by attaching fibrous plaster casts. Sometimes, even, ordinary real materials are used. This process, which gives relief and texture to the surfaces, has its simulacrum in the computer-graphics technique known as 'bump-mapping'. An image is drawn in shades of grey to represent the various degrees of relief, and attached to a surface. When the scene is rendered, the relief is used to modify the local orientation of the surface, and hence the way that it reflects light.

The third stage of preparing a set is to paint it. The corresponding computer-graphics technique is called (rather misleadingly) texture-mapping. A full-coloured image is mapped to the surface, and affects its local colour when it is rendered. The texture map can be generated in a computer painting program, but is more commonly scanned from a photograph. In set design it would frequently be obtained by scanning a painting, or a sample of the desired finish. Other computer-graphics techniques which would be of use are reflectance mapping (which deals with varying degrees of shininess), transparency mapping (for example, for dirty glass) and luminosity mapping (for example, for placing lighted windows on a distant building).

These techniques are not found in the simple architectural modellers mentioned earlier. Texture mapping is carried out very speedily by special hardware of the sort found in expensive graphics workstations; it is likely to be available on PCs in the near future. The other techniques are found in the more elaborate but slower rendering programs. They need to be foreground techniques in any system aimed at set design, where the way in which surfaces react to light is of prime importance.

Lighting

The simulation (and teaching) of lighting is the most challenging, but potentially the most rewarding area for research. Conventional computer rendering programs only begin to acknowledge the complexities of film lighting, and even the most advanced research software would be severely stretched.

Light sources used in film studios include tungsten, tungsten/halogen, metal/halide and carbon arc. The distinctions matter, because they affect the colour temperature of the light. The power of sources is typically 1 or 2 kilowatts, but may commonly vary from 200 watts to 15 kilowatts.

Sources are used in a range of different types of fittings. Open-face fittings have a reflector and source in a container, but no lens. They may be adjustable to some extent, and there are a variety of shapes. Sometimes up to a dozen open-face fittings are combined to form a modular array. These provide a diffuse light from a large-area source. Softlites and skylights use reflectors or diffusers to intercept the beam, and again provide large-area soft lighting.

The most commonly used closed fitting contains a reflector and a fresnel lens. It provides a widely adjustable beam with a soft edge, but coming from a fairly small source, so shadows are defined. Focus spots, on the other hand, have precise optics and an aperture plate capable of giving a precisely shaped beam from practically a point source.

It is interesting to compare this diversity of fittings with the types offered by conventional computer rendering programs. These typically offer a choice of three: a remote source (sun), a point source (naked bulb) and a spot. This last has an adjustable beam angle, and perhaps a variable rate of cut-off. However, altering the focus does not affect the brightness of the beam, as happens with a real fresnel spot. There is no simulation of large-area sources at all, nor any notion of colour temperature. What is needed is a catalogue of industry-standard fittings, each characterised by precise photometric data over the whole range of focus settings.

Fittings may be modified in many ways. The beam may be restricted by barn-doors or snoots. The colour can be modified by filters, the intensity and spread by diffusers or scrims. Dimmers (which are ubiquitous in theatre lighting) are used with restraint, as they alter the colour temperature.

Film lighting may be extensively modified after it leaves the lantern by reflectors (matt or metallic), diffusers (for example, of glass fibre, tracing paper or gauze), and gobos, which are devices used to cast shadows, or to keep light off places where it is not wanted. Gauzes may also be used, partially fogged by side lighting, to give an effect of distance to the background.

Control of intensity is occasionally by dimmers, but more often by choice of fitting, spreading the beam, fitting a scrim, or simply by moving the lamp further from the subject. The required level of light may be expressed photometrically (400-foot-candles), or perhaps in terms of the aperture that will be used on the camera (for example, T5.6, with some implied assumptions about the shutter speed, film stock, and processing options).

Conventional computer graphics do not provide a very adequate simulation of this variety of lighting strategies. The normal techniques are not photometrically accurate, and fail to deal with large-area sources, soft-edged shadows, diffusers and reflectors. Most importantly, they deal only with light received directly from the source, and not with light reflected from other surfaces in the set. In film and theatre lighting it is essential to take into account at least the first inter-reflection between surfaces (this is also a severe problem in architectural rendering of daylit interiors, where five or more levels of inter-reflection may be significant). Two techniques to solve this problem are currently at the research stage – radiosity and stochastic ray-tracing. Both are slow to calculate, but a variant of the first (progressive radiosity) can give an approximate rendering quickly, and then improve it over time by taking more inter-reflections into account. Curiously, most radiosity renderers deal only with large-area diffuse sources, though there is no real reason

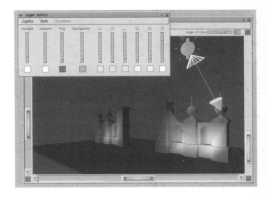

Direct manipulation of lights, with a simulated dimmer board.

why this should be so. There are known difficulties in combining radiosity with bump-mapping, which need to be overcome.

The ideal lighting simulator for film design will use industry-standard fittings, and produce a visual simulation showing shadows, modelling, colour and the balance of fill to key. It should be possible to introduce a simulated photometer, in order to measure the calculated light levels (incident or reflected). If, as is likely, the most accurate simulation is slow, there should be a range of faster approximations. Ideally it should be possible to position, focus and filter the lanterns, while seeing the effect immediately on the computer screen. Rapid feedback is invaluable to the practitioner, in enabling a design to be realised quickly, and to the student, in developing an intuition about how things behave.

Another mode of operation would be to use idealised lanterns, which can be positioned and focused to get the angles right, and then coloured and dimmed to balance the lighting, again with immediate feedback of the result. When the lighting has been fully composed, the idealised lights would be replaced by real lanterns of appropriate wattage, so as to achieve the same effect without the aid of dimmers.

Photography

One problem with photometrically accurate lighting simulation is that the range of brightness in the scene, as calculated, will vary as widely as it does in the real world, and will not be representable on the computer screen which has a dynamic range limited to about 1:30. Some technique is necessary to reduce the range, and it would most usefully be a simulation of the photographic parameters such as exposure, film stock and processing. Camera simulation includes positioning and orienting the camera, and picking the correct aspect ratio. The lens should (as with lanterns) be chosen from a catalogue of industry-standard types, which gives their focal length, and aperture range, both photometric (T) and optical (f). Zoom lenses need the range of focal lengths, and possibly details of how the apertures change over the range.

It should be possible to set the aperture from a simulated scene, perhaps by using a simulated 18% grey test card. Alternatively, the aperture can be set arbitrarily, and the resulting photographic image simulated. This simulation might include the effect of film-stock and processing options on sensitivity, latitude, gamma and colour rendering. It would be valuable also to simulate the effect of focusing, and of changing aperture on the depth of field, by selectively blurring parts of the image.

The camera simulation might also take account of filters of various types, such as neutral density, graduated, diffusing and colour correction. The last implies a detailed treatment of colour temperature, and would be important if location filming were to be taken into account.

Animation

As well as simulating a static shot, it is desirable to be able to render an action sequence as a short animation. The most obvious case is where the camera moves on a track or crane, but there are others, such as the simulation of zooms, focus pulling, changeable lighting, and moving properties or vehicles. Lights may move with the camera, or be attached to other objects (practical lights).

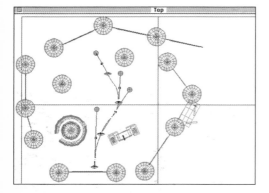

Setting up a crane shot animation, with (below) the start and end frames of the sequence.

The simulation of movement requires laying down a track (generally a curve in three dimensions), specifying how the camera orientation changes as it moves along the track, and controlling its speed, especially at the start and end of a movement.

As digital effects become more and more prominent in film-making, the production designer/art director will increasingly need to try things out at the design stage. So the simulations might well extend to include matting, chroma key, computer-controlled model photography, and indeed computer animation itself.

Conclusions

The initial impetus for this investigation came from the National Film and Television School, which educates and trains people in the disciplines involved in most aspects of screen production in a very practical way, by making films, video projects and television drama. The cost in time and materials of doing this is considerable, and has to a large extent to determine the experiences that can be offered to students. Student production designers normally have the opportunity to design and build for at least three productions, but with computer simulation could easily explore many more possibilities in style, scope and scale, creating a broader portfolio of work. Similarly, cinematographers could learn a great deal about the behaviour of light, lenses and film-stock in a variety of different circumstances alongside the practical workshops and actual shoots in which they participate at the school.

Our experiences with NFTS student productions indicate that it is quite possible, using normal architectural software, to get a good approximation to the visual 'feel' of a set. A simple model is useful to explore camera angles, and quickly shows up problems (for example, if the set is not tall enough) as well as new opportunities (angles that had not been thought of). Simulating lighting turned out to need a good deal of trickery, because the normal computer lighting model is so far from physical reality. Photographic simulation we did not attempt. But the overall impression was that, though it is possible to do these things, it is far from easy. Though the majority of the ambitions described in this paper have been realised piecemeal in commercial software, or at least in the research laboratory, they have not ever been put together in a way that the student film-maker could really use.

We have kept in the background the possibility that the same software might be used to simulate theatre or television design, and possibly other events such as exhibitions and rock shows. Theatre stage sets are designed for a more limited set of viewing positions than film or TV sets, but the geometry of the stage and the auditorium becomes an important part of the problem. Stage lighting uses hundreds of lanterns in fixed positions, but with elaborate computer-controlled dimmers, which enable the whole production to be lit. Film set-ups use fewer lights, other means of control, and may be reconstituted for every scene. Television studios seem to hold an intermediate position.

It is likely that software aimed at the educational objectives outlined in this paper would also be of use to commercial practitioners. One of the most interesting areas of use for the NFTS is in the negotiations which have to occur in the collaborative creative process. We see computer simulation being used in negotiations between designer and director, between cinematographer and director, and as a means of effective communication

Simulation of special effects photography.

between all three – whether in the same room, or as part of distance producing. Such computer-aided pre-visualisation should help to promote common understanding, and also to avoid expensive mistakes. For example, we have noticed that often far more of a set is built than is ever filmed, which could perhaps be avoided by simulating the shooting script. Similarly, the commissioning of special effects or computer animation will be helped if the art director can present a sketch simulation of what is required.

Acknowledgments

The staff of the National Film and Television School, particularly Maureen Thomas, and the Director, Henning Camre, Diana Charnley and Sharon Springel have been most helpful in providing information about film-making practice. I am deeply grateful to the production designers who have been most generous with their time in discussing particular projects – Stuart Craig (*Mary Reilly*), and Christopher Hobbs (*Cold Lazarus*).

Looking to the Future – Imagining the Truth

Zbig Rybczynski

Poland

When I was fifteen, I took an express train from Warsaw to Gdansk, to buy an old print in an antique shop. The return train was in the evening, so I had some time to spare. I went to the old Cathedral. Inside it was very empty, and from somewhere I heard the sound of a Bach fugue. I sat on the floor with my back against a column and gazed up at the distant ceiling. I'm not sure whether it really happened, or whether it was only in my imagination, but I saw a naked couple flying in the air, between the columns.

I began my career as a painter. Then, at the end of the 60s, I decided that painting was dead – I wanted movement, not stillness. So I turned to film. But I had a problem. On film, in general we record the 'real' – what is in front of the camera. But I was interested in recording things which don't exist in reality – though we are sure they are quite real. I was looking to record images which exist in our minds, in our dreams, in our consciousness, in our fantasy. That is the kind of 'real' I care about, and I am still searching for a new method of 'filming', which will allow me to create such images on the screen in such a way as to be totally convincing.

Photographic realism, the result of great discoveries – the lens, photography, film, television – is not the ultimate 'solution'. It is a 'version', a 'mechanical version' of the image, surely the most important step in the history of visualisation, but not the final one.

Images – of the city, for example – before the discovery of the lens are a very interesting study. In the World Chronicle, printed in Nuremberg in the fifteenth century – the first book with illustrations after Gutenberg had invented print – there are some extremely interesting views of cities. I find these images very realistic, much more realistic than photographs. Probably everyone could recognise Krakow, Vienna and London even today.

If I think of New York, in a split second I have an image of the city closer in concept to these old prints than to any existing photographs of New York. It is not unlike the image – a perfect mental image – of the ancient world we have today. I suspect we can all conjure up that kind of image – though we cannot photograph it. Antiquity. The Middle Ages. We recognise the image, the image exists – but we don't yet have the technology to film it, to show it, to transmit it to others. I really believe that we are now on the brink, with our modern technology, of making visible such images – of 'photographing' them, and seeing them on the screen.

And why stop there? It is fascinating to speculate. If we can record today photographic images of the present, there is no reason why we should not one day record photographic images from the past. They exist. When we look at the stars, we are seeing some really very old images. We don't yet have the technology to narrow the focus to, let's say, the year 1836 in England, to pick a specific location and view an image, let's say, in the apartment of Mr. and Mrs. Talbot – but, theoretically, I see no reason why we should not some day develop a device capable of such an achievement.

What we are seeing today, in this time of the 'information superhighway', is a move away from the photographic concept of 'realism' towards something much closer to what the image *is* at its origins. Although we can only catch glimpses of the next 'version' awaiting us, it has an – awful or beautiful? – name: digital computer graphics.

So, back in the late 60s, I decided to study at a film school, and to be a film director. But an angel gave me some advice – maybe misleading: 'Listen Zbig, anyone can be a film director. To be a real film-maker, I mean a real film director, you need to be … '

The angel gazed at the sky, as though searching for somebody, and with a delicate smile concluded: 'Somebody rather like … a director of photography. Film, you see, is a technology.'

The angel disappeared.

This is the only reason why I decided to study in the camera department. I have no idea why my first film was *Square* (1972). It was a mix of photography and animation and it took my whole vacation – sixteen hours a day. I analysed, through a film camera, a loop of thirty-six squarish black-and-white photographs representing a human being moving in a circle. What was the logic of my analysis? I decided to photograph the loop on film and repeat it thirty-six times. During every new repetition I divided the film window – which I made in the shape of a square – so that in every cycle there was an increasing number of subdivisions; today I would say different resolutions. I put a white square of paper in the subdivisions where in the photograph there was a part of a figure; where there was not, I put a black square. I had to rearrange the white and black squares at least a hundred thousand times. On the lens I put a colour filter, and then rotated it – but I don't want to bore you. What is most important about this is that not being aware of computer imaging – it was 1970 in Poland – I manufactured my own 'digital' processing on film. Strange that I needed twenty-six years of work – including my work during all my next twenty-five vacations – to come back to *Square* with full awareness and understanding of why.

My first thirteen years of film-making resulted in a short film, *Tango* (1980). Thirty-six characters from different stages of life – representations of different times – interact in one room, moving in loops, observed by a static camera. I had to draw and paint about 16,000 cell-mattes, and make several hundred thousand exposures on an optical printer. It took a full seven months, sixteen hours per day, to make the piece. The miracle is that the negative got through the process with only minor damage, and I made less than one hundred mathematical mistakes out of several hundred thousand possibilities. In the final result, there are plenty of flaws – black lines are visible around humans, jitters caused by the instability of film material resulting from film perforation and the elasticity of celluloid, changes of colour caused by the fluctuation in colour temperature of the projector bulb

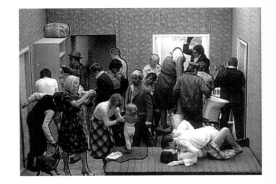

Tango

and, inevitably, dirt, grain and scratches. I received many awards, including an Oscar, but how big a step had I taken towards showing all those things which don't exist in front of the camera? A very small one indeed. How far did I run from painting? Not far at all. I produced a kind of 'oil-photo-painting with scratches', with some jerky motion inside the frame, but with a terrible, terrible static frame, and, and …

Such a labour of Sisyphus was not the solution. Between me and 'all those things' I wanted to show was a wall consisting of celluloid and the post-production process. So I looked in the direction of video. I packed my things, picked up a ticket, and landed in New York.

New York

The biggest advantage of electronic recording over film is that you can complete the whole process live, at the time of the shoot. And at your disposal there are hundreds of magic boxes – the monarch of them all a fantastic machine invented by Paul Vlahos; the Ultimatte, a technique for blue matting which automatically produces for you, in real time, an unlimited number of 'cell mattes', like those I made with such labour for *Tango*. So with all these boxes I developed a technique which allows me to play back a picture recorded earlier – perhaps a minute or a second before – and then record new components over it.

My great idea was to bring to the studio, for the camera, all existing video boxes, which worked together in synch – of course connected to each other by a thousand cables. On the actual set, we could shoot, edit and finish the whole work. And, most importantly, we could have a fantastic spontaneous idea – IT – and immediately see the result of IT. Then if we are not pleased with IT, we can erase IT for ever. This technique I called 'instant video'. I was rewarded by fantastic press, success, some small degree of fame in narrow professional circles, and a number of awards.

Here I have to pause for a moment. Since that time more than a decade has passed, and to the best of my knowledge still nobody else is working with this technique. Film directors still shoot on film or video and take IT – with all their fantastic ideas which can never be erased – to super-expensive post-production houses, whose decor is designed like the interior of a cabin in a UFO, where, during an editing session, you can order food and talk on the telephone, voluntarily spending countless hours there engaged in Sisyphus-like labours. Thousand of buttons on multitudes of consoles and computers are pressed, usually by mysterious 'editors'. Usually directors don't understand the function or reasons for all these buttons, so they are completely dependent on the mercy of the mysterious editors – and this causes great frustration. Very often directors see – on many monitors – that IT doesn't work. But by now it is too late for a new shoot – their only hope is the mysterious editors and all those thousands of buttons. Like dogs let loose gazing towards the horizon, directors gaze at the thousand buttons, at the editors, and at the monitors – desperately hoping that something interesting can be done to IT. Where is the right button? Where? In the cabin of the UFO, the atmosphere is nightmarish. At the back art directors bark angrily.

Apologies for the digression. Back to the subject.

Using my 'instant video' method, I made several productions and music videos. *Imagine* (1986) is one of them. It's a short video, made in High Definition – actually, the first High Definition production done in the United States.

The set I built consisted of one room, with two blue walls, stage left and stage right. I made the piece 'live', pushing my camera by hand, recording the same room over and over again, matching the far edge (stage left) to the new near edge (stage right) of the frame in sequence, starting each take in the middle at the last exposure. Thus the two live-action characters in the film appear to walk continuously through an almost endless series of rooms, and the illusion is that they walk through time as well as space. They start as tiny children playing, then as they enter each subsequent 'room' – which is in fact the same room, the set dressed a little differently – they have grown older, and the room reflects the changes in their life and relationship. At the same time, the illusion of all this happening in 'real' time is created by the panorama of buildings seen through the windows in the back wall of the rooms. This background, like neighbouring rooms, is matted in – I photographed it with a static camera in New York City. So, because this very real background seen through the windows is what we would expect to see if the rooms really existed in space next to each other, because the view is sequential but different out of each one, we are easily convinced that the rooms actually do open one upon another. The two characters pass from room to room at an even pace, while John Lennon's song reinforces the idea of imagination and time as a complex interaction. Seeing is believing, and we accept that this is real because the components of the images are true.

Obviously, I had made progress. The whole thing took three days. No scratches, no thousands of numbers, no thousands of cells. They, of course, were inside the machines. But, to create the images I needed in 1986, I had to build a set. Not a complete set, only a part of one, but still a full-scale set. There was no budget to speak of for the film – I made it as a test for High Definition. The crew of volunteers worked for nothing – but still it was a high-cost production. We needed a studio, lighting, building materials. And of course I saw a new wall ahead – though at quite a distance. But in general, yes, this was the right direction. In this way I could produce images which worked. But now I wanted them to be able to accommodate any kind of camera movement in space.

In order to gain real freedom in time and space, there were several problems I had to solve. I made *Imagine* by pushing the camera by hand – and it worked, because I pushed only in one direction. It was linear travelling – such a simple movement could be controlled by hand. But for any kind of complex motion you need a motion control system for the camera – a kind of very mobile crane, controlled by computer. So I examined all the existing motion control systems. I found out that these were not particularly useful for my purposes. They are heavy – gigantic constructions. They do not move in real time. And they can move only in space limited by the dimensions of a studio. So I made a series of films designed to analyse movement, to see exactly what it was I needed, what I would have to invent.

To make my film *Orchestra* (1989), I went to France from the United States with three tons of High Definition equipment and a simple motion control camera head. I photographed different locations – one of them Chartres Cathedral.

Imagine

185

Orchestra

Chartres Cathedral is very big, and very dark inside. I beamed about 250 kilowatts of light upwards, but still the light could not reach the roof. And the rest of the building was plunged in darkness. To expose the mandala pattern on the floor I had to remove all the chairs – there must have been a few thousand, or at least a few hundred of them. There were ugly white lamps suspended from the ceiling at intervals of about five metres, so when I used lighting, of course everything was overexposed. Terrible. It was two o'clock in the morning, so I greased somebody's palm, and we climbed up to a place we could reach the lights from and tried to move them. Then there turned out to be speakers stuck on the walls, and religious tracts. What could I do in the shot? Very little. I couldn't fly between the columns; I couldn't change the decor. So I sat on the floor and I decided to 'photograph' the flying couple I had seen in Gdansk in my mind's eye when I was fifteen.

Film-makers like to think that we can shoot pretty well wherever we like, more or less whenever we like. My own experience – I have, of course, worked on ordinary films in the normal way, two features and a number of documentaries —tell me that it can in fact be extremely difficult to organise a location shoot so that it really works. For example, when I did a shoot in Washington, DC, I had to have special permits, because it's a government area, and there are only certain specific points where you are allowed to set up tracks and camera equipment. Unfortunately, when I was trying to work there, these points only permitted me to shoot directly into the sun, and the buildings themselves were very dark. I wanted to film, for example, inside the Lincoln Memorial. You can't even get a permit to do that, because once some film crew damaged some bit of marble. So now nobody can shoot there – because it belongs not to the film industry, only to the nation.

So it isn't as easy as it sounds to shoot what you like when you like and where you like. How can we photograph public buildings which are not really accessible? Of course we can build a huge model like the ones Christopher Hobbs describes. We could build a model of King's College, Cambridge, say, in a studio which has a 100-metre by 40-metre stage, and use a gigantic, really enormous, motion control camera. But how much money would it cost? And what, really, can we photograph? Where is the landscape that provides the setting for the building? Where is the moon shining on those pristine turrets? Can this model breathe? Can it morph? No, even for a billion dollars it will never be made to come to life.

After a series of experiments across the whole area of visual 'motion', I came to the conclusion that I could get away from a real full-scale set altogether and generate the whole world of the action using small models. And that such a world would look extremely convincing.

In the course of my experiments I made some very interesting discoveries: that motion, visual motion, if I can call it that, gives us the possibility of photographing 'reality', in a very different way from what we know from our experience. I built a motion control system which allowed the camera to make any 'motion' in space, at any 'speed' – very complex and curious 'motions', some of which cannot exist in physical reality as we know it. For example, using this device, we can actually 'move' forwards at very high speed and then reverse immediately, without stopping or even slowing down.

We are used to the idea that we are observing the world – let's say the ceilings, walls, floors and other objects – at the same time, located at only one point of observation. All objects are then located at different points in space. But I decided to tear this perception apart and reverse it. At any given moment, we are looking at only one object, which is always located at the same point in space. Every object is associated with a unique position relative to the camera in space.

Compositing together – through the Ultimatte – different 'looks' at different objects, we can create very complex 'architecture'. Models representing floor, walls, ceiling, are set up at one location, in the same place in the studio. Let's call this our 'source'. Imagine looking at every 'source' from different positions. The effect of perspective would be achieved – when the camera is in the right place to look at the particular 'source' from the right distance and with the right pan, tilt, roll, and focus.

The upshot was that I built a device run through a PC, using very simple software. First, you have to design a move in space – just like saying to the gaffer, 'Could you just lay this track on the floor from here to there?' Then you have to explain what you are trying to film. In terms of the computer, this means what scale you are using and where an object should be located in your imaginary space. The program has to figure out how the camera has to position itself to photograph the 'source' so as to achieve a particular perspective. Then all I needed was a relatively small space in which to create lighting effects and place the 'sources'. The camera is positioned fully automatically. Every component of the image is photographed with a different motion. And surprisingly – this results in an amazing illusion – the camera's eye appears to make an absolutely specific motion through space, which was never in fact executed, which nine times out of ten could never be executed in physical space and time. This is the system I used for the production of *Kafka* (1992).

I always work with very low budgets, though I'm probably using the most expensive technology, which means that it was not possible for me to devote a lot of money to on-screen expenses – actors, props, details of the picture. All the money was spent on the studio, equipment and technological research. For *Kafka*, I assembled the first prototype of the camera control device. I couldn't do any real tests for the whole process, because I ran out of time and money. So every take was really a test of the system.

In *Kafka*, I constructed many interiors. And, eventually, I photographed 'my' cathedral. I found a way to deal with the Chartres' problem. I made two attempts at cathedral-building. I juxtaposed one column, about three feet high, with the pulpit in proportion, and a little bit of floor, plus one wall, which is repeated. The first cathedral was very far from perfect (the joins show in small details, minute breaks or differences in lighting-levels) but my second cathedral is quite convincing. All of the components were photographed with different movements of the camera – and the final assembled illusion is that they are all organic parts of the same whole.

Kafka

First I recorded the walls in a full take – only the walls. Then I recorded the columns farthest away. Then I came in closer and closer and closer, and, finally, onto the completed background, I recorded the actors. I made all recordings directly onto the final master. This process is the next stage of the 'instant video' technique.

Observing the screen, the viewer is convinced that the camera really makes the movements the eye accepts it as making – revolving completely through 360 degrees, whilst travelling within the cathedral. In actual fact, the camera was fixed while recording the actors. The program calculated a few very tiny motions, very different from a 360-degree travelling shot, which create the illusion of the movement. The zoom is working all the time – from 62 degrees to 4 degrees horizontally, the camera is panning and tilting, and changes elevation from zero to two metres during the movement – and yet all the parts of the building appear to be solidly connected.

The camera appears to travel at a height of about eighteen feet. Actually, it was on the ground, but still I got the illusion of a high viewpoint. The whole composition is built from about eighty layers, eighty components, which are recorded onto each other. Some takes involve very complex and long moves. In the last scene of the film, I tried a single take where the camera travels about two kilometres. I did not succeed in getting everything right, but the idea is there, like a sketch of a possibility. The camera travels along what appears to be a 330-metre corridor, then enters into another virtual set – 120 by 120 metres – and finally travels into the next long corridor. On HD it looks pretty good.

So how long does it take to build a screen cathedral, using this method; and to work through the *mise en scène* with the actors? The whole background for, let us say, a three-minute take, I recorded on day one, and the actors on day two. The whole film, which lasts one hour, was made using this method. It would have been impossible to create special effects of this kind, on film or video, with traditional methods, for any realistic budget.

The great joy of this kind of production is the speed at which you can work. I could make an artistic decision in the morning, and by about one o'clock at night it had come into existence, and was finished.

On average, in the U. S. A., to get a feature film finished, from the time you start the script, takes seven years. You have to plan every special effect, make drawings and build models and sets (as Diana Charnley describes, pp. 154-165), and you have to decide in advance about virtually every second of the filming. It is my dream to arrive at a mechanism which will allow spontaneous, creative film-making, so that, for example, you could make a fifty-minute special-effects movie in a day – no, let's be realistic, say a month.

At the core of human civilisation is a hope, a dream, a belief, that we humans may one day become a beautiful species, attain to a beautiful form of existence: though we know in our heart of hearts that this is not really likely to be. Through the centuries we keep trying to build a 'model' of that projection, what we dream about ourselves, of who we should be. The 'model' has nothing to do with reality; the 'model' represents a poor fantasy. This fantasy is, of course, like every fantasy, a bit naive and a bit kitschy. In it we are beautiful, immortal, with good hearts, standing on pedestals covered with gold, flowers and smiles. The pedestals are surrounded by vague rococo gardens.

Through the centuries, great artists visualised this concept in magnificent art forms with the most advanced technologies of their epochs. Their visions keep us going through the worst times. Every epoch adds a new element to the fantasy of the era just departed. A more beautiful finger, a more shapely ear, a more sentimental eye, a piece of lace, a piece of elegance, a piece of 'goodness'. And with time, in synch with the development of technology, the vision becomes more and more convincing to the audience. But the really important thing is that in every case the visions were produced by artists, completely from scratch – with nothing but their own hands, eyes, ears and brains. They had to study a great deal about their subject and their materials; and, if they needed a machine or some kind of construction to achieve their vision, they had to invent and then build it. The amount of suffering, energy and time which every creation took was immaterial to the creators.

Around the time that the artistic vision became very convincing, in terms of realism, on our planet there emerged correspondingly new technologies – among them, photography.

It is very interesting to eavesdrop on what Mrs. Talbot – the wife of the inventor of photography – said, as she watched the first photographs in history, the first photographs produced by her husband.

MR. TALBOT (*with enthusiasm*): Look, my dear! My invention is producing an image of our bucket, of our window, of our ladder, of the mound of straw in our courtyard. And also – a very lifelike image of you.

(*He gives his wife the first photograph of a human being. Mrs. Talbot looks for a moment at the first photograph*).

MRS. TALBOT: No! How can you call this the truth? (*She tears the first photograph into pieces*). 'My dear, I am sorry to say I do not see the significance of your invention. (*On her way out of the room, she stops for a moment in the doorway*). And, what is more, I can see no practical application whatever of your invention to the arts.

Of course, Mrs. Talbot was right. Even today we can see what she meant, if we compare the first photographs with images created by artists at that time, and earlier. Before the invention of photography we find not a single image where something or somebody is truly ugly, dirty, naked, pathological or dead. In photographs from the nineteenth century, suddenly an awful and meaningless world appears. People are terribly ugly – they look like dead bodies which have just risen from their graves. Even their clothing is covered with dirt and mud and cut by bad tailors. Not only the people, but also streets, buildings, towns, the whole world has a graveyard air. For Mrs. Talbot, the idea that we should be surrounded by images of the things we already have in front of us – a bucket, for example – or by images of ourselves as we really are – was, both from a logical and from an aesthetic point of view absolute nonsense. Mrs. Talbot was a great visionary. She saw right at the outset the danger her husband's invention might bring to our 'vision'. It has the potential to destroy it completely.

It took just over a hundred years from Mrs. Talbot's perspicacious observation for artists to proclaim 'cinéma vérité'. The ground was prepared. Within fifty years the television transmission of 'big events' commenced. The 'vision' was over. The 'truth' about ourselves started to blossom. The fairytale-like concept of a Cocteau landed in the trashcan. Suddenly we understood that we are already the most beautiful of species – just as we *are*. We don't need any improvement. What we feel in the depths of our hearts is completely wrong – we should no longer be worrying about that sort of thing. And of course modern artists really don't have to suffer any more, they can enjoy life just like anyone else – and, conversely, anyone else can very easily become an artist. Because the creative process became really, really simple. Just waiting for you is all this fantastic technology. You don't have to understand how it works. It just works – for you! All you have to do is look around, find something 'hot', set up your camera, and push the button.

If we could somehow compare numerically the success of the old, classical 'vision' with the success of the modern 'vision', it would be a devastating comparison for the artists of past generations. No one masterpiece created by them was ever so admired by an audience as the almost 'daily' creations of today. In the past – and the same is of course true today – nobody would be likely to spend longer than an hour, for example, looking at *The Last Judgement* by Michelangelo; or to listen for longer than two hours to a concerto by Mozart, or sit for longer than three hours watching a performance such as *Macbeth*. But in modern times millions of people, holding their breath and biting their nails, can sit and watch shows eight or ten hours long, without getting bored for a second. A successful, married real-estate businessman from New York has a lover! Did a judge, a candidate for the Supreme Court, give his secretary a glass of cognac containing one of his pubic hairs? How did a former marine sexually abuse his wife, before she cut off his penis? What will happen next in the O.J. trial?

The question arises: is the modern 'version' of reality really completely satisfying to us? I answer: No. There is still much to be done. But soon, we will overcome the last remainder of the 'old'.

Already, one of our most famous male artistes on his world tour sends a message – he publicly gropes his crotch on stage. In parallel, a famous female artiste informs whoever cares to know of her sexual preferences, during her world tour, while performing in bed on the stage. In New York City – for the moment only on cable TV – we can also see interviews conducted by and with completely naked people. What are the interviews about? About the future.

Is there an alternative form of art? Of course there is. Does the audience have the chance to see it? Of course it does. Where? In galleries, in museums of modern art, in avant-garde theatres, at multimedia exhibitions, in interactive virtual installations. Who is creating these forms of art, and what are they about? Hmm. To answer that question is not an easy task. The creators, I suppose, form our artistic elite – an intellectual elite. And the concept represents, I suppose, the 'vision' of that elite. But as to what the vision-concept is about, I really don't know. I can only speculate.

In days of old, artists were intellectuals and intellectuals were artists. And all of them were scientists. They worked on the development of the arts, new technologies and sciences – they were a real intellectual elite. Around the middle of the nineteenth century, the situation was changed drastically by the concept of 'specialisation'. From then on, technology was exclusively developed by maniac inventors, entrepreneurs, bureaucrats, military and political personnel. Science is developed exclusively by the scientists, art is exclusively created by the artists. Who belongs to the intellectual elite is no longer clear. But one thing is clear: the artist is fleeing from technology and science, like a devil from holy water.

If an artist touches technology – though note that only the most modern technology of the time is forbidden: the older kind is allowed to be touched – or if by chance an artist should invent a new technology, they are automatically disqualified from membership of the exclusive club. For example: Mr. Talbot, Mr. Eiffel, the Lumières – all are chance inventors! Of course they achieved something important, and it is proper that something should be written about them in technical books. But not in books about the arts, thank you! They cannot be permitted to rank with someone of the stature of a Van Gogh. An artistic hand cannot be permitted to produce a modern machine or build a new pyramid; an artistic eye cannot look into mathematical or physical formulae. Everything has become so complicated!

The belief in 'specialisation' – which in fact destroyed the old intellectual-artist-scientific elite – has caused terrible devastation in our culture. The belief in the mutual exclusivity of art and science has been taken seriously – as it still is – by some of the greatest minds of our time. Even Einstein played the violin in his closet only – just as a hobby.

It is a pity that Einstein, Chaplin, Jung, Kafka, Picasso, Joyce, to mention but a few out of potential hundreds, did not meet together in Hollywood and work together on the development of the most fascinating technology of the twentieth century – the technology of 'live pictures'.

Of course, the intellectual elite is making its voice heard today. Of course: crying out against atom bombs, politicians, the environment, fat, the Third World, crime – cold, digital, pseudo, commercial kitsch.

Probably, this cry was at the bottom of the avant-garde art of the last century, and doubtless the intellectual-artistic community has always had the best of intentions.

But why, today, is the audience not storming galleries of modern art? Why is modern art not on the next world tour, like the Rolling Stones? Why are there no groupies hanging around intellectuals? Today, intellectuals walk home *alone* after their performances. In *solitude* they place themselves on the couches in their homes. Today, in fact, the audience is manipulated by the 'stupid' media. Thinking such thoughts, the intellectuals switch on colour televisions and, with conceptual disapproval – but with real, simple, human curiosity – gaze at images transmitted live by satellite. Who is the new lover of the successful real estate businessman from New York? Did a judge give his secretary a glass of cognac containing one of his pubic hairs? What is new today in the O.J. trial? With pure fascination – no hypocrisy – a mass audience stares at the same screens, bored to death by the version of avant-garde art offered by intellectuals for the last hundred years at least.

Very often we can hear or read about the fear – intellectuals are crying about it – that in the near future the use of 'this all new digital technology' may be very dangerous for us: and, of course, for *our* civilisation. With it, we can forge the image of our reality and we can 'manipulate' the 'truth'. Well, this should not be our fear, my dear hypocrites: on the contrary, it should be our only hope. We should use it as soon as possible – before we are obliged to see the end: the naked 'truth' in gigantic close-up. The only problem is that 'this all-new digital technology' does not yet work properly in our field.

The trouble is that the inventors and scientists are discovering and inventing only what they are paid for, or what has taken their fancy, what happened to move their imaginations – I'm quite certain they are not thinking about forging or manipulating moving images for artistic purposes. At home, on television, they can watch such fascinating material! Why forge anything different? And even if an artist really did want to get down to it immediately, start today to 'forge' and 'to manipulate', it would not be possible: the tools are simply not available. The artists have to wait – thinking to themselves, 'Maybe "they" will soon get round to inventing and building something for us.'

In the last take of *Kafka*, the camera arrives at a landscape and stops there – it happens to be a cemetery. I recognise that in this take I also arrived at my second 'wall'. I was aware that too many things in the field of the picture make no sense today. Yet, at the time, there was nowhere else I could turn – not like my flight from film to video. Of course, a possible next 'step' lurked close by: computer graphics. But I was too aware that there was something wrong with computer graphics. Without the addition of a photographic image transmitted and recorded by video, computer graphics today makes no sense.

Experience suggested to me that there was some fundamental problem to be dealt with before I could use the potential of computer graphics. In all my work I have always used the technique of multi-composing, on film or on video, and in order to achieve the simplest effect I have usually had to do thousands of drawings. I had to deal with geometry, with mathematics – and in the process I made the observation that when I drew exactly what I intended the camera to see, defining accurately the edges of my frame, it was not in fact precisely what the camera actually recorded. I observed that the proportion of the picture which I drew did not correspond exactly with the proportion of the picture the camera actually sees. The frame window in the camera is very different from the window-frame formed by the lens in the world outside. At first I thought that this must be some kind of lens-aberration, but that turned out not to be the case.

I kept on analysing the way moving images work, and came to some important conclusions. For example, although, once we understand how to work with perspective, almost any location can be 'photographed' by computer, we need the lens to photograph humans. To me, the concept of making artificial images of human beings is pure science-fiction. I will not even attempt to do it – because I don't think we can possibly achieve it. To even begin we would have to understand the real nature of life, the human mind, the structure of the brain and how it works. How do you go about programming a personality? Maybe one day in the future we will find out. Meanwhile, we can create very convincing images of everything we know, can understand, or build. But how can we connect the images produced by the lens with computer graphics images, when they are so different in their construction?

The pictures produced by lenses look convincing; images produced by existing computer graphics software do not. We can recognise the difference in a split second. This is a problem which exercised my mind for a long time. One of the suspects which might be responsible for this effect of artificiality seemed to me to be the polygon concept which rules today's computer graphics theory. Once, when I was photographing a naked model, I decided to get really close, to examine the polygon concept from a very close angle. After detailed observation I became quite sure. Nowhere on the whole body of that model did I find a single polygon. How can we generate a proper picture of a 3D body if we take as a basis for the calculation something which bears no relation to the body?

The second suspect was the geometry of the picture. We know from our daily experience of reality, from our life, that in fact we see in a coherent way, not one which modifies the angles as we go, to follow the laws of perspective. To us, the three-dimensional surface of the world is a coherent whole which behaves consistently when we move in relation to it. We are accustomed to that concept, and we are very sensitive to the fact that when we move in space everything we observe changes in a consistent way, in a specific way which applies to every part of the image. The optical image, in general, has the same property. It makes no difference whether the lens is fish-eye, 45 degrees, a long lens or anything else. When we observe an image photographed by a lens in movement, we see coherent behaviour over the whole surface. In other words, every element is subject to the same deformation, wherever it is in the frame, over the entire surface of the image.

This is not the case in computer-graphics images produced with existing software. My own research made me interested in the whole question of the premises on which computer graphics software conceptualises the picture, in space and time. I looked closely at the graphic libraries, but I could not find any real scientific analysis of the principles I have just been outlining. On top of these conceptual shortcomings, you have to study the most advanced software for three years or so before you can use it yourself – even if you are not stupid. And when, in addition to that, I took into consideration that a really good computer plus software costs about one million dollars in today's market, and using it you can produce a few seconds worth of images per day, I came to the conclusion that that story is mostly cock-and-bull, or a scandal.

But still I wanted to make things better for myself and others, so I tried to study the issue of what an image actually is – and, believe it or not, I found that there exists very little scientific examination or knowledge of the subject. Here at the end of the twentieth century we really know almost nothing about the properties of the image. The last scientists who worked on this issue were the architects and painters of the fifteenth century. They discovered the principle of linear perspective which we are still using today, the formula written into all computer 3D graphics software. But my experiments showed that this concept is quite misleading – actually wrong.

I decided to hold a conference to try to focus the issue. The participants were Euclid, Pythagoras, Alberti, Descartes, Newton, Lobaczewski and Einstein. I opened the proceedings.

RYBCZYNSKI: Gentlemen, the question I should like to lay before you is the following: does a picture exist in the universe, independent of the human eye, of a lens, a screen? Independent in the sense that, let us say, kinetic energy exists independently from an apple falling from a tree? And, if such a picture does exist, is it possible to arrive at a definition, a formula to define it?

EINSTEIN: Fascinating question: I never thought about it.

NEWTON: Nor me …

DESCARTES: I was sure Alberti had a good definition …

ALBERTI: No, no, no. I just proposed a simple solution for painters, and …

Alberti casts a quick glance at the Greeks, then, with shame, drops his eyes to the floor.

ALBERTI: Anyway, I just used what the Greeks wrote.

EUCLID and PYTHAGORAS: We were occupied with fundamentals, not painters.

LOBACZEWSKI (*triumphant*):   I knew something was wrong with your fundamentals!

RYBCZYNSKI: Gentlemen! Do not let us waste time! I have a second question to propose: can we delineate the shape of a body with something other than a wire frame containing millions of polygons?

The full proceedings of the conference will, I hope, be published in the near future. More to the point, I left with a small piece of paper in my pocket containing the formula for the image and for the next stage of my work.

That small piece of paper was the ticket to continue my travels. I could use it to break through the wall that had stopped me on *Kafka*. But starting was a very complicated task. I had a company and my monthly overheads amounted to $125,000. I knew that I needed much more money to buy computers, build new hardware, pay top programmers, free myself from the daily grind.

Travelling on my new ticket, I shopped around with my ideas about imaging in the United States, Japan, France, England, Italy, even Spain. I spoke to the Gods of Technology, on whose desks shone telephones from which a single call is enough to start serious research. Every conversation began with a coffee served by a nice Heavenly Secretary. Every conversation ended something like this:

GOD OF TECHNOLOGY: OK, Zbig, your ideas are very interesting, but who are you actually?

ZBIG: I'm a film director.

ZBIG looks up to catch a delicate smile suffusing the faces of the GODS.

ZBIG: Oh, I'm sorry, not exactly – that is, I'm a director of photography.

ZBIG is dismayed to see the GODS' eyebrows move up their august countenances.

ZBIG: Oh, actually not quite – er … I'm a video maker? Anyway, I'm absolutely convinced that it is necessary to change a lot in the existing technology of electronic recording and image processing.

The GODS stand up, displaying their fangs.

GODS (*yelling*):   You're an artist, that's what you are, aren't you?

The HEAVENLY SECRETARY silently holds the door open for ZBIG.

GODS (*furious*):   So, go on – get back to your art!

Head down, ZBIG scuttles off in the direction indicated by the sternly pointing fingers of the GODS.

GODS: And you'd better be creative, Zbig!

Berlin

Finally, however, I had some luck. I found someone who understood me, in Germany – Mr. Paul Bielicki. I packed my things and moved to Berlin. With a little, but substantial, support from the German government and with a little faith from a German bank, we are developing, in Berlin, a studio – CFB Centrum – with the most advanced technology of its kind in the world. Richard Welnowski moved with me from the United States to Berlin – he is the chief engineer, whose knowledge in this field is matched by nobody else in the world. He has worked with me since I first decided to work with HD. We have been through all the ups and downs of this artistic/scientific journey together.

In Berlin we are now working on connecting images produced by the lens – via motion control – with computer graphics images. The marriage is made inside the computer. This is an example of spherical perspective. What is the advantage of doing everything inside the computer? It is that there I can do anything – I am not subject to the limitations imposed by 'real' space and time at all. For *Kafka*, I still had physically to create miniature models of columns. If I had wanted to use other shapes or modify anything in any way, it would have had to be made out of wood or whatever, in a workshop. But if I had a picture of a column generated by computer, I could transform and morph it during a movement of the camera, and if I could then place human beings in the world generated by that computer – then I should be very close to imaging those 'things which do not exist' in front of the lens.

Personally, I believe that software designers and computer designers are genuinely moving civilisation forwards. Theirs is the most creative story being told today. But for those of us who are truly interested in the future of our culture, it is necessary to re-examine the basis on which software and hardware for the creation of images are being developed. I think the science of special effects – I use the expression 'special effects', but one day they will be thought of as 'realism' – lags behind other technologies, just as the science of the image does.

For example, we can build an aeroplane which has sixteen million parts working in synch, mechanical parts and electronic parts, and aeroplanes very rarely crash. In a picture, the highest resolution we have today is, let's say, 5,000 pixels by 5,000 pixels or 2,000 pixels by 2,000 pixels. How many elements does that require to work together? Only a few million, even though every pixel has to be RGB, the right colour. A 'few million' are not the problem, computers can calculate them in a split second. The real problem is an intellectual one: what has to be calculated in every pixel-square? We have come full circle, back to my first film – back to square one (forgive the pun).

If today, using computers, we cannot produce images which are actually better than those a lens can photograph, it means we are confused in our concept of how to do it. Because, if we really understand the nature of pictures, of the image, creating such images with the aid of technology becomes a very easy task.

For example, in all my video productions I have always used the Ultimatte – the fantastic machine invented by Paul Vlahos – a device which allows us to make an extract with blue matte, and then combine the foreground with the background. It has a panel and the panel has some twenty buttons. The operator pushes combinations of buttons to achieve the matte.

Now, in my whole career in the United States, I only ever found two people who can actually do a good matte. One was in New York, the second is Richard Welnowski. In Europe, I haven't found a single person with enough experience to really be an expert - at least, so far I haven't had the luck to meet such a person. It's a question of operating all those twenty buttons in combination. But in the final analysis, a matte is very specific – there is only one possible result, only one way in which it is going to be convincing. In effect, the buttons might be said not to be necessary at all, since really there are so few variables.

But now there is a company developing digital software containing the equivalent of about 2,000 buttons. When they make a new version it will have 3,000 more. Suddenly, the problem is no longer how to achieve an illusion by combining two representations of reality convincingly by pushing 20 or 3,000 buttons, but how to build the desired image itself using computers. There is an ancillary problem – designing software which is not only functional, but also user-friendly. If this technology is really to extend horizons for film-makers, it has to be easy – easier than pressing those twenty real buttons people have so much difficulty with, not more difficult. It has to be simple. And it has to be built around the way we are accustomed to perceiving reality, how we act in life. This is a very important aspect of our work in Berlin. We want to develop software which takes you no more than two hours – well, perhaps two days – to learn, after which you will be able to design a very complex take, in the world where your stories happen.

I believe that if we can combine a proper understanding of how images function – and how they are perceived – with elegant software design, we will have moved very close to the kind of new 'realism' of the moving image I started to imagine in the 60s. We are developing a prototype for use on the PC. You can design your whole film, including architecture, landscape, actors' movements and camera movements, and you can see them in a kind of sketch form in real time, with sound. You can very quickly create something which functions rather like a cross between a story-board and a screenplay, a kind of treatment for the whole film. Then, in the studio, a very sophisticated device with the complete system can really execute the images from your treatment, making the necessary adjustments. The whole process operates like a fully mechanised studio. There is no crew in the traditional sense. There is no camera set-up. One machine can execute every

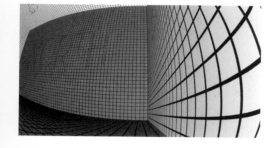

180 degrees perspectives using computational techniques developped by Centrum (Berlin)

movement in space you require. Work can be conducted in a very intensive way – a large amount of material can be recorded in a single day. The only decisions to be made during the 'shoot' are the creative ones.

We still have a lot of problems to solve. Good working powerful buffers for real-time storage don't yet exist, so we have to build them. The transition of data from camera to recorder, from recorder to buffer, from buffer to computer, from computer to buffer and from buffer to recorder still needs to be very much simplified. The computer for the processing of optically recorded pictures has to be simplified. The computer for generating artificial images has to be built from scratch. We also need to construct a new kind of lens, a zoom, with a field of view from 180 degrees to maybe 4 degrees which delivers the image having the same geometrical properties as a computer graphics 'lens'. We are developing a new method of composing different visual components into one coherent picture without a matte. We are also developing new methods of transfer between different formats: HDTV, PAL, NTSC, and FILM. By 1996, we hope that our 'machine' will already have produced impressive images.

I will be one step nearer to my kind of 'realism': to showing on the screen, solid and completely convincing as they are to our mind's eye, those things which are absolutely 'real', but do not offer themselves for capture by the photographic lens.

FILMOGRAPHY

d. = director; *w.* = writer; *w.d.* = writer director; *ph.* = cinematographer; *des.* = designer; *ed.* = editor; *p* = producer; *mus*=music

A

A bout de souffle
France 1959, *d.* Jean-Luc Godard; *w.* Jean-Luc Godard, François Truffaut (story); *ph.* Raoul Coutard; *des.* Claude Chabrol; *ed.* Cécile Decugis; *p.* Georges De Beauregard;

A nous la liberté
France 1930, *w.d.* René Clair; *ph* Georges Périnal; *des.* Lazare Meerson; *ed.* René Clair, René Le Henaff; *p.* Frank Clifford

Accattone
Italy 1961, *d.* Pier Paolo Pasolini; *w.* Sergio Citti (dialogue), Pier Paolo Pasolini; *ph.* Tonino Delli Colli; *des.* Flavio Mogherini; *ed.* Nino Baragli; *p.* Alfredo Bini

After Hours
USA 1985, *d.* Martin Scorsese; *w.* Joseph Minion; *ph.* Michael Ballhaus; *des.* Jeffrey Townsend; *ed.* Thelma Schoonmaker; *p.* Robert F. Colesberry, Griffin Dunne, Amy Robinson

L'Age d'Or
France 1930, *d.* Luis Buñuel; *w.* Luis Buñuel, Salvador Dali; *ph.* Albert Duverger; *des.* Pierre Schildknecht; *ed.* Luis Buñuel; *p.* Le Vicomte De Noailles

The Age of Innocence
USA 1993, *d.* Martin Scorsese; *w.* Edith Wharton (novel), Jay Cocks, Martin Scorsese; *ph.* Michael Ballhaus; *des.* Dante Ferretti; *ed.* Thelma Schoonmaker; *p.* Barbara De Fina

Algol
Germany 1920, *d.* Hans Werckmeister; *w.* Hans Brenert, Friedel Koehne; *ph.* Axel Graatkjaer, Hermann Kircheldorff; *des.* Walter Reimann

Alice
USA 1990, *w.d.* Woody Allen; *ph.* Carlo Di Palma; *des.* Santo Loquasto; *ed.* Susan E. Morse; *p.* Robert Greenhut

Alice Doesn't Live Here Anymore
USA 1974, *d.* Martin Scorsese; *w.* Robert Getchell; *ph.* Kent L. Wakeford; *des.* Toby Carr Rafelson; *ed.* Marcia Lucas; *p.* Audrey Maas, David Susskind

Alien
USA 1979, *d.* Ridley Scott; *w.* Ronald Shusett (story), Dan O'Bannon; *ph.* Derek Vanlint; *des.* Roger Christian, Leslie Dilley, Anton Furst, Michael Seymour; *ed.* Terry Rawlings, Peter Weatherley; *p.* Gordon Carroll, David Giler, Walter Hill

Alphaville
France/Italy 1965, *d.* Jean-Luc Godard; *w.* Jean-Luc Godard, *ph.* Raoul Coutard; *ed.* Agnès Guillemot; *p.* André Michelin

A propos de Nice
France 1930, *w.d.* Jean Vigo; *ph.* Boris Kaufman

American Boy: A Profile of Steven Prince
USA 1978, *d.* Martin Scorsese; *ph.* Michael Chapman; *ed.* Amy Jones, Bert Lovitt; *p.* Bert Lovitt

Un americano a Roma
Italy 1954, *d.* Steno [Stefano Vanzina]; *w.* Sandro Continenza, Lucio Fulci, Ettore Scola, Sordi, Steno; *ph.* Carlo Montuori; *ed.* Giuliana Attenni

Annie Hall
USA 1977, *d.* Woody Allen; *w.* Woody Allen, Marshall Brickman; *ph.* Gordon Willis; *des.* Mel Bourne; *ed.* Ralph Rosenblum; *p.* Charles H. Joffe, Jack Rollins

Another Woman
USA 1988, *d.* Woody Allen; *w.* Woody Allen; *ph.* Sven Nykvist; *des.* Santo Loquasto; *ed.* Susan E. Morse; *p.* Robert Greenhut

Applause
USA 1929, *d.* Rouben Mamoulian; *w.* Beth Brown (novel), Garrett Fort; *ph.* George J. Folsey; *ed.* John Bassler; *p.* Monta Bell, Jesse L. Lasky

Architectures d'aujourd'hui
France 1930–31, *d.* Pierre Chenal

L'Argent
France/Switzerland 1983, *d.* Robert Bresson; *w.* Robert Bresson, Leo Tolstoy (story); *ph.* Pasqualino De Santis, Emmanuel Machuel; *des.* Pierre Guffroy; *ed.* Jean Francois Naudon; *p.* Jean-Marc Henchoz

L'avventura
Italy/France 1959, *d.* Michelangelo Antonioni; *w.* Michelangelo Antonioni (also story), Elio Bartolini, Tonino Guerra; *ph.* Aldo Scavarda; *des.* Piero Poletto; *ed.* Eraldo Da Roma; *p.* Cino Del Duca, Amato Pennasilico, Luciano Perugia

B

Bananas
USA, 1971, *d.* Woody Allen; *w.* Woody Allen, Mickey Rose; *ph.* Andrew M. Costikyan; *des.* Ed Wittstein; *ed.* Ron Kalish, Ralph Rosenberg; *p.* Jack Grossberg

Barton Fink
USA, 1991, *d.* Joel Coen; *w.* Ethan Coen, Joel Coen; *ph.* Roger Deakins; *des.* Dennis Gassner; *ed.* Ethan Coen (as Roderick Jaynes), Joel Coen (as Roderick Jaynes); *p.* Ethan Coen, Graham Place.

Bâtir
France 1930–1, *d.* Pierre Chenal

Batman
USA 1989, *d.* Tim Burton; *w.* Sam Hamm, Warren Skaaren; *ph.* Roger Pratt; *des.* Anton Furst; *ed.* Ray Lovejoy; *p.* Peter Guber, Jon Peters

Der Bau der Lorrainebrücke in Bern
Germany 1928–30, *d.* Paul Schmid

La Belle et la bête
France 1946, *d.* Jean Cocteau; *w.* Jean Cocteau (story/dialogue), Jeanne-Marie Leprince de Beaumont (story); *ph.* Henri Alekan; *des.* Christian Berard; *ed.* Claude Ibéria; *p.* André Paulvé

Belle, ma povere
Italy 1957, *d.* Dino Risi

Bellissima
Italy 1951, *d.* Roberto Rossellini, Luchino Visconti; *w.* Suso Cecchi D'Amico, Francesco Rosi, Luchino Visconti, Cesare Zavattini; *ph.* Piero Portalupi, Paul Ronald; *ed.* Mario Serandrei

The Belly of an Architect
Italy/GB 1987, *w.d.* Peter Greenaway; *ph.* Sacha Vierny; *des.* Luciana Vedovelli; *ed.* John Wilson; *p.* Colin Callender, Walter Donohue

Berlin Alexanderplatz
Germany 1979, *d.* Rainer Werner Fassbinder; *w.* Alfred Döblin (novel), Rainer Werner Fassbinder; *ph.* Xaver Schwarzenberger; *ed.* Juliane Lorenz; *p.* Günter Rohrbach

Berlin, Symphonie Einer Großstadt
Germany 1927, *d.* Walter Ruttmann; *w.* Karl Freund, Carl Mayer, Walter Ruttmann; *ph.* Robert Baberske, Karl Freund, Reimar Kuntze, Laszlo Schäffer; *des.* Erich Ketelhut; *ed.* Walter Ruttmann

Berlin von unten
Germany 1928, *d.* A. Strasser

Bicycle Thieves/Ladri di biciclette
Italy 1949, *d.* Vittorio De Sica; *w.* Vittorio De Sica, Cesare Zavattini, Oreste Biancoli, Suso Cecchi D'Amico, Adolfo Franci; *ph.* Carlo Montuori

Black Rain
USA 1989, *d.* Ridley Scott; *w.* Craig Bolotin, Warren Lewis; *ph.* Jan de Bont; *des.* Norris Spencer; *ed.* Tom Rolf; *p.* Stanley R. Jaffe, Sherry Lansing,

Blade Runner
USA 1982, *d.* Ridley Scott; *w.* Philip K. Dick (novel *Do Androids Dream of Electric Sheep?*), Hampton Fancher, David Webb Peoples; *ph.* Jordan Cronenweth; *des.* Lawrence G. Paull; *ed.* Marsha Nakashima; *p.* Michael Deeley

Blow-Up
UK 1966, *d.* Michelangelo Antonioni; *w.* Michelangelo Antonioni, Tonino Guerra, Edward Bond, Julio Cortazar (story); *ph.* Carlo Di Palma; *des.* Assheton Gorton; *ed.* Frank Clarke; *p.* Carlo Ponti

Bonnie and Clyde
USA, 1967, *d.* Arthur Penn; *w.* Robert Benton, David Newman, Robert Towne (uncredited); *ph.* Burnett Guffey; *des.* Dean Tavoularis; *ed.* Dede Allen; *p.* Warren Beatty

Boxcar Bertha
USA 1972, *d.* Martin Scorsese; *w.* John William Corrington, Joyce Hooper Corrington; *ph.* John M. Stephens; *ed.* Buzz Feitshans; *p.* Roger Corman

Brazil
GB 1985, *d.* Terry Gilliam, *w.* Terry Gilliam, Charles McKeown, Tom Stoppard; *ph.* Roger Pratt; *des.* Norman Garwood; *ed.* Julian Doyle; *p.* Arnon Milchan

Broadway Danny Rose
USA 1983, *w.d.* Woody Allen; *ph.* Gordon Willis; *des.* Mel Bourne; *ed.* Susan E. Morse; *p.* Robert Greenhut

De Brug/The Bridge
Netherlands 1928, *d.* Joris Ivens

Die Büchse der Pandora/Pandora's Box
Germany 1928, *d.* Georg Wilhelm Pabst, *w.* Joseph Fleisler, Georg Wilhelm Pabst, Ladislaus Vajda, Frank Wedekind (plays *Erdgeist* and *Die Büchse der Pandora*); *ph.* Günther Krampf; *des.* Andrei Andreiev, Gottlieb Hesch; *p.* Seymour Nebenzal

Bullets Over Broadway
USA 1994, *d.* Woody Allen; *w.* Woody Allen, Douglas McGrath; *ph.* Carlo Di Palma; *des.* Santo Loquasto; *ed.* Susan E. Morse; *p.* Robert Greenhut

C

The Cabinet of Dr Caligari/Das Kabinett des Doktor Caligari
Germany 1919, *d.* Robert Wiene; *w.* Hans Janowitz. Carl Mayer; *ph.* Willy Hameister; *des.* Walter Reimann, Walter Roehrig, Hermann Warm; *p.* Erich Pommer

Cape Fear
USA 1991, *d.* Martin Scorsese; *w.* John D. MacDonald (novel *The Executioners*), Wesley Strick, James R. Webb; *ph.* Freddie Francis; *des.* Henry Bumstead; *ed.* Thelma Schoonmaker; *p.* Barbara De Fina

Casanova
Italy 1976, *d*. Federico Fellini; *w*. Giacomo Casanova (autobiography *Storia della mia vita*); Federico Fellini; Bernadino Zapponi; *ph*. Giuseppe Rotunno; *des*. Danilo Donati; *ed*. Ruggero Mastroianni; *p*. Alberto Grimaldi

Casino
USA 1995, *d*. Martin Scorsese; *w*. Nicholas Pileggi (also book *Casino: Love and Honor in Las Vegas*), Martin Scorsese; *des*. Dante Ferretti; *ed*. Thelma Schoonmaker; *p*. Barbara De Fina

Children At School
GB 1937, Gas, Light and Coke Company

The City
USA 1939, *d*. Ralph Steiner, *W.S*. Van Dyke

A City Reborn
GB 1945, Ministry of Information

Close Quarters
GB 1943, Crown Film Unit

Coastal Command
GB 1942, Crown Film Unit

Cold Lazarus
GB 1995 (TV), *d*. Renny Rye; *w*. Dennis Potter; *ph*. Ashley Rowe; *des*. Christopher Hobbs, Gary Williamson (from *Karaoke*); *ed*. Clare Douglas; *p*. Kenith Trodd, Rosemarie Whitman

The Color of Money
USA 1986, *d*. Martin Scorsese; *w*. Richard Price, Walter Tevis (novel); *ph*. Michael Ballhaus; *des*. Boris Leven; *ed*. Thelma Schoonmaker; *p*. Irving Axelrod, Barbara De Fina

La commare secca
Italy 1962, *d*. Bernardo Bertolucci; *w*. Bernardo Bertolucci, Sergio Citti, Pier Paolo Pasolini (also story); *ph*. Giovanni Narzisi; *ed*. Nino Baragli; *p*. Antonio Cervi

Un Condamné à mort s'est échappé/ A Man Escaped
France 1956, *d*. Robert Bresson; *w*. Robert Bresson, André Devigny (memoir); *ph*. Léonce-Henri Burel; *des*. Pierre Charbonnier; *ed*. Raymond Lamy; *p*. Alain Poiré, Jean Thuillier

Copy Cat
USA 1996, *d*. Jon Amiel; *w*. Ann Biderman, David Madsen (story), Frank Pierson; *ph*. László Kovács; *des*. Jim Clay; *ed*. Jim Clark, Alan Heim; *p*. Arnon Milchan, Mark Tarlov

Crimes and Misdemeanors
USA 1989, *w.d*. Woody Allen: *ph*. Sven Nykvist; *des*. Santo Loquasto; *ed*. Susan E. Morse; *p*. Robert Greenhut

The Crowd
USA 1928, *d*. King Vidor; *w*. Harry Behn, King Vidor (also story), John V.A. Weaver; *ph*. Henry Sharp; *des*. Cedric Gibbons, Arnold Gillespie; *ed*. Hugh Wynn; *p*. Irving Thalberg

The Crying Game
GB 1992, *w.d*. Neil Jordan; *ph*. Ian Wilson; *des*. Jim Clay; *ed*. Kant Pan; *p*. Stephen Woolley

D

Dear Diary/Caro diario/Journal intime
France/Italy 1993, *w.d*. Nanni Moretti; *ph*. Giuseppe Lanci; *des*. Marta Maffucci; *ed*. Mirco Garrone; *p*. Nella Banfi, Angelo Barbagallo, Nanni Moretti

Il deserto rosso
France/Italy 1964, *d*. Michelangelo Antonioni; w Michelangelo Antonioni, Tonino Guerra; *ph*. Carlo Di Palma; *ed*. Eraldo Da Roma; *p*. Antonio Cervi

The Devils
GB 1970, *d*. Ken Russell; *w*. Aldous Huxley (novel *The Devils of Loudon*), Ken Russell, John Whiting (play); *ph*. David Watkin; *des*. Robert Cartwright, Derek Jarman; *ed*. Michael Bradsell; *p*. Ken Russell, Robert H. Solo

Diary: Architects' Congress
1933, *d*. Lázló Maholy-Nagy

La dolce vita
Italy 1960, *d*. Federico Fellini; Frederico Fellini, Ennio Flaiano, Tullio Pinelli, Brunello Rondi; *ph*. Otello Martelli; *des*. Piero Gherardi; *p*. Franco Magli

Dr Mabuse der Spiele (Der Grosse Spieler + Inferno)
Germany 1922, *d*. Fritz Lang; *w*. Norbert Jacques (novel), Fritz Lang, Thea von Harbou; *des*. Carl Hoffman; *des*. Otto Hunte, Erich Ketelhut, Karl Stahl-Urach, Karl Vollbrecht; *p*. Erich Pommer

E

L'eclisse
France/Italy 1962, *d*. Michelangelo Antonioni; *w*. Michelangelo Antonioni, Elio Bartolini, Tonino Guerra, Ottiero Ottieri; *ph*. Gianni Di Venanzo; *des*. Piero Poletto; *ed*. Eraldo Da Roma; *p*. Raymond Hakim, Robert Hakim

L'Ecole des facteurs
France 1947, *w.d*. Jacques Tati; *ph*. Louis Félix; *ed*. Marcel Moreau; *p*. Fred Orain

Edward II
GB 1993, *d*. Derek Jarman; *w*. Ken Butler, Steve Clark-Hall, Derek Jarman, Christopher Marlowe (play), Stephen McBride, Antony Root; *ph*. Ian Wilson; *des*. Christopher Hobbs; *ed*. George Akers; *p*. Steve Clark-Hall

The Elephant Man
GB/USA 1980, *d*. David Lynch; *w*. Eric Bergren, Christopher DeVore, David Lynch, Ashley Montagu (book *The Elephant Man: A Study in Human Dignity*), Frederick Treves (book *The Elephant Man and Other Reminisces*); *ph*. Freddie Francis; *des*. Stuart Craig; *ed*. Anne V. Coates; *p*. Mel Brooks (uncredited), Jonathan Sanger

Emil und die Detektive
Germany 1931, *d*. Gerhard Lamprecht; *w*. Erich Kästner (novel, as Berthold Buerger), Billy Wilder; *ph*. Werner Brandes; *p*. Günther Stapenhorst

Les Enfants du paradis
France 1945, *d*. Marcel Carné; *w*. Jacques Prévert; *ph*. Marc Fossard, Roger Hubert; *des*. Léon Barsacq, Raymond Gabutti, Alexandre Trauner; *ed*. Madeleine Bonin, Henri Rust; *p*. Raymond Borderie, Fred Orain

Everything You Always Wanted to Know about Sex …
USA 1972, *d*. Woody Allen; *w*. Woody Allen, David Reuben (book); *ph*. David M. Walsh; *des*. Dale Hennesy; *ed*. Eric Albertson, James T. Heckert; *p*. Charles H. Joffe

F

Fantomas
France 1913, *w.d*. Louis Feuillade

Faust
Germany 1926, *d*. F. W. Murnau; *w*. Johann Wolfgang Goethe (story), Hans Kyser, Christopher Marlowe (story); *ph*. Carl Hoffmann; *des*. Robert Herlth, Walter Röhrig; *p*. Erich Pommer

Fear Eats the Soul
W. Germany 1974, *w.d*. Rainer Werner Fassbinder;

ph. Jürgen Jürges; *des*. Rainer Werner Fassbinder; *ed*. Thea Eymèsz; *p*. Christian Hohoff

Fellini Roma
Italy 1972, *w.d*. Federico Fellini; *ph*. Giuseppe Rotunno; *des*. Danilo Donati; *ed*. Ruggero Mastroianni; *p*. Turi Vasile

Feu Mathias Pascal
France 1925, *d*. Marcel L'Herbier; *w*. Marcel L'Herbier, Luigi Pirandello (novel); *ph*. Jimmy Berliet, F. Bourgassof, René Guichard, Jean Letort; *des*. Erik Aaes, Alberto Cavalcanti, Lazare Meerson

Field of Dreams
USA 1989, *d*. Phil Alden Robinson; *w*. W.P. Kinsella (book *Shoeless Joe*), Phil Alden Robinson; *ph*. John Lindley; *des*. Dennis Gassner; *ed*. Ian Crafford; *p*. Charles Gordon, Lawrence Gordon

Fires Were Started
GB 1943, Crown Film Unit, *d*. Humphrey Jennings; *ph*. C.M. Pennington-Richards; *ed*. Stewart McAllister

For the First Time
USA/W. Germany 1959, *d*. Rudolph Maté; *w*. Andrew Solt; *ph*. Aldo Tonti; Alexander Gruter

Die Frankfurter Kleinstwohnung
1927–8, *d*. P. Wolff

Die Frankfurter Küche
1927–8, *d*. P. Wolff

The French Connection
USA 1971, *d*. William Friedkin; *w*. Robin Moore (novel), Ernest Tidyman; *ph*. Owen Roizman; *ed*. Gerald B. Greenberg; *p*. Philip D'Antoni

G

Genuine
Germany 1920, *d*. Robert Wiene; *w*. Carl Mayer; *ph*. Willy Hameister; *p*. Erich Pommer

Una giornata particolare
Canada/Italy 1977, *d*. Ettore Scola; *w*. Maurizio Costanzo, Ruggero Maccari, Ettore Scola; *ph*. Pasqualino De Santis; *des*. Luciano Ricceri, *ed*. Raimondo Crociani; *p*. Carlo Ponti

Gloria
USA 1980, *w.d*. John Cassavetes; *ph*. Fred Schuler; *des*. René D'Auriac; *ed*. George Villasenor; *p*. Sam Shaw

Der Golem, wie er in die Welt kam
Germany 1920, *d*. Carl Boese, Paul Wegener; *w*. Henrik Galeen, Paul Wegener; *ph*. Karl Freund; *des*. Hans Poelzig, Kurt Richter

GoodFellas
USA 1990, d Martin Scorsese; *w*. Nicholas Pileggi (also novel *Wiseguy*), Martin Scorsese; *ph*. Michael Ballhaus; *des*. Kristi Zea; *ed*. Thelma Schoonmaker; *p*. Irwin Winkler

Il grido
Italy 1957, *d*. Michelangelo Antonioni; *w*. Michelangelo Antonioni, Elio Bartolini, Ennio DeConcini; *ph*. Gianni Di Venanzo; *ed*. Eraldo Da Roma; *p*. Franco Cancellieri

Guardie e ladri
Italy 1951, *d*. Steno [Stefano Vanzina]; *w*. Steno, Mario Monicelli; *ph*. Mario Bava

H

Hammett
USA 1983, *d*. Wim Wenders; *w*. Joe Gores (novel), Dennis O'Flaherty; Thomas Pope, Ross Thomas; *ph*. Joseph F. Biroc, Philip H. Lathrop; *des*. Eugene Lee, Dean Tavoularis;

ed. Marc Laub, Robert Q. Lovett, Barry Malkin, Randy Roberts; p. Ronald Colby, Don Guest, Fred Roos

Hannah and Her Sisters
USA 1986, w.d. Woody Allen; ph. Carlo Di Palma; des. Stuart Wurtzel; ed. Susan E. Morse; p. Robert Greenhut

Die Häuserfabrik der Stadt Frankfurt-am-Main
Germany 1927–8, d. P. Wolff

Der Hinterstreppe/Backstairs
Germany 1921, d. Leopold Jessner, Paul Leni; w. Carl Mayer; ph. Willy Hameister, Karl Hasselmann

Hoogstraat
Netherlands 1929, d. A. von Barsy

Housing Problems
GB 1935, d. F. Anstey, Ray Elton

Hudson Hawk
USA 1991, d. Michael Lehmann; w. Bruce Willis (story), Robert Kraft (story), Steven E. De Souza, ph. Dante Spinotti; des. Jackson De Govia; ed. Chris Lebenzon, Michael Tronick; p. Joel Silver

The Hudsucker Proxy
USA 1994, d. Joel Coen; w. Ethan Coen, Joel Coen, Sam Raimi; ph. Roger Deakins; des. Dennis Gassner; ed. Thom Noble; p. Ethan Coen

Husbands and Wives
USA 1992, w.d. Woody Allen; ph. Carlo Di Palma; des. Santo Loquasto; ed. Susan E. Morse; p. Robert Greenhut

I

The Icicle Thief/Ladri di saponette
Italy 1989, d. Maurizio Nichetti; w. Maurizio Nichetti, Mauro Monti; ph. Mario Battistoni; des. Ada Legori; ed. Rita Rossi, Anna Missoni; p. Ernesto Di Sarro

Images d'Oostende
Belgium 1930, d. H. Storck

Imagine
USA 1986, d. Zbig Rybczynski; mus. John Lennon

L'Inhumaine
France 1924, w.d. Marcel L'Herbier; ph. Roche, Georges Specht; des. Claude Autant-Lara, Alberto Cavalcanti, Pierre Chareau, Fernand Leger, Robert Mallet-Stevens

Interiors
USA 1978, w.d. Woody Allen; ph. Gordon Willis; des. Mel Bourne; ed. Ralph Rosenblum; p. Charles H. Joffe, Jack Rollins

Intervista
Italy 1987, d. Frederico Fellini; w. Gianfranco Angelucci, Federico Fellini; ph. Tonino Delli Colli; des. Danilo Donati; ed. Nino Baragli; p. Ibrahim Moussa

Italianamerican
USA 1974, d. Martin Scorsese; w. Lawrence D. Cohen, Mardik Martin; Martin Scorsese; ph. Alec Hirschfield; ed. Bert Lovitt; p. Elaine Attias, Saul Rubin

It's a Wonderful Life
USA 1946, d. Frank Capra; w. Frank Capra, Frances Goodrich, Albert Hackett, Philip Van Doren Stern (story), Jo Swerling; ph. Joseph F. Biroc, Joseph Walker; ed. William Hornbeck; p. Frank Capra

Ivan's Childhood/Ivanovo Detstvo
Soviet Union 1962, d. Andrei Tarkovsky; w. Vladimir Bogomolov, Mikhail Papava; ph. Vadim Yusov; des. Yevgeni Chernyayev; ed. Lyudmila Feyginova

J

Jour de fête
France 1949, d. Jacques Tati; w. Henri Marquet, Jacques Tati, René Wheeler; ph. Marcel Franchi, Jacques Mercanton, Jacques Sauvageot; des. René Moulaert; ed. Marcel Morreau; p. Fred Orain

K

Kafka
France/USA 1992, d. Steven Soderbergh; w. Lem Dobbs; ph. Walt Lloyd; des. Gavin Bocquet; ed. Steven Soderbergh; p. Harry Benn, Stuart Cornfield

Katzelmacher
W. Germany 1971, w.d. Rainer Werner Fassbinder; ph. Dietrich Lohmann; ed. Rainer Werner Fassbinder

The King of Comedy
USA 1983, d. Martin Scorsese; w. Paul D. Zimmermann; ph. Fred Schuler; des. Boris Leven; ed. Thelma Schoonmaker; p. Arnon Milchan

A Kiss Before Dying
USA 1991, d. James Dearden; w. James Dearden, Ira Levin (novel); ph. Mike Southon; des. Jim Clay; ed. Michael Bradsell; p. Robert Lawrence

L

The Ladies' Man
USA 1961, d. Jerry Lewis; w. Jerry Lewis, Bill Richmond; ph. W. Wallace Kelley; ed. Stanley E. Johnson; p. Jerry Lewis

The Lady from Shanghai
USA 1948, d. Orson Welles; w. Sherwood King (novel), Orson Welles; ph. Charles Lawton Jr.; ed. Viola Lawrence; p. Harry Cohn

Land of Promise
GB 1945, d. Paul Rotha

The Last Laugh/Der Letzte Mann
Germany 1924, d. F. Wilhelm Murnau; w. Carl Mayer; ph. Robert Baberske, Karl Freund; des. Robert Herlth, Walter Röhrig; p. Erich Pommer

The Last Temptation of Christ
USA 1988, d. Martin Scorsese; w. Nikos Kazantzakis (novel), Paul Schrader; ph. Michael Ballhaus; des. John Beard; ed. Thelma Schoonmaker; p. Barbara De Fina

The Last Waltz
USA 1978; d. Martin Scorsese; ph. Michael W. Watkins, Vilmos Zsigmond; des. Boris Leven; p. Robbie Robertson

Léon
France/USA 1994, w.d. Luc Besson; ph. Thierry Arbogast; des. Dan Weil; ed. Sylvie Landra; p. Luc Besson, Bernard Grenet (line)

Life Lessons (segment *New York Stories*)
USA 1989, d. Martin Scorsese; w. Richard Price; ph. Nestor Almendros, des. Kristi Zea; ed. Thelma Schoonmaker; p. Robert Greenhut

Little White Lies
USA 1989 (TV), d. Anson Williams; ph. Isidore Mankofsky; ed. Robert Pergament; p. Kevin Inch

The Long Day Closes
GB 1992, w.d. Terence Davies; ph. Michael Coulter; des. Christopher Hobbs; ed. William Diver; p. Olivia Stewart, Angela Toppings

Loser Takes All
GB 1956, d. Ken Annakin; w. Graham Greene; ph. Georges Périnal; des. Christopher Hobbs; ed. Jean Baker; p. John Stafford

Love and Death
USA 1975, d. Woody Allen; w. Woody Allen, Mildred Cram, Donald Ogden Stewart; ph. Ghislain Cloquet; des. Willy Holt; ed. George Hively, Ron Kalish, Ralph Rosenblum; p. Fred T. Gallo, Charles H. Joffe, Martin Poll

M

M
Germany 1931, d. Fritz Lang; wr. Fritz Lang, Thea von Harbou; ph. Fritz Arno Wagner, Karl Vash; des. Emil Hasler, Karl Vollbrech; p. Seymour Nebenzal

Mamma Roma
Italy 1962, w.d. Pier Paolo Pasolini; ph. Tonino Delli Colli; ed. Nino Baragli; p. Alfredo Bini

The Man with the Movie Camera/Chelovek s Kinoapparatom
Soviet Union 1929, w.d. Dziga Vertov; ph. Mikhail Kaufman; ed. Elisaveta Svilova

Manhatta
USA 1921, d. Paul Strand, Charles Sheeler

Manhattan
USA 1979, d. Woody Allen; w. Woody Allen, Marshall Brickman; ph. Gordon Willis; des. Mel Bourne; ed. Susan E. Morse; p. Charles H. Joffe

Manhattan Murder Mystery
USA 1993, d. Woody Allen; w. Woody Allen, Marshall Brickman; ph. Carlo Di Palma; des. Santo Loquasto; ed. Susan E. Morse; p. Robert Greenhut

Markt am Wittembergplatz
Germany 1929, d. W. Basse

Mary Reilly
USA 1995–6, d. Stephen Frears; w. Christopher Hampton, Valerie Martin (novel), Robert Louis Stevenson (novel *The Strange Case of Dr. Jekyll and Mr. Hyde*); ph. Philippe Rousselot; des. Stuart Craig; ed. Lesley Walker; p. Norma Heyman, Nancy Graham Tanen, Ned Tanen

Mean Streets
USA 1973, d. Martin Scorsese; w. Martin Scorsese, Mardik Martin; ph. Kent L. Wakeford; ed. Sidney Levin; p. Jonathan T. Taplin

Memphis Belle
GB/USA 1990, d. Michael Caton-Jones; w. Monte Merrick; ph. David Watkin; des. Stuart Craig; ed. Jim Clark; p. David Puttnam, Catherine Wyler

Menschen am Sonntag/People on Sunday
Germany 1930, d. Robert Siodmak, Edgar G. Ulmer, Fred Zinnemann; w. Robert Siodmak (source material), Billy Wilder; ph. Eugen Schüfftan

Le Mépris
France/Italy 1963, d. Jean-Luc Godard; w. Jean-Luc Godard, Alberto Moravia (novel *Il Disprezzo*); ph. Raoul Coutard; ed. Agnès Guillemot, Lila Lakshmanan; p. Georges De Beauregard, Joseph E. Levine, Carlo Ponti

The Merchant Of Four Seasons
W. Germany 1972, w.d. Rainer Werner Fassbinder; ph. Dietrich Lohmann; des. Kurt Raab; ed. Thea Eymèsz; p. Ingrid Caven (as Ingrid Fassbinder)

Metropolis
Germany 1925-6, d. Fritz Lang; w. Fritz Lang, Thea von

Harbou (novel); *ph.* Karl Freund, Günther Rittau; *des.* Otto Hunte, Erich Ketelhut, Karl Vollbrecht; *p.* Erich Pommer

A Midsummer Night Sex Comedy
USA 1982, *w.d.* Woody Allen; *ph.* Gordon Willis; *des.* Mel Bourne; *ed.* Susan E. Morse; *p.* Robert Greenhut

Mighty Aphrodite
USA 1995, *w.d.* Woody Allen; *ph.* Carlo Di Palma; *des.* Santo Loquasto; *ed.* Susan E. Morse; *p.* Robert Greenhut

Mignon è partita
Italy/France 1989, *d.* Francesca Archibugi; *w.* Francesca Archibugi, Gloria Malatesta, Claudia Sbarigia; *ph.* Luigi Verga; *ed.* Alfredo Muschietti; *p.* Leo Pescarolo, Guido De Laurentiis

Millers Crossing
USA 1990, *d.* Joel Coen; *w.* Ethan Coen, Joel Coen; *ph.* Barry Sonnenfeld; *des.* Dennis Gassner; *ed.* Michael R. Miller; *p.* Ben Barenholtz, Ethan Coen, Graham Place, Mark Silverman

Mirror/Zerkalo
Soviet Union 1974, *d.* Andrei Tarkovsky; *w.* Aleksandr Misharin, Andrei Tarkovsky; *ph.* Georgi Rerberg; *des.* Nikolai Dvigubsky; *ed.* Lyudmila Feyginova; *p.* Edward Weisberg

I misteri di Roma
Italy 1963, *d.* Cesare Zavattini

Mit der Pferdedroschke durch Berlin
Germany 1929, *d.* C. Frolich

Modern Times
USA 1936, *w.d.* Charles Chaplin; *ph.* Rollie Totheroh, Ira Morgan

Mon Oncle
France 1958, *d.* Jacques Tati; *w.* Jean L'Hôte, Jacques Lagrange, Jacques Tati; *ph.* Jean Bourgoin; *des.* Henri Schmitt; *ed.* Suzanne Baron; *p.* Fred Orain, Jacques Tati

Moskova
1925, *d.* Dziga Vertov (Mikhail Kaufman, 1927)

Mr Deeds Goes to Town
USA 1936, *d.* Frank Capra; *w.* Clarence Budington Kelland (novel *Opera Hat*), Robert Riskin; *ph.* Joseph Walker; *des.* Stephen Goosson; *ed.* Gene Havlick; *p.* Frank Capra

My Own Private Idaho
USA 1991, *d.* Gus Van Sant Jr.; *w.* William Shakespeare (play *Henry IV*), Gus Van Sant Jr.; *ph.* John J. Campbell, Eric Alan Edwards; *des.* David Brisbin; *ed.* Curtiss Clayton; *p.* Tony Brand (line), Laurie Parker

Les Mystères du château du Dé
France 1928, *d.* Man Ray

N

National Lampoon's European Vacation
USA 1985, *d.* Amy Heckerling; *w.* John Hughes (also story), Robert Klane; *ph.* Robert Paynter; *des.* Bob Cartwright; *ed.* Pembroke J. Herring; *p.* Matty Simmons

Nederlandsche Architectuur
Netherlands 1930, *d.* Mannus Franken

Neighbourhood 15, West Ham
GB 1945, Look & Learn Film Unit

Neon Bible
GB 1995, *d.* Terence Davies; *w.* Terence Davies, John Kennedy Toole (novel); *ph.* Michael Coulter; *des.* Christopher Hobbs; *ed.* Charles Rees; *p.* Elizabeth Karlsen, Olivia Stewart

Nestore l'ultima corsa
Italy 1993, *d.* Alberto Sordi; *w.* Rodolfo Sonego, Alberto Sordi; *ph.* Armando Nannuzzi; *ed.* Tatiana Casini Morigi

Die neue Wohnung
Germany 1930, *d.* Hans Richter

Neues Wohnen
Germany 1927–28, *d.* R. Paulick

New Builders
GB 1945, Ministry of Information

New Towns for Old
GB 1942, Ministry of Information

New York, New York
USA 1977, *d.* Martin Scorsese; *w.* Earl Mac Rauch, Mardik Martin; *ph.* László Kovács; *des.* Boris Leven; *ed.* Bert Lovitt, David Ramirez, Tom Rolf; *p.* Robert Chartoff, Irwin Winkler

New York, New York
USA 1957, *d.* Francis Thompson

New York Stories see **Life Lessons; Oedipus Wrecks**

Night on Earth
Japan/USA 1991, *w.d.* Jim Jarmusch; *ph.* Frederick Elmes; *ed.* Jay Rabinowitz; *p.* Jim Jarmusch, Rudd Simmons (line)

Nosferatu
Germany 1922, *d.* F.W. Murnau; *w.* Henrik Galeen, Bram Stoker (novel *Dracula*); *ph.* G¸nther Krampf, Fritz Arno Waner; *des.* Albin Grau; *p.* Enrico Dieckmann, Albin Grau

Nostalgia
Italy 1983, *d.* Andrei Tarkovsky; *w.* Tonino Guerra, Andrei Tarkovsky; *ph.* Giuseppe Lanci; *des.* Andrea Crisanti; *ed.* Erminia Marani, Amedeo Salfa; *p.* Franco Casati,

La notte
France/Italy 1960, *d.* Michelangelo Antonioni; *w.* Michelangelo Antonioni, Ennio Flaiano, Tonino Guerra; *ph.* Gianni Di Venanzo; *des.* Piero Zuffi; *ed.* Eraldo Da Roma; *p.* Emanuele Cassuto

Le notti di Cabiria
Italy 1957, *d* Federico Fellini; *w.* Federico Fellini, Ennio Flaiano, Pier Paolo Pasolini, Tullio Pinelli; *ph.* Otello Martelli, Aldo Tonti; *ed.* Leo Cattozzo; *p.* Dino De Laurentiis

The Nutrition Film: Enough to Eat
GB 1936, Gas, Light and Coke Company

O

Oedipus Wrecks (segment **New York Stories**)
USA 1989, *w.d.* Woody Allen; *ph.* Sven Nykvist; *des.* Santo Loquasto; *ed.* Susan E. Morse; *p.* Robert Greenhut

Oliver Twist
UK 1948, *d.* David Lean; *w.* Charles Dickens (novel), Stanley Haynes, David Lean; *ph.* Guy Green; *des.* John Bryan; *ed.* Jack Harris; *p.* Anthony Havelock-Allan, Ronald Neame

On Demande une brute
France 1932, *d.* Charles Barrois; *w.* Alfred Sauvy, Jacques Tati; *asst. d.* René Clément

On the Town
USA 1949, *d.* Stanley Donen, Gene Kelly; *w.* Betty Comden (also play), Adolph Green; *ph.* Harold Rosson; *ed.* Ralph E. Winters; *p.* Arthur Freed

On the Waterfront
USA 1954, *d.* Elia Kazan; *w.* Malcolm Johnson (articles), Budd Schulberg; *ph.* Boris Kaufman; *des.* Richard Day; *ed.* Gene Milford; *p.* Sam Spiegel

Orchestra
USA 1989, *d.* Zbig Rybczynski

Orlacs Hände/The Hands of Orlac
Austria 1924, *d.* R. Wiene

Orlando
France/GB/Italy/Netherlands/Russia 1993, *d.* Sally Potter; *w.* Sally Potter, Virginia Woolf (novel); *ph.* Alexei Rodionov; *des.* Ben van Os, Jan Roeles: *ed.* Hervè Schneid; *p.* Laurie Borg (line)

L'oro di Roma
Italy 1961, *d.* Carlo Lizzani, *ph.* Erico Menczer

Otto e mezzo/Eight and a Half
Italy 1963, *d.* Federico Fellini; *w.* Federico Fellini, Ennio Flaiano, Tullio Pinelli, Brunello Rondi; *ph.* Gianni Di Venanzo; *des.* Piero Gherardi; *ed.* Leo Cattozzo; *p.* Angelo Rizzoli

P

Paisà/Paisan
Italy 1946, *d.* Roberto Rossellini; *w.* Sergio Amidei, Federico Fellini, Alfred Hayes, Marcello Pagliero, Roberto Rossellini; *ph.* Otello Martelli; *ed.* Eraldo Da Roma; *p.* Mario Conti, Rod E. Geiger, Roberto Rossellini

Paris qui dort/The Crazy Ray (USA)
France 1924, *w.d./ed.* Renè Clair; *ph.* Maurice Dèsfassiaux, Paul Guichard; *p.* Henri Diamant-Berger

The Passenger
France/Italy/Spain/USA 1975, *d.* Michelangelo Antonioni; *w.* Michelangelo Antonioni, Mark Peploe (also story), Peter Wollen; *ph.* Luciano Tovoli; *ed.* Michelangelo Antonioni, Franco Arcalli; *p.* Carlo Ponti

Peeping Tom
UK 1960, *d.* Michael Powell; *w.* Leo Marks; *ph.* Otto Heller; *des.* Srthur Lawson; *ed.* Noreen Ackland; *p.* Michael Powell

Persona
Sweden 1966, *w.d.* Ingmar Bergman; *ph.* Sven Nykvist; *des.* Bibi Lindström; *ed.* Ulla Ryghe; *p.* Ingmar Bergman, Lars-Owe Carlberg

Pierrot le fou
France/Italy 1965, *d.* Jean-Luc Godard; *w.* Jean-Luc Godard; Lionel White (novel *Obsession*); *ph.* Raoul Coutard; *des.* Pierre Guffroy; *ed.* Françoise Collin; *p.* Georges De Beauregard

The Plan and the People
GB 1945, Ministry of Information

Playtime
France/Italy 1967, *d.* Jacques Tati; *w.* Jacques Lagrange, Jacques Tati; *ph.* Jean Badal, Andréas Winding; *des.* Eugène Roman; *ed.* Gérard Pollicand; *p.* René Silvera

The Poor Jenny
Germany 1912, *d.* Urban Gad

Poveri, ma belli
Italy 1957, *d.* Dino Risi

Proud City
GB 1945, Ministry of Information

The Public Enemy
USA 1933, *d.* William A. Wellman; *w.* John Bright (story *Beer and Blood*), Kubec Glasmon (story), Harvey F. Thew; *ph.* Devereaux Jennings; *ed.* Ed McCormick, Edward M. McDermott; *p.* Darryl F. Zanuck

The Purple Rose of Cairo
USA 1985, *w.d.* Woody Allen; *ph.* Gordon Willis;

des. Stuart Wurtzel; *ed.* Susan E. Morse; *p.* Robert Greenhut

Q

Queen of Hearts
GB/USA 1989, *d.* Jon Amiel; *w.* Tony Grisoni; *ph.* Mike Southon; *des.* Jim Clay; *ed.* Peter Boyle; *p.* Graham Benson (exec.), John Hardy, Caroline Hewitt (assoc.)

R

Racconti romani
Italy 1955, *d.* Gianni Amelio
Die Rache des Homunculus
Germany 1916, *d.* Otto Rippert; w, Robert Neuss, Otto Rippert; *ph.* Carl Hoffmann
Radio Days
USA 1987, *w.d.* Woody Allen; *ph.* Carlo Di Palma; *des.* Santo Loquasto; *des.* Santo Lo Quasto; *ed.* Susan E. Morse; *p.* Robert Greenhut
I ragazzi di Via Panisperna
Italy 1989, *d.* Gianni Amelio
Raging Bull
USA 1980, *d.* Martin Scorsese; *w.* Joseph Carter (book), Jake La Motta (book), Mardik Martin, Peter Savage (book), Paul Schrader; *ph.* Michael Chapman; *ed.* Gene Rudolf; *ed.* Thelma Schoonmaker; *p.* Robert Chartoff, Irwin Winkler
Rain or Shine
USA 1930, *d.* Frank Capra; *w.* James Gleason (also play), Maurice Marks; *ph.* Joseph Walker; *ed.* Maurice Wright; *p.* Harry Cohn
Raskolnikow/Crime and Punishment
Germany 1923, *d.* Robert Wiene; *w.* Fyodor Dostoyevsky (novel *Crime and Punishment*), Robert Wiene; *ph.* Willy Goldberger
Rear Window
USA 1954, *d.* Alfred Hitchcock; *w.* John Michael Hayes, Cornell Woolrich (novel); *ph.* Robert Burks; *des.* Hal Pereira, Joseph MacMillan Johnson; *ed.* George Tomasini
The Record of a Tenement Gentleman/Nagaya shinshiroku
Japan 1947, *d.* Yasujiro Ozu; *w.* Tadao Ikeda, Yasujiro Ozu; *ph.* Yuharu Atsuta; *ed.* Yoshi Sugihara
Regen/Rain
Netherlands 1929, *d.* Joris Ivens
Retour à la terre
France 1938, *w.* Jacques Tati
Rien que les heures
France 1926, *d.* Alberto Cavalcanti
Roma, città aperta/Rome, Open City
Italy 1946, *d.* Roberto Rossellini; *w.* Sergio Amidei, Federico Fellini, Roberto Rossellini; *ph.* Ubaldo Arata; *des.* Rosario Megna; *ed.* Eraldo Da Roma; *p.* Roberto Rossellini
Roma ore undici
Italy 1951, *d.* Giuseppe De Santis
Roman Holiday
USA 1952, *d.* William Wyler; *w.* John Dighton, Ben Hecht (uncredited), Ian McLellan Hunter (also story), Dalton Trumbo; *ph.* Henri Alekan, Franz Planer; *des.* Hal Pereira, Walter H. Tyler, *ed.* Robert Swink; *p.* William Wyler
The Roman Spring of Mrs Stone
USA 1961, *d.* JosÈ Quintero; *w.* Gavin Lambert,

Tennessee Williams (play); *ph.* Harry Waxman; *des.* Roger K. Furse; *ed.* Ralph Kemplen; *p.* Louis De Rochemont
Rome Adventure/Lovers Must Learn
USA 1962, *d.* Delmer Daves; *w.* Delmer Daves, Irving Fineman; *ph.* Charles Lawton Jr; *ed.* William H. Ziegler; *p.* Delmer Daves

S

The Sacrifice
France/Sweden 1986, *w.d.* Andrei Tarkovsky; *ph.* Sven Nykvist; *des.* Anna Asp; *ed.* Henri Colpi, Michal Leszczylowski, Andrei Tarkovsky; *p.* Anna-Lena Wibom
Lo sceicco bianco/The White Sheik
Italy 1952, *d.* Federico Fellini; *w.* Michelangelo Antonioni, Federico Fellini, Ennio Flaiano, Tullio Pinelli; *ph.* Arturo Galea; *ed.* Rolando Bebedetti; *p.* Luigi Rovere
Schatten/Warning Shadows
Germany 1922, *d.* Arthur Robison; *w.* Arthur Robison, Rudolf Schneider; *ph.* Fritz Arno Wagner; *des.* Albin Grau
Scherben/Shattered
Germany 1921, *d.* Lupu Pick; *w.* Carl Mayer, Lupu Pick
Scipione l'africano
Italy 1937, *d.* Carmine Gallone
Sciuscià
Italy 1946, *d.* Vittorio De Sica; *w.* Sergio Amidei, Adolfo Franci, C.G. Viola, Cesare Zavattini; *ph.* Anchise Brizzi; *des.* Ivo Battelli; *ed.* Niccolo Lazzari; *p.* Paolo William Tamburella
The Secret Garden
USA 1993, *d.* Agnieszka Holland; *w.* Frances Hodgson Burnett (novel), Caroline Thompson; *ph.* Roger Deakins, Jerzy Zielinski; *des.* Stuart Craig; *ed.* Isabelle Lorente; *p.* Fred Fuchs, Tom Luddy, Fred Roos
September
USA 1987, *w.d.* Woody Allen; *ph.* Carlo Di Palma; *des.* Santo Loquasto; *ed.* Susan E. Morse; *p.* Robert Greenhut
The Seven Hills of Rome
Italy/USA 1957, *d.* Roy Rowland; *w.* Giorgio Prosperi; *ph.* Tonino Delli Colli; *ed.* Gene Ruggiero; *p.* Lester Welch
Shadows and Fog
USA 1991, *w.d.* Woody Allen (also play *Death*); *ph.* Carlo Di Palma; *des.* Santo Loquasto; *ed.* Susan E. Morse; *p.* Robert Greenhut
The Shape of Things to Come
Canada 1979 (TV), *d.* George McCowan; *w.* Martin Lager
Siegfried/Die Nibelungen: Siegfried
Germany 1924, *d.* Fritz Lang; *w.* Fritz Lang, Thea von Harbou; *ph.* Carl Hoffmann, Günther Rittau, Walter Ruttmann; *des.* Otto Hunte, Karl Vollbrecht; *p.* Erich Pommer
The Singing Detective
GB 1986 (TV), *d.* Jon Amiel; *w.* Dennis Potter; *ph.* Ken Westbury; *des.* Jim Clay; *p.* John Harris, Kenith Trodd
Slags
GB 1983 (TV), *d.* Sandy Johnson; *des.* Christopher Hobbs
Sleeper
USA 1973, *d.* Woody Allen; *w.* Woody Allen, Marshall Brickman; *ph.* David M. Walsh; *des.* Dale Hennesy; *ed.* Ron Kalish, Ralph Rosenblum; *p.* Jack Grossberg, Charles H. Joffe
The Smoke Menace
GB 1937, Gas, Light and Coke Company

Soigne ton gauche
France 1936, *d.* René Clément; *w.* Jacques Tati; *p.* Fred Orain
Solaris
Soviet Union 1972, *d.* Andrei Tarkovsky; *w.* Friedrich Gorenstein, Stanislaw Lem (novel); Andrei Tarkovsky; *ph.* Vadim Yusov; *des.* Mikhail Romadin; *ed.* Lyudmila Feyginova; *p.* Viacheslav Tarasov
I soliti ignoti
Italy 1959, *d.* Mario Monicelli; *w.* Suso Cecchi D'Amico, Agenore Incrocci, Mario Monicelli, Furio Scarpelli; *ph.* Gianni Di Venanzo; *des.* Piero Gherardi; *ed.* Adriana Novelli; *p.* Franco Cristaldi
Sotto il sole di Roma
Italy 1948, *d.* Renato Castellani; *w.* Sergio Amidei, Renato Castellani, Emilio Cecchi, Ettor e Maria Margadonna, Fausto Tozzi; *ph.* Domenico Scala
Sous les toits de Paris
France 1930, *d.* René Clair; *w.* René Clair; *ph.* Georges Périnal, Georges Raulet; *des.* Lazare Meerson; *ed.* René Le Henaff
Square/Kwadrat
Poland 1972, *d.* Zbig Rybczynski
Die Stadt von morgen
1929–30, *d.* M. von Goldbeck, E. Kotzer
Stalker
Soviet Union 1979, *d.* Andrei Tarkovsky; *w.* Arkadi Strugatsky, Boris Strugatsky; *ph.* Alexander Knyazhinsky; *des.* Andrei Tarkovsky; *p.* Alexandra Demidova
Der Stand der Dinge/The State of Things
Portugal/USA/W. Germany 1982, *d.* Wim Wenders; *w.* Robert Kramer, Josh Wallace, Wim Wenders; *ph.* Henri Alekan, Fred Murphy, Martin Schäfer; *ed.* Peter Przygodda, Barbara von Weitershausen; *p.* Chris Sievernich
Star Wars
USA 1977, *d.* George Lucas; *w.* George Lucas; *ph.* Gilbert Taylor; *des.* John Barry; *ed.* Richard Chew, Paul Hirsch, Marcia Lucas; *p.* Gary Kurtz
Stardust Memories
USA 1980, *w.d.* Woody Allen; *ph.* Gordon Willis; *des.* Mel Bourne; *ed.* Susan E. Morse; *p.* Robert Greenhut, Jack Rollins
La strada
Italy 1954, *d.* Federico Fellini; *w.* Federico Fellini, Tullio Pinelli, Ennio Flaiano; *ph.* Otello Martelli
Die Strasse/The Street
Germany 1923, *d.* Karl Grune; *w.* Karl Grune, Julius Urgiß; *ph.* Karl Hasselmann
Sunrise
USA 1927, *d.* F.W. Murnau; *w.* Hermann Sudermann (story *Die Reise Nach Tilsit*), Carl Mayer (story); *ph.* Charles Rosher, Karl Struss; *des.* Rochus Gliese; *ed.* Harold D. Schuster; *p.* William Fox
Sylvester
Germany 1923, *d.* Lupu Pick

T

Take the Money and Run
USA 1969, *d.* Woody Allen; *w.* Woody Allen, Mickey Rose; *ph.* Lester Shorr, Fouad Said; *des.* Fred Harpman; *ed.* Ralph Rosenblum; *p.* Charles Joffe

Tango
Poland 1980, *d*. Z. Rybczynski
Target for Tonight
UK 1942, Crown Film Unit
Taxi Driver
US 1976, *d*. Martin Scorsese; *w*. Paul Schrader; *ph*.
Michael Chapman; *des*. Charles Rosn; *ed*. Marcia Lucas;
p. Michael Phillips, Julia Phillips
Le tentazioni del Dottor Antonio
Italy 1962, *d*. F. Fellini
The Thief of Baghdad
US 1924, *d*. Raoul Walsh, *w*. Lotta Woods, Douglas
Fairbanks, *ph*. Arthur Edeson; *des*. William Cameron
Menzies
Things to Come
GB 1936, *d./des*. William Cameron Menzies
Three Coins in the Fountain
USA 1955, *d*. Jean Negelesco; *w*. John Patrick, John H.
Secondari (novel); *ph*. Milton Krasner
Toby Dammit (segment **Tre passi nel delirio/Spirits of the
Dead**)
France/Italy 1968, *d*. Federico Fellini (segment *Toby
Dammit*), Louis Malle (segment *William Wilson*), Roger
Vadim (segment *Metzengerstein*); *w*. Daniel Boulanger,
Federico Fellini, Louis Malle, Edgar Allan Poe (stories),
Roger Vadim, Bernadino Zapponi; Tonino Delli Colli
(segments *William Wilson* and *Toby Dammit*), Claude
Renoir (segment *Metzengerstein*), Giuseppe Rotunno
(segment *Toby Dammit*); *des*. Ghislain Uhry; *ed*. Franco
Arcalli
Tokyo Story
Japan 1953, *d*. Yasujiro Ozu; . Kogo Noda, Yasujiro Ozu;
ph. Yuharu Atsuta; *des*. Tatsuo Hamad, Itsuo Takshit; *ed*.
Yoshiyasu Hamamura; *p*. Tasheki Yamamoto
Toto, Peppino e ... la dolce vita
Italy 1961, *d*. S. Corbucci
La Tour
France 1928, *d*. René Clair
Tout va bien
France 1972, *d*. Jean-Luc Godard; Jean-Pierre Goran,
Jean-Luc Godard; *ph*. Armand Marco; *des*. Jacques
Dugied; *ed*. Kenout Peltier; *p*. J. P. Rassan
Trois chantiers
France 1930–31, *d*. Pierre Chenal
20 Million Miles to Earth
USA 1957, *d*. Nathan Juran; *w*. Bob Williams, Chris
Knopf; *ph*. Irving Lippmann; *des*. Harry Hausen; *p*.
Charles Shneer
2001: A Space Odyssey
GB/USA 1968, *d*. Stanley Kubrick; *w*. Stanley Kubrick,
Arthur C. Clarke (story); *ph*. Geoffrey Unsworth, John
Alcott; *des*. Tony Masters, Harry Lange, Ernie Archer; *ed*.
Ray Lovejoy; *p*. Victor Lindon, Stanley Kubrick
Two Weeks in Another Town
USA 1962, *d*. Vincente Minelli; *w*. Charles Schnee, Irwin
Shaw (novel); *ph*. Milton Krasner

U

Umberto D
Italy 1952, *d*. Vittorio De Sica; *w*. Vittorio De Sica, Cesare
Zavattini; *ph*. G. R. Aldo; *des*. Virgilio Marchi; *ed*. Eraldo
Da Roma; *p*. Vittorio De Sica, Giuseppe Amato, Carlo
Rizzoli
Until the End of the World
Australia/Germany/France 1991, *d*. Wim Wenders; *w*. Wim
Wendersb (story), Peter Carey, Solveig Dommartin (story);
ph. Robby Muller; *des*. Thierry Flamand, Sally Campbell;
ed. Peter Przygodda; *p*. Jonathan Taplin

V

Les Vacances de Monsieur Hulot/Mr Hulot's Holiday
France 1953, *d*. Jacques Tati; *w*. Jacques Tati, Henri
Marquet; *ph*. Jacques Mercanton, Jean Mouselle; *des*.
Henri Schmitt, Roger Briacourt; *ed*. Jacques Grassi, Ginou
Bretoneiche, Suzanne Baron; *p*. Fred Orain
Vivre sa vie
France 1962, *w.d*. Jean-Luc Godard; *ph*. Raoul Coutard
Vordertreppe–Hintertreppe/ Frontstairs–Backstairs
Germany 1915, dir. Urban Gad

W

The Way of the Dragon
USA 1973, *d*. Bruce Lee
When We Build Again
GB 1942, Ministry of Information
Where There's Soap, There's Life
GB 1920s, Bermondsey M.B.C.
Who's That Knocking at My Door?
USA 1969, *d*. Martin Scorsese
Why Does Herr R. Run Amok?
West Germany 1969, *w.d*. Rainer Werner Fassbinder,
Michael Fengler (improvised), *ph*. Dietrich Lohmann
Wie wohnen wir gesund und wirtschaftlich?
Germany 1927–8, *d*. R. Paulick
The Wild Bunch
USA 1969, *d*. Sam Peckinpah; *w*. Walon Green; *ph*. Lucien
Ballard; *des*. Edward Carrere; *ed*. Lou Lombardo; *p*. Phil
Feldman
The Wizard of Oz
US 1939, *d*. Victor Fleming, King Vidor (uncredited); *w*.
Noel Langley, Florence Ryerson, Edgar Allan Woolf, L.
Frank Baum (novel); *ph*. Harold Rosson; *des*. Cedric
Gibbons, William A. Horning; *ed*. Blanche Sewell; *p*.
Mervyn LeRoy
Wo wohnen alte Leute?
Germany 1931, *d*. E. Bergmann-Michel
The Wolves of Willoughby Chase
GB 1988, *d*. Stuart Orme; *w*. William M. Akers, Joan
Aiken (novel); *des*. Christopher Hobbs; *ed*. Martin Walsh;
p. Mark Forstater
The Wonder Ring
Switzerland 1955, *d*. S. Brakhage
The Wrong Man
USA 1957, *d*. Alfred Hitchcock; *w*. Maxwell Anderson,
Angus MacPhail; *ph*. Robert Burks; *des*. Paul Sylbert,
William L. Kuehi; *ed*. George Tomasini; *p*. Alfred
Hitchcock

Z

Zabriskie Point
USA 1969, *d*. Michelangelo Antonioni; *w*. Michelangelo
Antonioni, Fred Gardner, Sam Shepard, Tonino Guerra,
Clare Peploe; *ph*. Alfio Contini; *des*. Dean Tavoularis; *ed*.
Franco Arcalli; *p*. Carlo Ponti
Zelig
USA 1983, *w.d*. Woody Allen; *ph*. Gordon Willis; *des*.
Speed Hopkins; *ed*. Susan E. Morse; *p*. Robert Greenhut

INDEX

films about 37, 43
  identifiable, in films 44
  location shoot, cathedral 186
  newsreels about 37
  photographic simulation, cathedral
    187–8
  see also architecture
Bullets over Broadway (1994) 75, 81, 82
Bullock, Nicholas 6–7, 45(n10), 52–60,
  61(n14)
'bump-mapping' 176, 176, 178
Buñuel, Luis 96
businesses, use of film 52

C

The Cabinet of Dr Caligari see Das
  Kabinett des Doktor Caligari
CAD (computer-aided design) 126, 174–5
  see also computer graphics; set design
Cahiers du Cinéma 63, 65, 66, 67, 69,
  78(n8)
Les Cahiers du Mois 33, 33(n10)
'Caligarism' 14, 15
Calvino, Italo 77
Cambridge Centre for Communications
  Systems Research 3
camera
  motion control system 185
  positioning prior to realisation 156
'camera eye' ('Kino-Eye') 22, 26
caméra-stylo 125
Camre, Henning 152–3, 180
Canudo, Ricciotto 29, 33(n6)
Cape Fear (1991) 82
Capra, Frank 73
Carné, Marcel 65, 172
Carpenter Center, Harvard University,
  computer graphics kit 135
cartoons, animated 38, 39
  see also animation
Cartwright, Robert 172
Casanova (1976) 169, 169, 172
Casino (1995) 82
Cassavetes, John 78(n15)
  see also Gloria
Castellani, Renato 97(n14)
Castle Drogo (Lutyens) 169
cathedrals, filming 186, 187–8
Cavalcanti, Alberto 2, 7, 18, 19–20,
  27(n12), 79(n22)
CD-ROM
  games, and architecture 120–1
  see also computer graphics;
    multimedia
CFB Centrum, Berlin 195
Chaplin, Charlie 64, 68(n1)
Chapman, Jay 18, 27(n12)
characters
  in architectural films 44
  computer graphics images 192
  as focus for city films 19, 20
  relationship to set design 31
Chareau, Pierre 163

Charnley, Diana 103, 152, 154–65, 180
Chartres Cathedral, as example of location
  shooting 186
Chenal, Pierre 2, 37, 42–4
Children at School (1937) 53
Chinese architecture 132, 135
Chion, Michel 69, 73–4, 78(n8, 9)
Christie, Ian 78
Churchill, Winston, and post-war housing
  57
CIAM (Congrès International de
  l'Architecture Moderne) 6, 35–6, 36
CICI (Congrès International du Cinéma
  Indépendant) 6, 35–6, 36
Cinecittà 94–5, 94, 96(n1), 99(n31)
cinema
  audience after First World War 34–5
  construction, focus in films 98(n28)
  relationship to urban culture 10
  see also film
Cinéma & Architecture 46(n27)
Cinéma pur 20
cinema vans 53, 53
cinéma vérité 9, 22, 189
Cinematograph Exhibitors Assocation 55
Cité de la Musique, Paris 120
city
  'city film' 6, 8–26
  'city symphonies' 10, 19, 23–5, 77,
    79(n22)
  film cartolina 85–6
  iconography 84–5
  images and photographs 182
  insider's view 88–9
  metaphors for 12
  modern city 49–99
  outsider's view 85–8
  planning, as symbol of power 87
  rain in city films 24, 73
  street film 8–11, 13, 16–18
  urban integration 72–3
  urban planning, films on 45(n15)
  virtual city 123–79, 146–7
  as a woman 77
  see also metropolis; 'urbanity';
city poems 18–23
A City Reborn (UK 1945) 55
The City (UK 1939) 45(n15)
The City (USA 1939) 45(n15)
Clair, René 2, 7, 19, 24–5, 65
Clay, Jim 164, 165(n)
Clement, René 68(n2)
Close Quarters (1943) 54
Club des amis du 7ième art 29
Coastal Command (1942) 54
Cocteau, Jean 132, 136(n1, 3)
  see also La Belle et la bête
Codelli, Lorenzo 45(n6)
Coen Brothers 154
Cold Lazarus (1995) 171, 171, 172, 180
Cole, G.D.H. 58, 61(n19)
The Color of Money (1986) 82
colour
  black and white films 30–1

expressionistic, as motif 78(n12)
  and lighting 176–7
  of New York 70–8
  Tati 67
  and use of digital images in
    architecture 128
colportage 9, 25
La commare secca (1962) 98(n19)
commissioning of films, influence 36–7
communication, using film for 55
composition, Mallet-Stevens 31
computer graphics
  animation 133
  deformation of images 193
  kit
    applications 134–6
    terminology 133–4
  and the notion of the image 183
  problems of 192–3
  in set design 174
  see also CAD (computer-aided
    design); CD-ROM; multimedia
computer simulation, film applications
  156, 174–80, 176, 179
conceptual space 43, 44
concrete, use in film sets 32
Congrès International de l'Architecture
  Moderne (CIAM) 6, 35–6, 36
Congrès International du Cinéma
  Indépendant (CICI) 6, 35–6, 36
Connelly, Chuck 79(n26)
la conque 120
Conrad, Peter 75, 78(n14)
construction, films about 37, 43
Constructivists 22, 25
Copy Cat (1995–6) 162–3
Corbett, Harvey Wiley 11
Corbucci, Sergio 95
Corbusier, Le see Le Corbusier
corporatism, and Playtime 51
County of London plan 54–5, 59
Craig, Stuart 165(n), 180
Crali, Tullio Nose-diving on the City
  (1939) 90
CREATEC (Creative Media Arts and
  Technologies Centre), London 3
'creative geography' 71
creative process, changing 189–90
Crimes and Misdemeanors (1989) 73, 76,
  76, 81, 82
The Crowd (1928) 76, 78(n15)
Crown Film Unit 53, 54, 60(n8)
The Crying Game (1992) 164, 164
cubism
  in architecture 40
  cubist villa, Mallet-Stevens 33
  cubist-like portrait, Taxi Driver 72
  in film 144
  Ruttmann and 21
Czwiklitzer, Christophe 46(n17)

D

Daidalos 45(n2)

Dalrymple, I. 60(n8)
dams, construction filmed 43
Daney, Serge 70, 78(n1)
dark expressionism 13–16
Daves, Delmer 96(n1)
Davies, Richard Llewelyn 54
Davies, Terence 172
De Niro, Robert 72
De Renzi, Mario 90, 92
De Santis, Giuseppe 97(n11)
De Sica, Vittorio 62, 88–9, 97(n11)
De Stijl 29
Dear Diary (1993) 92–3, 92
deconstruction, filmic 24, 42
La Défense 65, 65, 119
Del Debbio, Enrico 86
Denby, Elizabeth 56
Il deserto rosso (1964) 109, 111
design see architectural design; CAD
  (computer-aided design); interior
  design; production design; set design;
  three-dimensional design
designer-client relationship, and the
  Internet 143
detail
  architectural, La Belle et la bête 132
  Blade Runner 167
  building, in Die neue Wohnung 42
  Mayer 15, 16
  Ozu 109
  production design 160
  Rain 24
  Sander 108
  Scorsese 71
  Tati 67
deus ex machina, metropolis as 12
Deutsche Bauzeitung 45(n11)
2 mille 36 Joiseaux (video) 129, 129, 130
The Devils (1970) 171, 172
Diamant-Berger, Henri 29
Diary: Architects' Congress (1933) 36
digital techniques
  3D design 138–43
  in architectural design 124
  and art 191–2
  use in architectural education 126–30
Directorate of Army Education 60(n10)
disegno effects 16
Disneyland 170
distribution
  films on architecture 38
  MOI films 61(n16)
Divoire, Fernand 33(n6)
documentary film
  actualités 8
  Berlin as 'documentary' film 22–3
  British post-war 52–60
  development of style in early cinema 9
  early film on modern architecture 34–
    45
  mass communication by 55
  propaganda 52–3
  social force 52
  see also realism